12th
BLUE BOOK
Dolls & Values®

by Jan Foulke

photographs by Howard Foulke

Published by Hobb
Hobby
House   Gran
Press

D0448677

Other Titles by Author:

Blue Book of Dolls & Values®
2nd Blue Book of Dolls & Values®
3rd Blue Book of Dolls & Values®
4th Blue Book of Dolls & Values®
5th Blue Book of Dolls & Values®
6th Blue Book of Dolls & Values®
7th Blue Book of Dolls & Values®
8th Blue Book of Dolls & Values®
9th Blue Book of Dolls & Values®
10th Blue Book of Dolls & Values®
11th Blue Book of Dolls & Values®

Focusing on Effanbee Composition Dolls

Focusing on Treasury of
Mme. Alexander Dolls

Focusing on Gebrüder Heubach Dolls

Kestner: King of Dollmakers

Simon & Halbig Dolls: The Artful Aspect

Doll Classics

Focusing on Dolls

China Doll Collecting

Doll Buying & Selling

German 'Dolly' Collecting

The registered trademarks, the trademarks and the copyrights appearing in this book belong to the company under whose name they appear, unless otherwise noted.

The doll prices given within this book are intended as value guides rather than arbitrarily set prices. Each doll price recorded here is actually a compilation. The retail prices in this book are recorded as accurately as possible but in the case of errors, typographical, clerical or otherwise, the author and publisher assume no liability nor responsibility for any loss incurred by users of this book.

COVER (left to right): #2 BARBIE® in Commuter Set. *Sidney Jeffrey Collection.* (For further BARBIE® information see pages 77-82.) 14in (36cm) composition *Scootles*, all original. *H & J Foulke, Inc.* (For further information see page 110.) 18in (46cm) Bru *Bébé Gourmand*. (For further information see page 103.) *Private Collection.*

TITLE PAGE: 18in (46cm) Bru *Bébé Gourmand*. (For further information see page 103.) *Private Collection.*

BACK COVER: #3 Ponytail BARBIE® wearing Roman Holiday #968. *Courtesy of McMasters Doll Auctions.* (See photograph, page 77. For further information see pages 78 and 79). 16in (41cm) *Snow White,* all original. *H & J Foulke, Inc.* (For further information see page 22.)

**ADDITIONAL COPIES AVAILABLE @ $17.95 plus postage
FROM
HOBBY HOUSE PRESS, INC.
1 CORPORATE DRIVE
GRANTSVILLE, MD 21536
1-800-554-1447**

© 1995 by Jan and Howard Foulke

Printed in the United States of America

ISBN: 0-87588-440-7

Doll collecting continues to increase in popularity every year. The great number of collectors entering the field has given rise to larger and more frequent doll shows, more dealers in dolls, more books on dolls, thicker doll magazines and more doll conventions and seminars, as well as an overwhelming offering of new dolls by mass-production companies and individual artists. This explosion has also increased the demand for old dolls and discontinued collector's dolls, causing prices to rise as more collectors vie for the same dolls.

With the average old doll representing a purchase of at least several hundred dollars, today's collectors must be as well informed as possible about the dolls they are considering as additions to their collections. Since the first *Blue Book of Dolls & Values* was published in 1974, our objectives have remained the same:

- To present a book that will help collectors to identify and learn more about dolls.
- To provide retail prices as a guide for buyers and sellers of dolls.

Since every edition of the *Blue Book* has sold more copies than the previous one, we can only conclude that these objectives are in line with the needs of the doll lovers, collectors, dealers and appraisers who keep buying the latest editions of our book.

The dolls presented in this book are listed alphabetically by maker, material or the trade name of the individual doll. An extensive index has been provided to help in locating a specific doll. Of course, in a book this size, not every doll ever made can be discussed, but we have tried to include a broad spectrum of dolls that are available, desirable, interesting and popular, and even some that are rare.

For each doll we have provided historical information, a description of the doll, a copy of the mark or label, the retail selling price and a photograph or picture reference to a previous edition of the *Blue Book* because there is not enough space to show a photograph of each doll in each edition.

The price for a doll listed in this price guide is the retail value of a doll fulfilling all of the criteria discussed in the following chapter if it is purchased from a dealer.

In some cases the doll sizes given are the only ones known to have been made, but in the cases of most of the French and German bisque, china, papier-mâché and wood dolls, sizes priced are chosen at random and listed sizes must not be interpreted as definitive. It is impossible to list every doll in every possible size, especially for dolls that range from 6 to 42 inches (15 to 106cm). The user will need to call a little common sense into play to interpolate a price for an unlisted size.

The historical information given for some of the dolls would have been much more difficult to compile were it not for the original research already published by Dorothy S., Elizabeth A. and Evelyn J. Coleman; Johana G. Anderton; and Jürgen and Marianne Cieslik.

The data for retail prices was gathered during 1994 and 1995 from antique shops and shows, auctions, doll shops and shows, advertisements in collectors' periodicals, lists from doll dealers, and purchases and sales

26in (70cm) E 12 J, all original. *Private Collection.* (For additional information see page 222.)

The international market has been an important factor in the change of domestic doll prices during the past few years. International interest has added a whole new dimension to the American doll market as increasing awareness of antique dolls in Germany, France, Switzerland, Holland, Denmark and other countries is causing a great exodus and a depletion of our supply of antique dolls.

Of particular interest in the international arena are German bisque character children, German bisque babies by Kestner, Kämmer & Reinhardt, and Hertel, Schwab & Co., German bisque closed-mouth shoulder heads, German bisque "dolly" faces (particularly small sizes) by Kestner, Kämmer & Reinhardt, and Handwerck, Käthe Kruse dolls and German celluloid dolls. This interest has caused continued price increases in these categories.

All prices given for antique dolls are for those of good quality and condition, but showing normal wear, and appropriately dressed in new or old clothing, unless other specifications are given in the description accompanying that particular doll. Bisque or china heads should not be cracked, broken or repaired, but may have slight making imperfections such as speckling, surface lines, darkened mold lines and uneven coloring. Bodies may have repairs or be nicely repainted, but should be old and appropriate to the head. A doll with old dress, shoes and wig will generally be valued at higher than quoted

reported by both collectors and dealers. This information, along with our own valuations and judgments, was computed into the range of prices shown in this book. When we could not find a sufficient number of dolls to be sure of giving a reliable range, we marked those prices with two asterisks ("**").

In setting a price for each doll, we use a range to allow for the variables of originality, quality and condition that must be reflected in the price. As collectors become more sophisticated in their purchases, fine examples of a doll, especially those which are all original or with period clothing, can bring a premium of up to 50% more than prices quoted for ordinary examples. Sometimes a doll will bring a premium price because it is particularly cute, sweet, pretty or visually appealing, making an outstanding presentation. There is no way to factor this appeal into a price guide.

prices because these items are in scarce supply and can easily cost more than $65 each if purchased separately.

Prices given for modern dolls are for those in overall good to excellent condition with original hair and clothing, except as noted. Composition may be lightly crazed, but should be colorful. Hard plastic and vinyl must be perfect, with hair in original set and crisp, original clothes. A never-played-with doll in original box with labels would bring a premium price.

The users of this book must keep in mind that no price guide is the final word. It cannot provide an absolute answer as to what to pay. This book should be used only as an aid in purchasing a doll. The final decision must be yours, for only you are on the scene, actually examining the specific doll in question. No book can take the place of actual field experience. Doll popularity can cycle; prices can fluctuate; regional variations can occur. Before you buy, do a lot of looking. Ask questions. Most dealers and collectors are glad to talk about their dolls and pleased to share their information with you.

11in (28cm) K & R 116 character. *H & J Foulke, Inc.* (For additional information see page 231.)

24in (61cm) 143 Kestner child. *H & J Foulke, Inc.* (For additional information see page 239.)

6

ACKNOWLEDGEMENTS

For their encouragement and support, we again wish to thank our friends, customers, fellow dealers and fans, as well as doll collectors around the world.

Special thanks to:

Those who allowed us to use photographs of their dolls or who provided special information for use in this edition. Their help is greatly appreciated. Richard Wright, Richard Saxman, Rhoda Shoemaker, Kay and Wayne Jensen, Cathy Kiefer, Ruth Noden, Becky Lowe, Mary Barnes Kelley, Betty Harms, June and Norman Verro, Carol Corson, Joanna Ott, Matthew McKeeby, Ruth Covington West, Nancy A. Smith, Joan Kindler, Barbara Manhart, Rosemary Dent, Eleanora Miller, Gayle Elam, Jane Mann, Jim Fernando, Sidney Jeffrey, Peggy Bealefield of Doodlebug Dolls, Joyce Watson of McMasters Doll Auctions, Richard W. Withington, Inc. and H & J Foulke, Inc.

Those who shared their doll collections but wished to remain anonymous are greatly appreciated.

The Colemans, who allowed some marks to be reproduced from their book, *The Collector's Encyclopedia of Dolls*.

Gary and Mary Ruddell of Hobby House Press, Inc., with whom we have worked for more than 20 years.

Howard, for his beautiful photographs.

All of these people helped make this book possible.

Jan Foulke
June 1995

Out-of-print editions of the *Blue Book® of Dolls & Values* have become collectors' items. Out-of-print books can be found at doll shows or auctions. The following prices are for clean books with light wear on covers and corners.

Blue Book® of Dolls & Values	**$135**
2nd Blue Book® of Dolls & Values	**110**
3rd Blue Book® of Dolls & Values	**75**
4th Blue Book® of Dolls & Values	**75**
5th Blue Book® of Dolls & Values	**45**
6th Blue Book® of Dolls & Values	**35**
7th Blue Book® of Dolls & Values	**25**
8th Blue Book® of Dolls & Values	
9th Blue Book® of Dolls & Values	
10th Blue Book® of Dolls & Values	

INVESTING IN DOLLS

With the price of the average old doll representing a purchase of at least several hundred dollars in today's doll market, the assembling of a doll collection becomes rather costly. Actually, very few people buy dolls strictly as an investment; most collectors buy a doll because they like it. It has appeal to them for some reason: perhaps as an object of artistic beauty, perhaps because it evokes some kind of sentiment, perhaps because it fills some need that they feel or speaks to something inside them. It is this personal feeling toward the doll which makes it of value to the collector.

However, most collectors expect to at least break even when they eventually sell their dolls. Unfortunately, there is no guarantee that any particular doll will appreciate consistently year after year; however, the track record for old or antique dolls is fairly good. If you are thinking of the future sale of your collection, be wary of buying expensive new or reproduction dolls. They have no track record and little resale value. Collectible dolls of the last 30 years are a risky market. Alexander dolls are a case in point. After many years of doubling their value the minute they were carried from the toy store shelves, dolls of the 1960s and 1980s have slid in price so that many are now bringing only 25 - 50% of their cost to collectors.

Because most collectors have only limited funds for purchasing dolls, they must be sure they are spending their dollars to the best advantage. There are many factors to consider when buying a doll, and this chapter will give some suggestions about what to look for and what to consider. Probably the primary tenet is that a collector who is not particularly well-informed about a doll should not consider purchasing it unless he or she has confidence in the person selling the doll.

MARKS

Fortunately for collectors, most of the antique bisque, some of the papier-mâché, cloth and other types of antique dolls are marked or labeled. Marks and labels give the buyer confidence because they identify the trade name, the maker, the country of origin, the style or mold number, or perhaps even the patent date.

Most composition and modern dolls are marked with the maker's name and sometimes also the trade name of the doll and the date. Some dolls have tags sewn on or into their clothing to identify them; many still retain original hang tags.

Of course, many dolls are unmarked, but after you have seen quite a few dolls, you begin to notice their individual characteristics and can often determine what a doll possibly is. When you have had some experience buying dolls, you begin to recognize an unusual face or an especially fine quality doll. Then there should be no hesitation about buying a doll marked only with a mold number or no mark at all. The doll has to speak for itself, and the price must be based upon the collector's frame of doll reference. That is, one must relate the face and quality to those of a known doll maker and make price judgments from that point.

QUALITY

The mark does not tell everything about a doll. Two examples from the same mold could look entirely different and carry vastly different prices because of the quality of the work done on the doll, which can vary from head to head, even with dolls made from the same mold by one firm. To command top price, a bisque doll should have lovely bisque, decoration, eyes and hair. Before purchasing a doll, the collector should determine whether the example is the best available of that type.

7in (18cm) Alexander storybook character. *H & J Foulke, Inc.* (For additional information see page 19.)

5-1/4in (13cm) French all-bisques, all original court costumes. *H & J Foulke, Inc.* (For additional information see page 36.)

16-1/2in (43cm) Unmarked bisque character man. *Gladyse Hills Hilsdorf Collection.*

14in (36cm) composition *Scootles*, all original. *H & J Foulke, Inc.* (For further information see page 110.)

14in (36cm) head circumference *Bye-Lo Baby* with 1923 incised date. *H & J Foulke, Inc.* (For further information see page 107.)

16-1/2in (42cm) Celluloid girl with Turtle Mark, all original. *H & J Foulke, Inc.* (For further information see page 114).

Even the molding of one head can be much sharper with more delineation of such details as dimples or locks of hair. The molding detail is especially important to notice when purchasing dolls with character faces or molded hair.

The quality of the bisque should be smooth; dolls with bisque which is pimply, peppered with tiny black specks or unevenly colored or which has noticeable firing lines on the face would be second choices at a lower price. However, collectors must keep in mind that porcelain factories sold many heads with small manufacturing defects because companies were in business for profit and were producing expendable play items, not works of art. Small manufacturing defects do not devalue a doll. It is perfectly acceptable to have light speckling, light surface lines, firing lines in inconspicuous places, darkened mold lines, a few black specks or cheek rubs. The absolutely perfect bisque head is a rarity.

Since doll heads are hand-painted, the artistry of the decoration should be examined. The tinting of the complexion should be subdued and even, not harsh and splotchy. Artistic skill should be evident in the portrayal of the expression on the face and in details such as the lips, eyebrows and eyelashes, and particularly in the eyes, which should show highlights and shading when they are painted. On a doll with molded hair, individual brush marks to give the hair a more realistic look would be a desirable detail.

If a doll has a wig, the hair should be appropriate if not old. Dynel or synthetic wigs are not appropriate for antique dolls; a human hair or good quality mohair wig should be used. If a doll has glass eyes, they should be old with natural color and threading in the irises to give a lifelike appearance.

If a doll does not meet all of these standards, it should be priced lower than one that does. Furthermore, an especially fine example will bring a premium over an ordinary but nice model.

CONDITION

Another important factor when pricing a doll is the condition. A bisque doll with a crack on the face or extensive professional repair involving the face would sell for one-quarter or less than a doll with only normal wear. An inconspicuous hairline would decrease the value somewhat, but in a rare doll it would not be as great a detriment as in a common doll. As the so-called better dolls are becoming more difficult to find, a hairline is more acceptable to collectors if there is a price adjustment. The same is true for a doll which has a spectacular face — a hairline would be less important to price in that doll than in one with an ordinary face.

Sometimes a head will have a factory flaw which occurred in the making, such as a firing crack, scratch, piece of kiln debris, dark specks, small bubbles, a ridge not smoothed out or light surface lines. Since the factory was producing toys for a profit and not creating works of art, heads with slight flaws were not all discarded, especially if flaws were inconspicuous or could be covered. If factory defects are not detracting, they have little or no effect on the value of a doll.

It is to be expected that an old doll will show some wear. Perhaps there is a rub on the nose or cheek, a few small "wig pulls" or maybe a chipped earring hole; a Schoenhut doll or a Käthe Kruse may have some scuffs; an old papier-mâché may have a few age cracks; a china head may show wear on the hair; an old composition body may have scuffed toes or missing fingers. This wear is to be expected and does not necessarily affect the value of a doll. However, a doll in exceptional condition will bring more than "book" price.

Unless an antique doll is rare or you particularly want that specific doll, do not pay top price for a doll that needs extensive work: restringing, setting eyes, repairing fingers, replacing body parts, new wig or dressing. All of these repairs add up to a considerable sum at the doll hospital, possibly making the total cost of the doll more than it is really worth.

Composition dolls in perfect condition are becoming harder to find. Because their material is so susceptible to the atmosphere, their condition can deteriorate literally overnight. Even in excellent condition, a composition doll nearly always has some fine crazing or slight fading. It is very difficult to find a composition doll in mint condition and even harder to be sure that it will stay that way. However, in order for a composition doll to bring "book" price, there should be a minimum of crazing, very good coloring, original uncombed hair and original clothes in very good condition. Pay less for a doll that does not have original clothes and hair or that is all original but shows extensive play wear. Pay even less for one with heavy crazing and cracking or other damages. For composition dolls that are all original, unplayed with, in original boxes and with little or no crazing, allow a premium of about 50% over "book" price.

Hard plastic and vinyl dolls must be in excellent condition if they are at "book" price. The hair should be perfect in the original set: clothes should be completely original, fresh and unfaded. Skin tones should be natural with good cheek color. Add a premium of 25-50% for mint dolls never removed from their original boxes.

BODY

In order to command top price, an old doll must have the original or an appropriate old body in good condition. If a doll does not have the correct type of body, the buyer ends up not with a complete doll but with parts that may not be worth as much as one whole doll. As dolls are becoming more difficult to find, more are turning up with "put together" bodies. Many dolls are now entering the market from old collections assembled years ago. Some of these contain dolls which were "put together" before there was much information available about correct heads and bodies. Therefore, the body should be checked to make sure it is appropriate to the head, and all parts of the body should be checked to make sure that they are appropriate to each other. A body with mixed parts from several makers or types of bodies is not worth as much as one with correct parts.

Minor damage or repair to an old body does not affect the value of an antique doll. An original body carefully repaired, recovered or even, if necessary, completely repainted is preferable to a new one. An antique head on a new body would be worth only the value of its parts, whatever the price of the head and new body, not the the full price of an antique doll. A rule of thumb is that an antique head is generally worth about 40-50% of the price of the complete doll. A very rare head could be worth up to 80%.

If there is a choice of body types for the same bisque head, a good quality ball-jointed composition body is more desirable than a crudely made five-piece body or stick-type body with only pieces of turned wood for upper arms and legs. Collectors prefer jointed composition bodies over kid ones for dolly-faced dolls, and pay more for the same face on a composition body.

Occasionally the body adds value to the doll. In the case of bisque heads, a small doll with a completely jointed body, a French fashion-type with a wood-jointed body, a *Tête Jumeau* head on an adult body or a character baby head on a jointed toddler-type body would all be higher in price because of their special bodies.

As for the later modern dolls, a composition doll on the wrong body or with a body that is cracked, peeling and in poor condition would have a greatly reduced value. The same is true of a vinyl doll with replaced parts, body stains or chewed-off fingers.

8in (20cm) Alexander **Wendykins** #462, bent-knee walker. *Rhoda Shoemaker Collection.* (For further information see page 30.)

14in (35cm) Effanbee composition **Patsy**, all original. *H & J Foulke, Inc.* (For further information see page 159.)

Chase cloth girl with bobbed hair. *H & J Foulke, Inc.* (For further information see page 119.)

32in (81cm) Patent Washable, superior quality, all original. *Private Collection.* (For further information see page 143.)

24in (61cm) unmarked composition mama doll, all original. *H & J Foulke, Inc.* (For further information see page 138.)

18in (46cm) Hertel, Schwab & Co. 141 character girl with glass eyes. *Mary Barnes Kelley Collection.* (For further information see page 196.)

CLOTHING

It is becoming increasingly difficult to find dolls in old clothing because, as the years go by, fabrics continue to deteriorate. Consequently, collectors are paying more than "book" price for an antique doll if it has appropriate old clothes, shoes and hair. Even faded, somewhat worn, or carefully mended original or appropriate old clothes are preferable to new ones. As collectors become more sophisticated and selective, they realize the value of old doll clothing and accessories. Some dealers are now specializing in these areas. Good old leather doll shoes will bring more than $75 per pair; a lovely Victorian white-work doll dress can easily cost $75; an old dress for a French fashion lady, $300 and more. Good old doll wigs can bring from $25 to $250.

However, when clothing must be replaced and appropriate old clothing cannot be obtained, new clothes should be authentically styled for the age of the doll and constructed of fabrics that would have been available when the doll was produced. There are many reference books and catalog reprints showing dolls in original clothing, and doll supply companies offer patterns for dressing old dolls.

To bring top price, a modern doll must have original clothes. It is usually fairly simple to determine whether or not the clothing is original and factory made. Some makers even placed tags in the doll's clothing. Replaced clothing greatly reduces the price of modern dolls. Without the original clothing, it is often impossible to identify a modern doll because so many were made using the same face mold.

TOTAL ORIGINALITY

Today totally original dolls are becoming rare. It is often difficult to determine whether the head and body and all other parts of a doll, including wig, eyes and clothes, have always been together. Many parts of a doll may have been changed and clothing and accessories could have been added over the years. Many dolls labeled "all original" are simply wearing contemporary clothing and wigs. Some collectors and dealers are "embellishing" more expensive dolls by taking original clothing and wigs from cheaper dolls to further enhance the value of the more cost-ly ones. Dolls with trunks of clothing and in boxed sets are particularly vulnerable to this type of raiding.

Collectors should examine clothes and accessories carefully before they pay ul-tra-high prices for such ensembles. Of course, when these ensembles are genuine, they are the ultimate in doll collecting.

AGE

The oldest dolls do not necessarily command the highest prices. A lovely old china head with exquisite decoration and very unusual hairdo would bring a price of several thousand dollars but not as much as a 20th century German bisque char-acter child. Many desirable composition dolls of the 1930s and *BARBIE*® dolls of the 1960s are selling at prices higher than older bisque dolls of 1890 to 1920. So, in determining price, the age of the doll may or may not be significant.

SIZE

The size of a doll is usually taken into account when determining a price. Gen-erally, the size and price for a certain doll are related: a smaller size is lower, a larg-er size is higher. However, there are a few exceptions. The 11in (28cm) *Shirley Temple* and tiny German dolly-faced dolls on fully-jointed bodies are examples of small dolls that bring higher prices than their larger counterparts.

AVAILABILITY

The price of a doll is directly related to its availability in most cases. The harder a doll is to find, the higher will be its price. Each year brings more new doll collectors than newly discovered, desirable old dolls; hence, the supply of old dolls is diminished. As long as the demand for certain antique and collectible dolls is greater than the supply, prices will rise. This explains the great increase in prices of less common dolls, such as the K & R and other German character children, early china heads and papier-mâchés, composition personality dolls, Sasha dolls and some Alexander dolls that were made for only a limited period of time. Dolls that are fairly common, primarily the German dolly-faces and the later china head dolls made over a long period of production, show a more gentle increase in price.

POPULARITY

There are fads in dolls just as in clothes, food and other aspects of life. Dolls that have recently risen in price because of their popularity include the early Jumeaus, all-bisques, German character children, *Patsy* family dolls, *Shirley Temples*, large composition babies, early *BARBIE*® dolls, composition personality dolls and hard plastic dolls. Some dolls are popular enough to tempt collectors to pay prices higher than the availability factor warrants. Although *Shirley Temples*, *Tête Jumeaus*, *Bye-Los*, *Hildas*, K & R 117, and some plastic Alexander dolls are not rare, the high prices they bring are due to their popularity. American cloth dolls and Greiners are in a soft period, so many bargains can be found in this category.

DESIRABILITY

Some very rare dolls do not bring a high price because they are not particularly desirable. There are not many collectors looking for them. Falling into this category are the dolls with shoulder heads made of rubber or rawhide. While an especially outstanding example will bring a high price, most examples bring very low prices in relationship to their rarity.

UNIQUENESS

Sometimes the uniqueness of a doll makes price determination very difficult. If a collector has never seen a doll exactly like it before, and it is not cited in a price guide or even shown in any books, deciding what to pay can be a problem. In this case, the buyer has to use all available knowledge as a frame of reference for the unknown doll. Perhaps a doll marked "A.M. 2000" or "S & H 1289" has been found, and the asking price is 25% higher than for the more commonly found numbers by that maker. Or perhaps a black *Kamkins* is offered for twice the price of a white one, or a French fashion lady with original wardrobe is offered at 60% more than a redressed one. In cases such as these, a collector must use his or her own judgment to determine what the doll is worth.

VISUAL APPEAL

Perhaps the most elusive aspect in pricing a doll is its visual appeal. Sometimes, particularly at auction, we have seen dolls bring well over their "book" value simply because of their look. Often this is nothing more than the handiwork of someone who had the ability to choose just the right wig, clothing and accessories to enhance the doll's visual appeal and make it look particularly cute, stunning, beautiful or otherwise especially outstanding.

Sometimes, though, the visual appeal comes from the face of the doll itself. It may be the way the teeth are put in, the placement of the eyes, the tinting on the face or the sharpness of the molding. Or it may not be any of these specific things; it may just be what some collectors refer to as the "presence" of the doll, an elusive indefinable quality which makes it the best example known!

SELLING A DOLL

So many times we are asked, "How do I go about selling a doll?," that it seems a few paragraphs on the topic are in order. The first logical step is to look through the **Blue Book** to identify the doll and to ascertain a retail price. Work from there to decide what you might ask for your doll. It is very difficult for a private person to get a retail price for a doll.

Be realistic about the condition. If you have a marked 18in (46cm) *Shirley Temple* doll with combed hair, no clothing, faded face with crazing and a piece off of her nose, do not expect to get the book price of $900 for her because that would be a retail price for an excellent doll, all original, in pristine unplayed-with condition if purchased from a dealer. Your very used doll is probably worth only $50 to $75 because it will have to be purchased by someone who wants to restore it.

If you have an antique doll with a perfect bisque head but no wig, no clothes and unstrung, but with all of its body parts, you can probably expect to get about half of its retail value depending upon how desirable the particular doll is. If your doll has a perfect bisque head with original wig, clothing and shoes, you can probably get up to 75% of its retail value.

As to actually selling the doll, there are several possibilities. Possibly the easiest is to advertise in your local paper. You may not think there are any doll collectors in your area, but there probably are. You might also check your local paper to see if anyone is advertising to purchase dolls; many dealers and collectors do so. Check the paper to find out about antique shows in your area. If anyone has dolls, ask if they would be interested in buying your doll. Also, you could inquire at antique shops in your area for dealers who specialize in dolls. You will probably get a higher price from a specialist than a general antique dealer because the former are more familiar with the market for specific dolls. A roster of doll specialists is available from The National Antique Doll Dealers Association, Inc., P.O. Box 50446, Kalamazoo, MI 49005.

You could consign your doll to an auction. If it is a common doll, it will probably do quite well at a local sale. If it is a more rare doll, consider sending it to one of the auction houses that specializes in selling dolls; most of them will accept one doll if it is a good one, and they will probably get the best price for you. It would probably be worth your while to purchase a doll magazine from your local book store, doll shop or newsstand; most doll magazines include ads from auction houses, doll shows and leading dealers. You could advertise in doll magazines, but you might have to ship the doll and guarantee return privileges if the buyer does not like it.

If you cannot find your doll in the **Blue Book**, it might be a good idea to have it professionally appraised. This will involve your paying a fee to have the doll evaluated. We provide this service and can be contacted through the publisher. Many museums and auction houses also appraise dolls.

ALABAMA INDESTRUCTIBLE DOLL

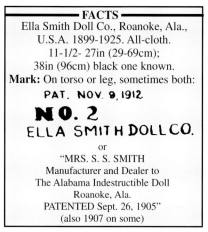

FACTS

Ella Smith Doll Co., Roanoke, Ala.,
U.S.A. 1899-1925. All-cloth.
11-1/2- 27in (29-69cm);
38in (96cm) black one known.
Mark: On torso or leg, sometimes both:

PAT. NOV. 9, 1912

NO. 2
ELLA SMITH DOLL CO.

or

"MRS. S. S. SMITH
Manufacturer and Dealer to
The Alabama Indestructible Doll
Roanoke, Ala.
PATENTED Sept. 26, 1905"
(also 1907 on some)

18in (46cm) *Alabama Indestructible Doll.*
Courtesy of Richard W. Withington, Inc.

Early Alabama Baby: All-cloth painted with oils, tab-jointed shoulders and hips, flat derriere for sitting; painted hair with circular seam on head, molded face with painted facial features; applied ears; painted stockings and shoes (a few with bare feet); appropriate clothes; all in good condition, some wear acceptable, no repaint or touch up.

11in (28cm)	$ 1400 - 1600
14-15in (36-38cm)	1400 - 1600
21-24in (53-61cm)	2500 - 3000
Black, 14-19in (36-48cm)	6600**
Wigged, 24in (61cm)	3500**

Later doll: molded ears, bobbed hairdo.

14-15in (36-38cm)	800 - 1000
21-24in (53-61cm)	2000 - 2500
Black, 14-19in (36-48cm)	3000

**Not enough price samples to compute a reliable average.

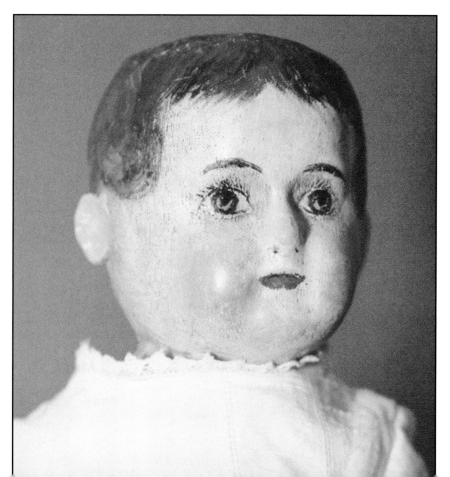

MADAME ALEXANDER

13in (33cm) cloth baby, all original. *H & J Foulke, Inc.*

FACTS

Alexander Doll Co. Inc.,
New York, N.Y., U.S.A.
1923 - on, but as early
as 1912 the Alexander
sisters were designing
doll clothes and dressing
dolls commercially.
Mark: Dolls themselves
marked in various ways,
usually "ALEXAN-
DER." Clothing has a
white cloth label with
blue lettering sewn into
a seam which says
"MADAME ALEXAN-
DER" and usually the
name of the specific
doll. Cloth and other
early dolls are unmarked
and identifiable only by
the clothing label.

CLOTH

Cloth Character Dolls: Ca. 1933 through the 1930s. All-cloth with one-piece arms and legs sewn on; mohair wig, molded mask face of felt or flocked fabric, painted eyes to the side, original tagged clothes. Produced characters from *Little Women*, Charles Dickens, Longfellow and other literary works, as well as storybook characters. (See page 20 for *Little Women* photograph.)

16in (41cm) only:

Fair	**$200 - 250**
Good	**350 - 400**
Excellent	**650 - 700**

20in (51cm) **Alice:**

Fair	**200 - 250**
Good	**350 - 400**
Excellent	**650 - 700**

Bunny Belle:

13in (33cm) mint, at auction **$ 700**

Cloth Baby: Ca. 1936.

13in (33cm) very good	**$250 - 300**
17in (43cm) very good	**425 - 475**

Cloth Dionne Quintuplet: Ca. 1935. (For photograph see *6th Blue Book*, page 18.)

17in (43cm) very good	**$ 800**
24in (61cm) very good	**1100 - 1200**

Susie Q. & Bobby Q.: Ca. 1938. (For photograph see *6th Blue Book*, page 19.)

12-16in (31 - 41cm) very good

$ 600 - 650

Little Shaver: 1942. Yarn hair. Very good condition. (For photograph see *10th Blue Book*, page 34.)

10-12in (25 - 31cm)	**$ 350 - 400**
20in (51cm)	**500 - 550**

Kamkins-type (hard felt face). Very good condition.

20in (51cm) **$ 550 - 650**

COMPOSITION

Dionne Quintuplets: 1935. All-composition with swivel head, jointed hips and shoulders, toddler or bent-limb legs (some babies have cloth bodies with composition lower limbs); wigs or molded hair, sleep or painted eyes; original tagged clothing, all in excellent condition.

7-8in (18 - 20cm)	$ 250 - 275
Matched set	1500
10in (25cm) baby	325 - 350
11-12in (28 - 31cm) toddler	375 - 425
14in (36cm) toddler	475 - 525
16in (41cm) baby with cloth body	450
20in (51cm) toddler	650 - 700
23-24in (58 - 61cm) baby with cloth body	550 - 650
Pins, each	90 - 100

Each Quint has her own color for clothing:
Yvonne - pink
Annette - yellow
Cecile - green
Emelie - lavender
Marie - blue

Children: Ca. 1935 to mid 1940s. All-composition with one-piece head and body on smaller ones and separate head on larger ones, jointed shoulders and hips; mohair wig, painted eyes; original tagged clothes; all in excellent condition. (For photograph see page 8.)
7-9in (18 - 23cm)

Foreign Countries	$ 175 - 200
Storybook Characters	200 - 250 up
Special Outfits	250 up
Birthday Dolls	325 - 375
Bride and Bridesmaids	225 each

Little Colonel: 1935.
13in (33cm) 550 - 650
Unnamed Girl: Dimples, sleep eyes. Ca. 1935. 13in (33cm) 325 - 350
Nurse: Ca. 1935. (For photograph see *11th Blue Book*, page 19.)
13in (33cm) 600 - 700
Betty: Ca. 1935. Painted or sleep eyes, wigged or molded hair.
13in (33cm) 325 - 350
19in (48cm) 675 - 725
Topsy Turvy: Ca. 1936.
7-1/2in (19cm) 185 - 210

19in (48cm) ***Betty***, all original. *H & J Foulke, Inc.*

20in (51cm) ***Dionne Quintuplet Emelie***, all original. *H & J Foulke, Inc.*

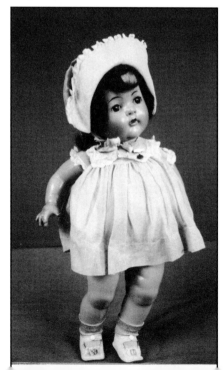

16in (41cm) cloth *Little Women*, all original. *H & J Foulke, Inc.* (For further information see page 18.)

16in (41cm) *Little Genius*, all original. *H & J Foulke, Inc.* (For further information see page 22.)

13in (33cm) *Princess Elizabeth*, all original. *H & J Foulke, Inc.* (For further information see page 22.)

16in (41cm) **McGuffey Ana**, all original.
H & J Foulke, Inc. (For further information
see page 22.)

16in (41cm) **Snow White**, all original.
H & J Foulke, Inc. (For further information see page 22.)

16in (41cm) **Special Girl**, all original. *H & J
Foulke, Inc.* (For further information see
page 23.)

MADAME ALEXANDER COMPOSITION *continued*

Marionettes: 1935. Character faces.
10-12in (25 - 30cm)

Tony Sarg	$ 225 - 250
Disney	350 - 400

Babies: 1936-on. "Little Genius (See photograph on page 20)," "Baby McGuffey," "Precious," "Butch," "Bitsey." Composition head, hands and legs, cloth bodies; molded hair or wigged, sleep eyes, open or closed mouth; original tagged clothes; all in excellent condition.

11-12in (28-31cm)	$ 225 - 250
16-18in (41-46cm)	375 - 425
24in (61cm)	475 - 525

Pinky, 16-18in (41-46cm) $ 425 - 475

Princess Elizabeth Face: All-composition, jointed at neck, shoulders and hips; mohair or human hair wig, sleeping eyes, open mouth; original tagged clothes; all in excellent condition.
Mark: On head:
"PRINCESS ELIZABETH
ALEXANDER DOLL CO."

Clothing tagged with individual name of doll.

Princess Elizabeth, 1937. (For photograph see page 20.)

13in (33cm) Betty face	$ 300 - 350
16-18in (41-46cm)	425 - 475
22-24in (56-61cm)	550 - 600
27in (69cm)	750 - 800

McGuffey Ana, 1937, braids. (For photograph see page 21.)
9in (23cm) painted eyes,

Wendy face	$ 325 - 375
11in (28cm) closed mouth	375 - 425
15-16in (38-41cm)	475 - 525
20-22in (51-56cm)	600 - 700

Snow White, 1937, closed mouth, black hair. (For photograph see page 21.)

13in (33cm)	$ 400 - 425
16-18in (41-46cm)	500 - 600

Flora McFlimsey, 1938. (For photograph see *11th Blue Book*, page 21.)
15in (38cm) $ 650 - 700

Kate Greenaway, 1938.
16-18in (41-46cm) $ 550 - 600

Wendy Ann Face: All-composition, jointed at neck, shoulders and hips; human hair or mohair wig, sleeping eyes, closed mouth; original tagged clothes; all in excellent condition.

Wendy Ann, 1936. (For photograph see *9th Blue Book*, page 28.)

9in (23cm) painted eyes	$ 300 - 325
14in (36cm) swivel waist	400 - 450
21in (53cm)	600 - 700

Scarlet O'Hara, 1937, black hair, blue or green eyes. (For photograph see *11th Blue Book*, page 21.)

11in (28cm)	$ 500 - 550
14in (36cm)	650 - 750
18in (46cm)	900 - 1000
21in (53cm)	1200 - 1400

Note: Sometimes the name is spelled "Scarlet"; other times "Scarlett."

Bride & Bridesmaids, 1940. (For photograph see *9th Blue Book*, page 28.)

14in (36cm)	$ 275 - 300
18in (46cm)	400 - 450

Portraits, 1940s.
21in (53cm) $ 1500 up

Carmen (Miranda), 1942 (black hair). (For photograph see *7th Blue Book*, page 30.):

9in (23cm) painted eyes	$ 250 - 275
14-15in (36-38cm)	350 - 400

Fairy Princess or **Fairy Queen,** 1942. (For photograph see *8th Blue Book*, page 28.)
18in (46cm) $ 500 - 600

Armed Forces Dolls, 1942. (For photograph see *7th Blue Book*, page 29.)
WAAC, WAVE, WAAF, Soldier, Marine
14in (36cm) $ 600 - 700

Miss America, 1939.
14in (36cm) $ 550 - 650

Sleeping Beauty, Cinderella. Ca. 1941. (For photograph see *11th Blue Book*, page 21.)
14in (36cm) $ 375 - 425

Special Face Dolls:

Dr. Dafoe, 1936. (The Quintuplets' doctor). (For photograph see *11th Blue Book*, page 23.)

14in (36cm)	$	**1200 up**

Jane Withers, 1937.

13in (33cm) closed mouth	$	**850 - 900**
15-16in (38-41cm)		**1000 - 1100**
21in (53cm)		**1500**

Sonja Henie, 1939. (For photograph see *10th Blue Book*, page 39.) 14in (36cm) can be found on Wendy-Ann body with swivel waist.

14in (36cm)	$	**450 - 500**
18in (46cm)		**700 - 800**
21in (53cm)		**900 - 1000**

Jeannie Walker, 1941. (For photograph see *10th Blue Book*, page 39.)

13 - 14in (33 - 36cm)	$	**475 - 525**
18in (46cm)		**650 - 700**

Baby Jane, 1935.

16in (41cm)	**$850 - 950**

Special Girl, 1942, cloth body. (For photograph see page 21.)

22in (56cm)	**$450 - 550**
16in (41cm)	**400**

Margaret Face: All-composition, jointed at neck, shoulders and hips; human hair, mohair, or floss wig, sleeping eyes, closed mouth; original tagged clothes; all in excellent condition.

Margaret O'Brien, 1946. (For photograph see page 24.) (dark braided wig):

14in (36cm)	$	**650 - 750**
18in (46cm)		**850 - 950**

Karen Ballerina, 1946. (For photograph see *8th Blue Book*, page 29.) (blonde wig in coiled braids):

18in (46cm)	$	**650 - 750**

Alice-in-Wonderland, 1947. (For photograph see *11th Blue Book*, page 23.)

14in (36cm)	$	**400 - 450**
18in (46cm)		**500 - 550**

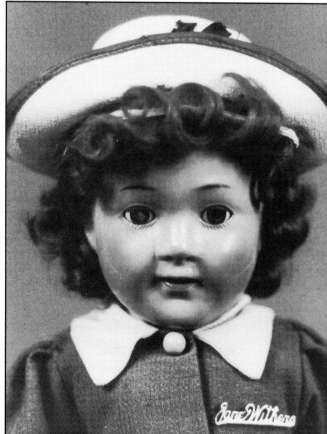

17in (43cm) *Jane Withers*, all original. *H & J Foulke, Inc.*

14in (36cm) *Margaret O'Brien*, all original. *H & J Foulke, Inc.* (For further information see page 23.)

18in (46cm) **Wendy Bride**, all original. *H & J Foulke, Inc.* (For further information see page 26.)

18in (46cm) **Snow White**, #1835, 1952, all original. *H & J Foulke, Inc.* (For further information see page 26.)

HARD PLASTIC
Margaret Face: 1948-on. All-hard plastic, jointed at neck, shoulders and hips; lovely wig, sleep eyes, closed mouth; original tagged clothes; all in excellent condition.

Babs, 1948 - 1949.*

14in (36cm)	$	500 - 600

Bride, Pink, 1950.

14in (36cm)	600 - 650

Cinderella, 1950.*

14in (36cm)	650 - 700

Cynthia (black), 1952 - 1953.

14in (36cm)	750 - 850

Fairy Queen, 1947 - 1948.*

14in (36cm)	550 - 600

Glamour Girls, 1953.*

18in (46cm)	1250

Godey Ladies, 1950.*

14in (36cm)	1100 - 1200

Margaret O'Brien, 1948.*

14in (36cm)	800 - 900

Margaret Rose, 1948-1953.*

14in (36cm)	500 - 600

Mary Martin, 1950.

14in (36cm)	750 - 850

Nina Ballerina, 1949-1951.

14in (36cm)	500 - 600
18in (46cm)	650 - 700

Prince Charming, 1950.

14in (36cm)	700 - 750

Prince Philip, Ca. 1950.*

18in (46cm)	750 - 850

Queen Elizabeth, 1953.

18in (46cm) with cape	1250
no cape	750 - 850

Snow White, 1952. (For photograph see page 25.)

14in (36cm)	550 - 650
18in (46cm)	800 - 900

Story Princess, 1954 - 1956.

14in (36cm)	550 - 650

Wendy-Ann, 1947 - 1948.

18in (46cm)	700 - 800

Wendy Bride, 1950.* (For photograph see page 25.)

14in (36cm)	400 - 450
18in (46cm)	500 - 600

Wendy (from Peter Pan set), 1953.

14in (36cm)	500 - 600

Maggie Face: 1948 - 1956. All hard plastic, jointed at neck, shoulders and hips; good quality wig, sleep eyes, closed mouth, original tagged clothes; all in excellent condition.

Alice in Wonderland, 1950 - 1951.*

17in (43cm)	$	600 - 650

Annabelle, 1952.*

15in (38cm)	475 - 525

Glamour Girls, 1953.*

18in (46cm)	1250

Godey Man, 1950.*

14in (36cm)	900 - 1000

John Powers Models

14in (36cm)	1500

Kathy, 1951.*

14in (36cm)	650 - 700

Margot Ballerina, 1953.

14in (36cm)	500 - 600

Maggie, 1948 - 1953.*

14in (36cm)	450 - 500
17in (43cm)	575 - 625

Me and My Shadow, 1954.

18in (46cm)	1200

Peter Pan, 1953.*

15in (38cm)	700 - 800

Polly Pigtails, 1949.

14in (36cm)	475 - 525
17in (43cm)	600 - 700

Rosamund Bridesmaid, 1953.*

15in (38cm)	475 - 525

Little Women: 1948-1956. All hard plastic, jointed at neck, shoulders and hips; synthetic wig, sleep eyes, closed mouth, original tagged clothes; all in excellent condition. Some models have jointed knees.
"Maggie" face: "Jo" and "Beth."
"Margaret" face: "Amy," "Marme" and "Meg."

14-15in (36-38cm)	
Floss hair, 1948 - 1950	$ 425 - 475 each
Amy, loop curls.	525
Dynel hair	325 - 375 each
Little Men, 1952	850 each

*For photographs see *Treasury of Mme. Alexander Dolls.*

14in (36cm) *Marme*, all original. *H & J Foulke, Inc.*

12in (31cm) *Baby Genius*, all original. *H & J Foulke, Inc.*

Babies: 1948-1951. Hard plastic head, hands and legs; cloth body; synthetic wig, sleep eyes, closed mouth; original tagged clothes; excellent condition.

"Baby Genius":

12in (31cm)	$ 225 - 250
16-18in (41-46cm)	325 - 350

Cissy: 1955-1959. Head, torso and jointed legs of hard plastic, jointed vinyl arms; synthetic wig, sleep eyes, closed mouth, pierced ears; original tagged clothes; all in excellent condition with perfect hair and rosy cheeks.

(For photograph see page 28.)

21in (53cm)

Street clothes	$ 375 - 425
Gowns	475 up
Elaborate fashion gowns	700 up
Queen	750 - 850
Bride	475 - 575
Lady in Red #2285, at auction	2090
Pink gown #2100, at auction	1870
Godey Portrait	1650
Ice Capades	1870

21in (53cm) *Cissy*, #2017, 1956, all original. *H & J Foulke, Inc.*
(For further information see page 27.)

Winnie and Binnie: 1953-1955. All-hard plastic, walking body, later with jointed knees and vinyl arms; lovely wig, sleep eyes, closed mouth; original tagged clothes; all in excellent condition.

15in (38cm)	**$ 300 - 350**
18in (46cm)	**400 - 450**
25in (63cm)	**500**

Mary Ellen,

31in (79cm)	**550 - 600**

Sweet Violet, fully-jointed body, 1954.

18in (46cm)	**1000 up**

18in (46cm) *Sweet Violet*, fully-jointed hard plastic body, all original. *H & J Foulke, Inc.*

12in (31cm) *Lissy Beth*, all original. *H & J Foulke, Inc.*

Alexander-Kins: 1953-to present. All hard plastic, jointed at neck, shoulders and hips; synthetic wig, sleep eyes, closed mouth; original clothes; all in excellent condition. (For photograph, see page 12.)
7-1/2–8in (19-20cm)
1953, straight leg non-walker
1954-1955, straight-leg walker
1956-1964, bent-knee walker
1965-1972, bent knee
1973-current, straight leg

Wendy, basic (panties, shoes and socks), through 1964, boxed.	$	275 - 325
Wendy, in dresses, 1953-1964		350 - 450
in riding habit		325 - 375
Wendy Ballerina, 1957-1965		350 - 450
Quizkin, 1953	$	450 - 550
Little Women, set of 5, 1956-1964		1000 - 1200

Wendy in Special Outfits:

Billy or Bobby	$	450 - 500
Parlor Maid		800 up
Prince Charles		800 up
Princess Ann		800 up
My Shadow		1000
Cherry Twin, each		900
Little Minister, 1957		1500
Groom, 1956-1972		450
Bride, 1955-1960		350
Baby Clown, 1955		1200 up
Nurse, 1956-1965		450 - 500
Parlour Maid, 1956		1000 up

Lissy: 1956-1958. All-hard plastic, jointed at neck, shoulders, hips, elbows and knees; synthetic wig, sleep eyes, closed mouth; original clothes; all in excellent condition.

12in (31cm)	$	300 - 400
Boxed with trousseau		1200 - 1500
Kelly, 1959*		400 - 500
Little Women, 1957-1967		200 - 250
Southern Belle, 1963*		1000 up
McGuffey Ana, 1963*		1000 up
Laurie, 1967*		450
Pamela, 1962-1963*		
Boxed with wigs		900 - 1000

Elise: 1957-1964. All-hard plastic with vinyl arms, completely jointed; synthetic wig,

sleep eyes, closed mouth; original tagged clothes; all in excellent condition. (For photograph see *11th Blue Book*, page 28.)
16-1/2–17in (42-43cm)

Street clothes	$	300
Gowns		375 up
Bride, Ballerina		350
Elaborate fashion gowns		500 up
Sleeping Beauty		550 - 600
Vinyl head, 1964		250

(For photograph see page 32.)

Cissette: 1957-1963. All hard-plastic, jointed at neck, shoulders, hips and knees; synthetic wig, sleep eyes, closed mouth, pierced ears; original tagged clothes; all in excellent condition with perfect hair and rosy cheeks. (For photographs see *Treasury of Mme. Alexander Dolls*, pages 79 - 84.)
Mark: None on doll
On dress tag: "Cissette"

10in (25cm) Cissette	$	225 up
Basic Cissette, mint and boxed		
		200 - 225
Gold Ballerina		450 - 500
Portrettes, 1968-1973		450 - 500
Gibson Girl, 1962-1963		700 - 800
Gold Rush, 1963		1200 - 1500
Jacqueline, 1962		475 - 575
Portrettes, 1986 to present		50 - 100
Sleeping Beauty, 1959-1960		350 - 450
Margot, 1961		300 - 400

Shari Lewis: 1959. All-hard plastic with slim fashion body; auburn hair, brown eyes, closed mouth; original tagged clothes; all in excellent condition. (For photographs see *5th Blue Book*, page 17.)

14in (36cm)	$	400 - 500
21in (53cm)		600 - 700

Maggie Mixup: 1960-1961. All-hard plastic, fully-jointed; red straight hair, green eyes, closed mouth, freckles; original tagged clothes; all in excellent condition. (For photograph see *6th Blue Book*, page 32.)

16-1/2–17in (42-43cm)	$	350 - 400
8in (20cm)		450 - 550
8in (20cm) angel		800 - 1000
Little Lady Gift Set		500 - 600

* For photographs see *Treasury of Mme. Alexander Dolls*, pages 74-78.

VINYL

Kelly Face: 1958-on. Vinyl character face with rooted hair, vinyl arms, hard plastic torso and legs, jointed waist; original tagged clothes; all in excellent condition. (For photograph see *9th Blue Book*, page 37.)

Kelly, 1958-1959.	
15in (38cm)	$ 225 - 250
Pollyana, 1960-1961.	
15in (38cm)	225 - 250
Marybel, 1959-1965.	
15in (38cm), in case	275 - 325
Edith, 1958-1959.	
15in (38cm)	225 - 250
Elise, 1962. (For photograph see page	
32.) 15in (38cm)	275 - 325

Jacqueline: 1961-1962. Vinyl and hard plastic; rooted dark hair, sleep eyes, closed mouth; original tagged clothes; all in excellent condition.

21in (53cm), Suit	$ 550 - 650
Riding habit	525 - 575
Brocade gown	650 - 700

Caroline: 1961-1962. Hard plastic and vinyl; rooted blonde hair, smiling character face; original tagged clothes; in excellent condition.

15in (38cm)	$250 - 300
Riding Habit	350

Janie: 1964-1966. Vinyl and hard plastic with rooted hair, impish face, pigeon-toed and knock-kneed; original tagged clothes; all in excellent condition.

12in (31cm)	$ 225 - 250
Lucinda, 1969-1970	250 - 275
Rozy, 1969	275 - 300
Suzy, 1970	275 - 300

Brenda Starr: 1964. Vinyl and hard plastic with rooted red hair, sleeping eyes; adult body; original tagged clothes; all in excellent condition. (For photograph see page 33.)

12in (31cm)	$ 225

Smarty: 1962-1963. Hard plastic and vinyl, smiling character face with rooted hair, knock-kneed and pigeon-toed; original tagged clothes; in excellent condition.

12in (31cm)	$ 200 - 250
with baby	300 - 350
Katie (black), 1965	350 - 400
Brother	225 - 275

Polly Face: 1965. All-vinyl with rooted hair, jointed at neck, shoulders and hips; original tagged clothes; all in excellent condition.

17in (43cm)	
Polly	$ 225 - 275
Leslie (black)	
(See photograph on page 33.)	300 - 400

Mary Ann Face: 1965 to present. Vinyl head and arms, hard plastic torso and legs; appropriate synthetic wig, sleep eyes; original clothes; all in excellent condition.

14in (35cm) only:	
Easter Girl, 1968.	$ 750 - 850
Scarlett #1495, flowered gown, 1968	
	450 - 500
Disney Snow White, 1967-1977.	
	400 - 450
Jenny Lind, 1970-1971.	350 - 400

Discontinued Dolls	
1965-1982	$ 100 - 200
1982-1992	50 - 90

Babies: 1960s to present. Vinyl head, arms and legs, cloth body; sleeping eyes, appropriate synthetic hair; original tagged clothes; all in excellent condition.

Baby Lynn, 1973-1976.	
20in (51cm)	$ 100 - 125
Mary Cassatt Baby, 1969-1970.	
20in (51cm)	175 - 225
Black Pussy Cat, 20in (51cm)	75 - 100
Slumbermate, closed eyes, 1951.	
13in (33cm)	150
Black Baby Ellen, 1965-1972.	
14in (35cm) all vinyl	75 - 100
Baby Brother, 1977-1979.	
20in (51cm)	75 - 100

16in (41cm) *Elise*, #1720, 1964, vinyl head, all original. *H & J Foulke, Inc.* (For further information see page 31.)

16in (41cm) *Leslie*, #1651, 1965, all original. *H & J Foulke, Inc.* (For further information see page 31.)

12in (31cm) *Brenda Starr*, #915, 1964, all original and boxed. *H & J Foulke, Inc.* (For further information see page 31.)

Sound of Music: Hard plastic and vinyl with appropriate synthetic wigs and sleep eyes; original tagged clothes; all in excellent conditon.

Small set, 1965-1970.

8in (20cm) Friedrich	$	175 - 200
8in (20cm) Gretl		175 - 200
8in (20cm) Marta		175 - 200
10in (25cm) Brigitta		200
12in (31cm) Maria		275
10in (25cm) Louisa		275
10in (25cm) Liesl		200

Large set*, 1971-1973.

11in (28cm) Friedrich	$	175 - 200
11in (28cm) Gretl		175 - 200
11in (28cm) Marta		175 - 200
14in (36cm) Brigitta		175 - 200
17in (43cm) Maria		275
14in (36cm) Louisa		250
14in (36cm) Liesl		175 - 200
11in (28cm) Kurt (sailor)		350

*Allow considerably more for sailor outfits.

Coco: 1966. Vinyl and hard plastic, rooted blonde hair, jointed waist, right leg bent slightly at knee; original tagged clothes; all in excellent condition. This face was also used for the 1966 portrait dolls.

21in (53cm)	$	1800 - 2000
1966 Portrait Dolls		1800 - 2000

Elise: 1966-1991. Redesigned vinyl face, rooted hair; original tagged clothes; all in excellent condition. (For photograph see *11th Blue Book*, page 34.)

17in (43cm)

Elise	$	125 - 175
Marlo, 1967		500 - 600
Maggie, 1972-1973		200 - 250

Peter Pan Set: 1969. Vinyl and hard plastic with appropriate wigs and sleep eyes; original tagged clothes; all in excellent condition.

14in (36cm) Peter Pan	$	200 - 225
14in (36cm) Wendy		200 - 225
12in (31cm) Michael		250
10in (25cm) Tinker Bell		300

Nancy Drew Face: 1967-1992. Vinyl head and arms, hard plastic torso and legs; appropriate synthetic wig, sleep eyes; original tagged clothes; all in excellent condition.

12in (31cm) only:

Nancy Drew, 1967	$	200 - 225
Renoir Child, 1967		150 - 200
Pamela with wigs, 1962 - 1963		500
Romantic Couples		75 - 100 pair

First Ladies: 1976-1989. Hard plastic and vinyl with rooted synthetic hair individually styled and sleep eyes; original tagged clothes; in mint condition. "Martha" and "Mary Ann" faces.

14in (36cm)	$	60 - 90

HENRI ALEXANDRE

H.A. Bébé: 1889-1891. Perfect bisque socket head, closed mouth, paperweight eyes, pierced ears, good wig; jointed composition and wood body; lovely clothes; all in good condition.

Mark:

17-19in (43-48cm)   **$ 5500 - 6500****

Bébé Phénix: 1889-1900. Perfect bisque head, closed mouth, paperweight eyes, pierced ears, good wig; composition body sometimes with one-piece arms and legs; well dressed; all in good condition.
Mark: Red Stamp Incised

PHÉNIX
★ 95

Approximate Size Chart:
*81 = 10in (25cm)
*84 = 12in (31cm)
*85 = 14in (36cm)
*88 = 17in (43cm)
*90 = 18in (46cm)
*92 = 19-21in (48-53cm)
*93 = 22in (56cm)
*94 = 23-24in (58-61cm)
*95 = 23-25in (58-64cm)

13-14in (33-36cm)	$ 2650 - 3000
17-18in (43-46cm)	3600 - 4000
22-23in (56-58cm)	4500 - 5000

Open Mouth:
    17-19in (43-48cm) $ 2000 - 2200

**Not enough price samples to compute a reliable range.

FACTS

Henri Alexandre, Paris, France, 1888-1892; Tourrel 1892-1895; Jules Steiner and successors 1895-1901. Bisque head, jointed composition body.
Designer: Henri Alexandre.
Trademark: Bébé Phénix.

24in (61cm) *Phénix Bébé*
★ 94. *H & J Foulke, Inc.*

ALL-BISQUE DOLLS (So-Called French)

All-Bisque French Doll: Jointed at shoulders and hips, swivel neck, slender arms and legs; good wig, glass eyes, closed mouth; molded shoes or boots and stockings; appropriately dressed; all in good condition, with proper parts. (For additional photograph, see page 8.)

5in (13cm)	$ 1050 - 1150*
6in (15cm)	1800 - 2000*
With bare feet,	
5in (13cm)	1250 - 1350*
6in (15cm)	1900 - 2100*
8in (20cm)	4200 - 4500**

With jointed elbows and knees,	
5-1/2in (14cm)	3500**
With jointed elbows,	
5-1/2in (14cm)	2400 - 2600**
Painted eyes,	
4–4-1/2in (10-12cm)	
all original	750 - 850

*Allow extra for original clothes.

**Not enough price samples to compute a reliable range.

FACTS
Various French and/or German firms. Ca. 1880-on. Various small sizes, 4-10in (10-25cm). Smiling-faced dolls made by Simon & Halbig for the French trade.
Mark: None, sometimes numbers.

6-1/4in (16cm) French all-bisque, rare with brown wig. *H & J Foulke, Inc.*

ALL-BISQUE DOLLS (German)

All-Bisque with molded clothes: Ca. 1890-on. Many by Hertwig & Co. Jointed at shoulders (sometimes hips), molded and painted clothes or underwear; molded and painted hair, sometimes with molded hat, painted eyes, closed mouth; molded shoes and socks (if in underwear often barefoot); good quality work; all in good condition, with proper parts.

Children:

3-1/2-4in (9-10cm)	$ 115- 150
5-6in (13-15cm)	175 - 225
7in (18cm)	250 - 275

Punch, Judy and other white bisque characters:

3-4in (8-10cm)	$ 95 - 110

Characters, fine quality; clown, acrobat, oriental and others:

4in (10cm)	$ 325 - 375

┌─────────── **FACTS** ───────────┐

Various firms including Amberg; Alt, Beck & Gottschalck; Kestner; Kling; Simon & Halbig; Hertel, Schwab & Co.; Bähr & Pröschild; Limbach; Ca. 1880-on. Various small sizes, most under 12in (31cm).

Mark: Some with "Germany" and/or numbers; some with paper labels on stomachs.

└─────────────────────────────────┘

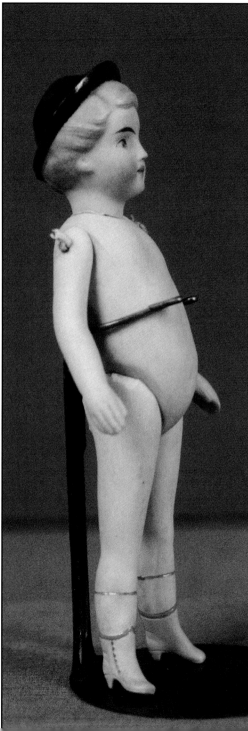

7in (18cm) early face, molded hat, swivel neck. *H & J Foulke, Inc.* (For further information see page 38.)

All-Bisque Slender Dolls: Ca. 1880-on. Jointed usually by wire or pegging at shoulders and hips, stationary neck, slender arms and legs; good wig, glass eyes, closed mouth; molded shoes or boots and stockings; dressed or undressed; many in regional costumes; all in good condition, with proper parts. (For photograph see *11th Blue Book,* page 38.)

3in (8cm)	$	225 - 250
3-3/4-4in (9-10cm)		185 - 210
5-6in (13-15cm)		300 - 350
Swivel neck:		
4in (10cm)		325 - 375
5-1/2in-6in (14-15cm)		525 - 575
4in (10cm) 10a or 39/11		225 - 250
5-1/2in (14cm) 13a		325 - 350
Black or Mulatto:		
4-4-1/2in (10-12cm)		325 - 375
Swivel neck:		
5in (13cm)		500

All-Bisque with painted eyes: Ca. 1880-1910. Jointed at shoulders, stiff or jointed hips, stationary neck; molded and painted hair or mohair wig, painted eyes, closed mouth; molded and painted shoes and stockings; fine quality work; dressed or undressed; all in good condition, with proper parts.

1-1/4in (3cm) crocheted clothes		
	$	65 - 85
1-1/2-2in (4-5cm)		75 - 85
4-5in (10-13cm)		175 - 200
6-7in (15-18cm)		225 - 275
Swivel neck:		
2-1/2in (6cm) all original		150 - 175
3-1/4in (8cm) molded hair		225 - 250
4-5in (10-13cm)		225 - 275
Early round face, bootines:		
4-5in (10-13cm)		225 - 275
6–6-1/2in (15-16cm)		325 - 375
8in (20cm)		650 - 675
Early face, molded hat, swivel neck:		
7in (18cm)		2750 - 3000**
Black stockings, tan slippers:		
6in (15cm)		375 - 425

** Not enough price samples to compute a reliable range.

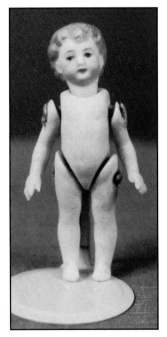

3-1/4in (8cm) molded hair, swivel neck. *H & J Foulke, Inc.*

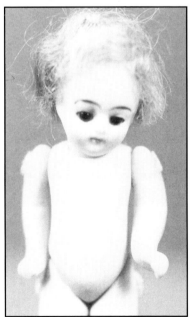

3-1/2in (9cm) early face, pink shirred hose. *H & J Foulke, Inc.*

ALL-BISQUE DOLLS (GERMAN) *continued*

6-1/4in (16cm) early girl with bootines.
H & J Foulke, Inc.

5in (13cm) girl with yellow boots.
H & J Foulke, Inc.

Early face, pink or blue shirred hose:

4-1/2in (12cm)	$ 185 - 210
6in (15cm)	350 - 375
8in (20cm)	575 - 625

Early face (molded hair):

3-3/4in–4-1/2in (9-11cm)	160 - 185
6-7in (15-18cm)	275 - 325

Molded hat: (For photograph see *11th Blue Book*, page 37.)

3-3/4in (9cm)	300 - 325

All-Bisque with glass eyes: Ca. 1890-1910. Very good quality bisque, jointed at shoulders, stiff or jointed hips; good wig, glass eyes, closed mouth (sometimes open); molded and painted shoes and stockings; dressed or undressed; all in good condition, with proper parts. Very good quality.

3in (8cm)	$ 275 - 325*
4-1/2–5in (11-13cm)	275 - 325*
6in (15cm)	350 - 375*
7in (18cm)	400 - 450*
8in (20cm)	500 - 550*
9in (23cm)	700 - 800
10in (25cm)	900 -1000
12in (31cm)	1300 -1400

Early style model, stiff hips, shirred hose or bootines:

3in (8cm)	$ 325
4-1/2in (11cm)	325 - 350
6in (15cm)	500 - 550
7in (18cm)	625 - 675
8-1/2in (21cm)	850 - 950

* Allow $50-100 extra for yellow boots or unusual footwear and/or especially fine quality.

8in (20cm) early Simon & Halbig-type girl with open mouth. *H & J Foulke, Inc.* (For further information see page 42.)

7-1/2in (19cm) girl with long black stockings, tan slippers. *H & J Foulke, Inc.* (For further information see page 42.)

5-1/2in (14cm) early Kestner with bare feet. *H & J Foulke, Inc.* (For further information see page 42.)

6-1/2in (17cm) 816 baby. *H & J Foulke, Inc.* (For further information see page 42.)

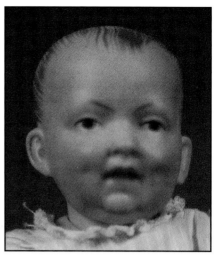

6-1/2in (17cm) 257 girl. *H & J Foulke, Inc.* (For further information see page 43.)

4in (10cm) 260 baby with molded clothes. *H & J Foulke, Inc.* (For further information see page 42.)

ALL-BISQUE DOLLS (GERMAN) *continued*

All-Bisque with swivel neck and glass eyes: Ca. 1880-1910. Swivel neck, loop strung or pegged shoulders and hips; good wig, glass eyes, closed or open mouth; molded and painted shoes or boots and stockings; dressed or undressed; all in good condition, with proper parts. Very good quality. (See photographs on page 40.)

3-1/4in (8cm)	$	350 - 375
4–4-1/2in (10-12cm)		`375 - 425*
5-6in (13-15cm)		550 - 650*
7in (18cm)		750 - 800*
8in (20cm)		900 - 1000*
9in (23cm)		1100 - 1200*
10in (25cm)		1300 - 1500

Early Kestner or S&H-type:

5in (13cm)	$	1250 - 1350
6in (15cm)		1450 - 1650
8in (20cm)		2100 - 2300
10in (25cm)		2800 - 3000

With swivel waist:

5-1/2–6in (14-15cm)	5000**

With jointed knee:

8in (20cm)	3850 - 4000

#102 (So-called: "Wrestler"):

6-1/2in (16cm)	1350 - 1500
8-1/2in (22cm)	1850 - 2000
9-1/2in (24cm)	2200 - 2400

#120 (Bru-type face):

8-1/2in (22cm)	2500**

Bare feet:

5-1/2–6in (14-15cm)	1800 - 1950
8in (20cm)	2600 - 2800
12in (31cm)	4500 - 5000**

Round face, bootines:

6in (15cm)	1000 - 1100
8in (20cm)	1650 - 1850

Long black stockings, tan slippers,

7-1/2in (19cm)	950

Simon & Halbig 886 and 890: See page 331.

*Allow $100-150 extra for yellow boots or unusual footwear.

All-Bisque Baby: 1900-on. Jointed at shoulders and hips with curved arms and legs; molded and painted hair, painted eyes; not dressed; all in good condition, with proper parts.

2-1/2–3-1/2in (6-9cm)	$	75 - 95
4in (10cm)		150 - 175
5in (13cm)		175 - 195

Fine early quality blonde molded hair: (For photograph see *11th Blue Book*, page 41.)

3-1/2–4-1/2in (9-11cm)	160 - 185
6-7in (15-18cm)	250 - 300
9in (23cm)	600 - 700
13in (33cm)	900 - 1100
5-6in (13-15cm) immobile	150 - 175

All-Bisque Character Baby: Ca. 1910. Jointed at shoulders and hips, curved arms and legs; molded hair, painted eyes, character face; undressed; all in good condition, with proper parts.

3-1/2in (9cm)	$	95 - 110
4-1/2–5-1/2in (11-14cm)		175 - 225
7in (18cm)		275 - 325
8in (20cm)		375 - 425

#830, #391, and others with glass eyes:

4-5in (10-13cm)	275 - 325
6in (15cm)	400 - 450
8in (20cm)	600 - 650

Swivel neck, glass eyes:

6in (15cm)	550 - 575
8in (20cm)	725 - 775
10in (25cm)	950 - 1000

Swivel neck, painted eyes:

5 - 6in (13 - 15cm)	325 - 375
8in (20cm)	475 - 525
11in (28cm)	775 - 875

#260, Molded clothes: (For photograph see page 41.)

4in (10cm)	250 - 275

**Not enough sample prices to compute a reliable average.

Later All-Bisque with glass eyes: Ca. 1910 on. Many of pretinted pink bisque. Jointed at shoulders and hips; good wig, glass eyes, closed or open mouth; molded and painted black one-strap shoes and stockings; dressed or undressed; all in good condition, with proper parts.

Good smooth bisque:

4 - 5in (10 - 13cm)	$ 150 - 185
6in (15cm)	225 - 250
7in (18cm)	300

Grainy bisque:

4-1/2in (12cm)	95
6in (15cm)	150

All-Bisque Character Dolls: 1913-on. Character faces with well-painted features and molded hair. All in good condition with proper parts.

Pink bisque:

2-3in (5-8cm)	$ 50 - 60
5in (13cm)	95
Thumbsucker, 3in (8cm)	225 - 250
Girl with molded hair bow loop,	
2-1/2in (6cm)	65 - 75
Chubby, 4-1/2in (11cm)	200 - 210
6in (15cm)	325 - 375
HEbee, SHEbee, 6in (15cm)	600
7in (18cm)	700 - 800
Peterkin, 5-6in (13-15cm)	250 - 275
Little Imp, 5in (13cm)	125 - 150
Orsini girls, 5in (13cm)	
glass eyes	1250 - 1450
painted eyes	900
Happifats,	
4in (10cm) boy and girl	500 - 600 pair
Happifats Baby,	
3-3/4in (10cm)	275 - 300
Baby Bud, glass eyes, wig and box,	
7in (18cm) at auction	1300

All-Bisque with character face: Ca. 1915. Jointed at shoulders and hips; smiling character face, closed or open mouth; molded and painted shoes and stockings; dressed or undressed; all in good condition, with proper parts. Very good quality.

#150 open/closed mouth with two painted teeth, dimples. (For photograph see *9th Blue Book*, page 49.)

Glass eyes:

5-6in (13-15cm)	$ 350 - 450
8-9in (20-23cm)	700 - 800

Painted eyes:

4-1/2–5-1/2in (11-14cm)	**175 - 225**
7in (18cm)	**300 - 350**

#602 Kestner, swivel neck glass eyes (For photograph see *10th Blue Book*, page 59.)

5-1/2–6in (14-15cm)	**550 - 650**

#155, 156, smiling face. (For photograph see *8th Blue Book*, page 48.)

6-7in (15-18cm)	**450 - 550**

#167, 168 7in (18cm) **350**

#79 pierced nose, (For photograph see page 45.) 4-1/2in (12cm) **500**

#790, 791, 792

5-1/2–6in (14-15cm)	**450 - 500**

#160 molded hair,

5-1/2–6in (14-15cm)	**300 - 350**

#177, Kestner toddler, 8in (20cm) **800 - 850**
#178, Kestner toddler, 8in (20cm) **950 - 1000**

5in (13cm) Orsini *ViVi*, painted eyes. *H & J Foulke, Inc.*

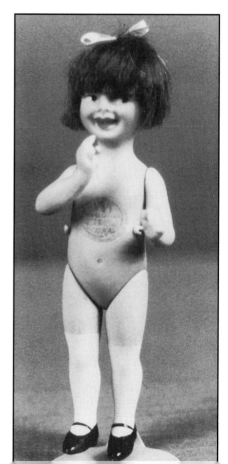

5-3/4in (15cm) 790 character boy. *H & J Foulke, Inc.*

Later All-Bisque with painted eyes: Ca. 1920. Many by Hertwig. Some of pretinted bisque. Jointed at shoulders and hips, stationary neck; mohair wig or molded hair, painted eyes, closed mouth; molded and painted one-strap shoes and white stockings; dressed or undressed; all in good condition, with proper parts. (For photograph see *10th Blue Book, page 60.*)

3-1/2in (9cm)	$ 70 - 80
4-1/2–5in (12-13cm)	100 - 110
6-7in (15-18cm)	160 - 185
8in (20cm)	225 - 250
Swivel neck,	
6-1/2in (16cm)	225 - 250

All-Bisque "Flapper" (tinted bisque): Ca. 1920. Jointed at shoulders and hips; molded bobbed hair with loop for bow, painted features; long yellow stockings, one-strap shoes with heels; dressed or undressed; all in good condition, with proper parts, very good quality. (For photograph see *11th Blue Book*, page 44.)

5in (13cm)	$275 - 300
6-7in (15-18cm)	375 - 425
Standard quality,	
4-5in (10-13cm)	135 - 165

All-Bisque Baby: Ca. 1920. Pink bisque, so-called "Candy Baby," jointed at shoulders and hips, curved arms and legs; painted hair, painted eyes; original factory clothes; all in good condition, with proper parts.

2-1/2–3in (6-8cm)	$ 85 - 95

All-Bisque "Flapper:" Ca. 1920. Pink bisque with wire joints at shoulders and hips; molded bobbed hair and painted features; painted shoes and socks; original factory clothes; all in good condition, with proper parts.

3in (8cm)	$ 75 - 95
Molded hats	200 - 225
Molded bunny ears cap	350
Aviatrix	225
Swivel waist, 3-1/2in (9cm)	350

4-1/2in (11cm) 79 character with pierced nose. *H & J Foulke, Inc.*

All-Bisque Nodder Characters: Ca. 1920-on. Many made by Hertwig & Co. Nodding heads, elastic strung, molded clothes; all in good condition. Decoration is usually not fired, so it wears and washes off very easily. Marked "Germany."

3-4in (8-10cm)	$	50 - 60
Comic characters		75 up*
Dressed Animals		150 - 175
Dressed Teddy Bears		200 - 225
Santa		200 - 225
Dutch Girl, 6in (15cm)		150 - 165
"Hitler Youth" boy and girl		350 pair

3-1/2in (9cm) "Hitler Youth" boy and girl nodders. *H & J Foulke, Inc.*

All-Bisque Immobiles: Ca. 1920. All-bisque figures with molded clothes, molded hair and painted features. Decoration is not fired, so it wears and washes off very easily. Marked "Germany." (For photographs see *10th Blue Book*, page 19.)

Adults and children,	
1-1/2–2-1/4in (4-6cm)	$ 35 - 45
Children, 3-1/4in (8cm)	55 - 65
Santa, 3in (8cm)	125 - 135
Children with animals on string,	
3in (8cm)	150 - 165

Jointed Animals: Ca. 1910-on. All-Bisque animals, wire-jointed shoulders and hips; original crocheted clothes.

Rabbit, 2–2-3/4in (5-7cm)	$ 475 - 525
Bear, 2–2-1/2in (5-6cm)	500 - 550
Frog, Monkey, Pig,	600 - 700
Bear on all fours,	
3-1/4in (8cm)	225

*Depending upon rarity.

Immobile Indian family, adults 2-1/4in (6cm). *H & J Foulke, Inc.*

ALL-BISQUE DOLLS (MADE IN JAPAN)

Baby:
  White, 4in (10cm) $ **30 - 33**
  All original elaborate outfit   **50 - 65**
  Black, 4-5in (10-13cm)   **55 - 65**
Betty Boop-type:
  4-5in (10-13cm)   **20 - 25**
  6-7in (15-18cm)   **32 - 38**
Child:
  4-5in (10-13cm)   **25 - 28**
  6-7in (15-18cm)   **35 - 45**
Comic Characters,
  3-4in (8-10cm)   **25 up***
Mickey Mouse   **50 - 60**
Bride & Groom, boxed set,
  4in (10cm)   **40 - 50**
Stiff Characters:
  3-4in (8-10cm) $ **5 - 10**
  6-7in (15-18cm)   **30 - 35**
Cho-Cho San, 4-1/2in (12cm)   **70 - 80**
Nodders, 4in (10cm)   **25 - 35**
Orientals, 3-4in (8-10cm)   **20 - 25**

Queue San, 4in (10cm)   **70 - 80**
Marked "Nippon" Characters,
  4-5in (10-13cm)   **65 - 75**
Three Bears, boxed set   **175 - 200**
Snow White, boxed set   **350 - 450**
Black Character Girl, molded hair bow
  loop 4-1/2in (12cm)   **40 - 50**
Old Woman in Shoe,
  boxed set   **150 - 175**
Two-face Baby
  (crying and sleeping)   **150 - 175**
Shirley Temple, 5in (13cm)   **95 - 110**
Circus Set, boxed, 11 pieces   **150 - 175**
Three Little Pigs   **40 - 50 each**

*Depending upon rarity.

FACTS

Various Japanese firms. Ca. 1915-on. **Mark:** "Made in Japan" or "NIPPON."

4in (10cm) character baby, all original. *H & J Foulke, Inc.*

ALT, BECK & GOTTSCHALCK

China Shoulder Heads: Ca. 1880. Black or blonde-haired china head; old cloth body with china limbs; dressed; all in good condition. Mold numbers such as 784, 1000, 1008, 1028, 1046, 1142, 1210.

Mark:

1008 ✗9

Also ✗ or *No* in place of ✗

15-17in (38-43cm)	$ 300 - 350
20in (51cm)	375 - 425
22-24in (56-61cm)	450 - 500
28in (71cm)	550 - 600

Bisque Shoulder Head: Ca. 1880. Molded hair, painted or glass eyes, closed mouth; cloth body with bisque lower limbs; dressed; all in good condition. Mold numbers, such as 890, 990, 1000, 1008, 1028, 1064, 1142, 1254, 1288, 1304.
Mark: See above.

Painted eyes:

15-17in (38-43cm)	$ 375 - 425*
22-23in (56-58cm)	525 - 575*

Glass eyes:

14-16in (36-41cm)	550 - 650*
22in (56cm)	1100*

#998 molded bonnet. (For photograph see *11th Blue Book*, page 49.)
18in (46cm) at auction $ 1300

Boy with molded blue cap,
17in (43cm) $ 850
#882 head only, glass eyes 300
#974 long blonde shoulder-length hair,
27in (69cm) at auction 1150

* Allow extra for unusual or elaborate hairdo or molded hat.

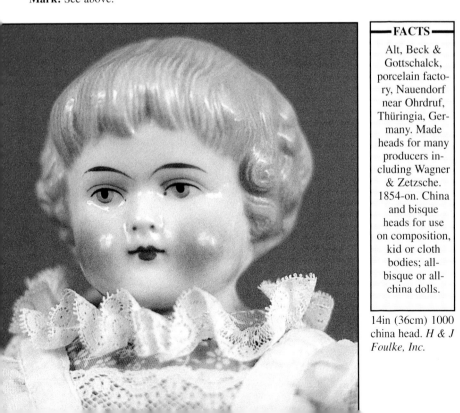

FACTS

Alt, Beck & Gottschalck, porcelain factory, Nauendorf near Ohrdruf, Thüringia, Germany. Made heads for many producers including Wagner & Zetzsche. 1854-on. China and bisque heads for use on composition, kid or cloth bodies; all-bisque or all-china dolls.

14in (36cm) 1000 china head. *H & J Foulke, Inc.*

19in (48cm) 1288 bisque shoulder head. *H & J Foulke, Inc.*

21in (53cm) 1235 girl, open mouth, all original. *H & J Foulke, Inc.* (For further information see page 50.)

26in (67cm) 1111 lady. *H & J Foulke, Inc.* (For further information see page 50.)

Bisque Shoulder Head: Ca. 1885-on. Turned shoulder head, mohair or human hair wig, plaster dome or bald head, glass sleeping or set eyes, closed mouth; kid body with gusseted joints and bisque lower arms, or cloth body with kid lower arms; dressed; all in good condition. Mold numbers, such as 639, 698, 912, 1032, 1123, 1235. (See photograph on page 49.)

Mark:

6 3 9 ✗ 6

with DEP after 1888

15-17in (38-43cm)	$	**800 - 900**
21-23in (53-58cm)		**1200 - 1300**
25-26in (64-67cm)		**1500 - 1600**
27in (69cm), all original, boxed,		
at auction		**1760**

#1111, lady face. (For photograph see page 49.)
26in (67cm)   **1500****

#911, 916, swivel neck. (For photograph see *10th Blue Book*, page 20.)
19 - 22in (48 - 56cm) $ **2100 - 2300**
With open mouth:
Mark:

6 9 8 ½ Germany Dep № 10

16-18in (41-46cm)	$	**525 - 575**
21-23in (53-58cm)		**700 - 750**

Child Doll: Perfect bisque head, good wig, sleep eyes, open mouth; ball-jointed body in good condition; appropriate clothes.
Mark:

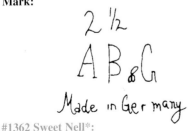

2 ½
A B & G
Made in Germany

#1362 Sweet Nell*:
14-16in (36-41cm)	$	**425 - 475**
19-21in (43-53cm)		**525 - 550**
23-25in (58-64cm)		**650 - 750**

29-30in (74-76cm)	**1000 - 1100**
36in (91cm)	**1600 - 1700**

(*Allow 10-15% extra for Flapper body.)

#911, closed mouth: (For photograph see *10th Blue Book*, page 20.)
22in (56cm) composition body
                    2500-3000**

#630, closed mouth:
23in (68cm)   **2200 - 2500****
#630, open mouth:
17in (43cm)   **625 - 675**
#989, closed mouth: (For photograph see *9th Blue Book*, page 362. Now this mold is attributed to ABG.)
18in (46cm)   **3000 - 3500**
#938, closed mouth:
21in (53cm) at auction   **3800**

All-Bisque Girl: 1911. Chubby body, loop strung shoulders and hips, inset glass eyes open/closed mouth, painted eyelashes, full mohair or silky wig; molded white stockings, blue garters, black Mary Janes. (For photograph see *9th Blue Book*, page 56.)
Mark:

8 3
——
2 2 5
2 +

Also #100, 125 or 150 in place of 225
Bottom number is centimeter size.
5-6in (13-15cm)	$	**250 - 275**
7in (18cm)		**325 - 375**
8in (20cm)		**450 - 500**

All-Bisque Baby:
8-1/2in (21cm) $ **850**

**Not enough price samples to compute a reliable range.

ALT, BECK & GOTTSCHALCK *continued*

Character: 1910-on. Perfect bisque head, good wig, sleep eyes, open mouth; some with open nostrils; composition body; all in good condition; suitable clothes.

Mark:

#1322, 1352, 1361:
10-12in (25-31cm)	$ 350 - 400*
16-18in (41-46cm)	525 - 575*
22-23in (56-58cm)	850 - 900*

#1357: (For photograph see *11th Blue Book*, page 52.)
14in (36cm)	850 - 950

#1407 Baby BoKaye:
8in (20cm)	1300 - 1400

#1431 Orsini, earthenware baby:
18-20in (46-51cm)	700 - 800

* Allow $50 extra for flirty eyes or toddler body.

22in (56cm) 1362 *Sweet Nell.*
H & J Foulke, Inc.

LOUIS AMBERG & SON

FACTS

Louis Amberg & Son, New York, N.Y., U.S.A. 1907-on (although Amberg had been in the doll business under other names since 1878).

Newborn Babe: 1914, reissued 1924. Designed by Jeno Juszko. Bisque head of an infant with painted hair, sleep eyes, closed or open mouth; soft cloth body with celluloid, rubber or composition hands; appropriate clothes; all in good condition. Mold **886** by Recknagel. Mold **371** with open mouth by Marseille.

Mark:

L · A · & · S ·
371 · 3/0 D · R · G · M ·
Germany

THE ORIGINAL
NEWBORN BABE
(C) Jan. 9th 1914 — No. G 45520

AMBERG DOLLS
(The World Standard)

Length:
9-10in (23-25cm)	$	375 - 425
13-14in (33-36cm)		500 - 600
17in (43cm)		700 - 750

Charlie Chaplin: 1915. Composition portrait head with molded and painted hair, painted eyes to the side, closed full mouth, molded mustache; straw-filled cloth body with composition hands; original clothes; all in good condition with wear.

Mark: cloth label on sleeve:

"CHARLIE CHAPLIN DOLL
World's Greatest Comedian
Made exclusively by Louis Amberg
& Son, N.Y.
by Special Arrangement with
Essamay Film Co."

14in (36cm)	**$ 600**

Composition Mibs: 1921. Composition shoulder head designed by Hazel Drucker with wistful expression, molded and painted blonde or reddish hair, blue painted eyes, closed mouth; cloth body with composition arms and legs with painted shoes and socks; appropriate old clothes; all in good condition. (For photograph see *10th Blue Book*, page 359.)

Mark: None on doll; paper label only:

"Amberg Dolls
Please Love Me
I'm Mibs"

16in (41cm)	**$ 850 - 950****

Baby Peggy: 1923. Composition head, arms and legs, cloth body; molded brown bobbed hair, painted eyes, smiling closed mouth; appropriately dressed; all in good condition. (For photograph see *11th Blue Book*, page 56.)

20in (51cm)	**$ 650 - 750****

** Not enough price samples to compute a reliable range.

14in (36cm) *Charlie Chaplin. H & J Foulke, Inc.*

15in (38cm) *Newborn Babe*, marked head and body. *H & J Foulke, Inc.*

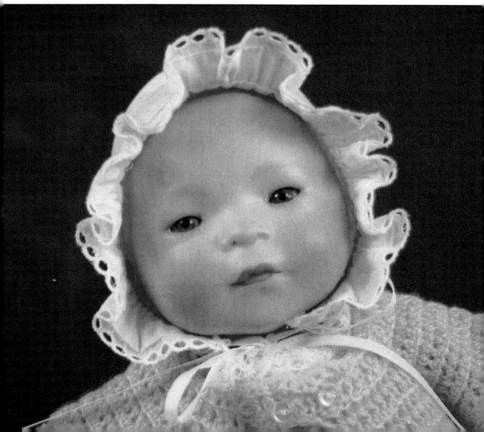

Baby Peggy: 1924. Perfect bisque head by Armand Marseille with character face; brown bobbed mohair wig, brown sleep eyes, closed mouth; composition or kid body, fully-jointed; dressed or undressed; all in very good condition.

Mark:

> "19 © 24"
> LA & S NY
> Germany
> —50—
> 982/2"

also:

973 (smiling socket head)
972 (pensive socket head)
983 (smiling shoulder head)
982 (pensive shoulder head)
20in (51cm) shoulder head
$ **2000 - 2200**
18-22in (46-56cm) socket head
2500 - 2850

All-Bisque Character Children: 1920s. Made by a German porcelain factory. Pink pretinted bisque with molded and painted features, molded hair; jointed at shoulders and hips; molded stockings with blue garters, brown strap shoes, white stockings.

4in (10cm)	$	**125**
5-6in (13-15cm)		**160 - 185**

Girl with molded bow, (For photograph see *11th Blue Book*, page 54.)

6in (15cm)	**325 - 375**

Girl with downward gaze, glass eyes, wig. (For photograph see *11th Blue Book*, page 56.)

5-1/2in (14cm)	**425 - 450**

Mibs:

3in (8cm)	**225 - 250**
4-3/4in (12cm)	**350 - 375**

Baby Peggy:

3in (8cm)	**225 - 250**
5-1/2in (14cm)	**350 - 375**

Baby Peggy, 973 socket head. *Courtesy of Elizabeth Burke.*

20in (51cm) composition head
Vanta Baby with original
label. *H & J Foulke, Inc.*

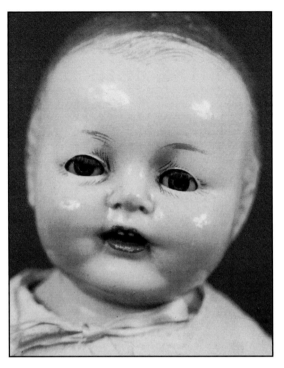

Vanta Baby: 1927. A tie-in with Vanta baby
garments. Composition or bisque head with
molded and painted hair, sleep eyes, open
mouth with two teeth (closed mouth and
painted eyes in all-composition small dolls);
muslin body jointed at hips and shoulders,
curved composition arms and legs; suitably
dressed; all in good condition.
Mark: Bisque Head

> Vanta Baby
> L A⍟S · 3/0 D·R·G·M·
> Germany.

Composition head,
20in (51cm) $ 325 - 375
Bisque head,
20-22in (51-56cm)   **900 - 1000**

Sue, Edwina or It: 1928. All-composition
with molded and painted hair, painted eyes;
jointed neck, shoulders and hips, a large
round ball joint at waist; dressed; all in very
good condition. (For photograph see *7th
Blue Book*, page 59.)
Mark:

> "AMBERG"
> PAT.PEND.
> L.A. & S. © 1928"

14in (36cm)   **$ 425 - 475**

Tiny Tots Body Twists: 1928. All-composition with jointed shoulders and a large round
ball joint at the waist; molded and painted
hair in both boy and girl styles, painted eyes;
painted shoes and socks; dressed; all in good
condition. (For photograph see *11th Blue
Book*, page 57.)
Mark: tag on clothes:

> "An Amberg Doll with
> BODY TWIST
> all its own
> PAT. PEND. SER. NO.
> 32018"

8in (20cm)   **$ 175 - 195**

AMERICAN CHARACTER

FACTS

American Character Doll Co., New York, N.Y., U.S.A. 1919-on.
Trademark: Petite.

Marked Petite or American Character Mama Dolls: 1923-on. Composition head, arms and legs, cloth torso; mohair or human hair wig, sleep eyes, closed or open mouth; original clothes; all in good condition. (For photograph see *9th Blue Book*, page 61.)

16-18in (41-46cm)	**$ 225 - 265**
24in (61cm)	325 - 375

Baby Petite:

12in. (31cm)	**$ 200**

Campbell Kid: 1923. Designed by Grace Drayton; sometimes called *Dolly Dingle*. All composition with swivel head, jointed shoulders and hips; molded and painted hair, eyes to side, watermelon mouth; original clothes; all in good condition. (For photograph see *4th Blue Book*, page 86.)

12in (31cm)	**$ 550 - 650****

Puggy: 1928. All-composition chubby body jointed at neck, shoulders and hips; molded and painted hair, painted eyes to the side, closed mouth, pug nose, frowning face; original clothes; all in good condtion. (For photograph see *11th Blue Book*, page 58.)
Mark:

"A PETITE DOLL"

12in (31cm)	**$ 500 - 550**

Marked Petite Girl Dolls: 1930s. All-composition jointed at neck, shoulders and hips (some with cloth torsos); human hair or mohair wig, lashed sleeping eyes, closed or open mouth with teeth; original clothes; all in good condition.

16-18in (41-46cm)	**$ 265 - 295**
24in (61cm)	325 - 375

Sally: 1930. Painted eyes and molded hair or wigged with sleeping eyes; original clothes.

12in (31cm)	**$ 225 - 250**
16in (41cm)	250 - 275
18in (46cm) **Sally-Joy**	300 - 325

**Not enough price samples to compute a reliable range.

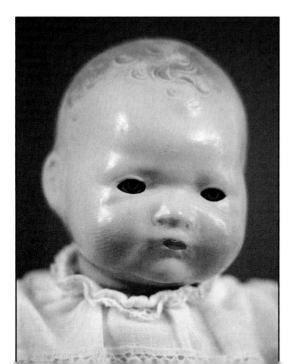

12in (31cm) *Baby Petite. H & J Foulke, Inc.*

18in (46cm) *Sweet Sue*, all original. *H & J Foulke, Inc.* (For further information see page 58.)

12in (31cm) *Tiny Tears*, all original.
Doddlebug Dolls.

10-1/2in (26cm) *Toni. Private Collection.*

Carol Ann Beery, 1935. "Two-Some Doll" with special crown braid
16-1/2in (42cm)
$ 500 - 600

Toodles: Hard rubber baby, molded hair, sleep eyes; drinks and wets; original clothes; excellent condition. (For photograph see *11th Blue Book*, page 59.)
18-1/2in (47cm)
$ 225 - 250

Tiny Tears: 1950s. Hard plastic head, sleep eyes, tear ducts, molded hair; drinks and wets; rubber or vinyl body; original clothes; excellent condition. (For photograph see *11th Blue Book*, page 59.)
12in (31cm)   **$ 150 - 165**
18in (46cm)   **200 - 225**

Sweet Sue: 1953. All-hard plastic or hard plastic and vinyl, some with walking mechanism, some fully-jointed including elbows, knees and ankles; original clothes; all in excellent condition. (For photograph see page 57.)
Marks: "A.C."
"Amer. Char."
14in (36cm)   **$ 225 - 250**
18-20in (46-51cm)   **275 - 300**
24in (61cm)   **325 - 375**

Sweet Sue Sophisticate, vinyl head
20in (51cm)   **$ 225 - 250**

Toni, vinyl head:
10-1/2in (26cm)   **$150 - 200***

*Depending upon costume.

Eloise: Ca. 1955. All-cloth with molded face, painted side-glancing eyes, smiling mouth, yellow yarn hair; flexible arms and legs; original clothing; in excellent condition. Designed by Bette Gould from the fictional little girl "Eloise" who lived at the Plaza Hotel in New York City. (For photograph see *11th Blue Book*, page 60.)
Mark: Cardboard tag
21in (53cm)   **$350 - 400**

Betsy McCall: 1957. All-hard plastic with legs jointed at knees; rooted Saran hair on a wig cap, round face with sleep eyes, plastic eyelashes; original clothes; all in excellent condition.
Mark:

8in (20cm)
Dressed   **$ 165 - 185***
Basic (undergarment, shoes and
    socks)   **150**

Betsy McCall: 1960. All-vinyl with rooted hair, lashed sleep eyes, round face, turned-up mouth; slender arms and legs; original clothes; all in excellent condition. (For photograph see *11th Blue Book*, page 61.)
Mark:

McCALL
19©56
CORP.

14in (36cm)   **$ 250 - 275**
20in (51cm)   **300 - 325**
30-36in (76-91cm)   **500 - 550**

*Allow extra for unusual outfits.

8in (20cm) **Betsy McCall**, all original. *H & J Foulke, Inc.*

ARRANBEE

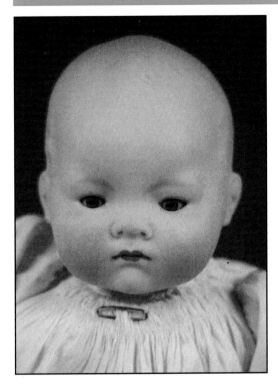

18in (46cm) incised "ARRAN-BEE" baby. *H & J Foulke, Inc.*

FACTS

Arranbee Doll Co., New York, N.Y., U.S.A. 1922-1960.
Mark: "ARRANBEE" or "R & B."

My Dream Baby: 1924. Perfect bisque head with solid dome and painted hair, sleep eyes, closed or open mouth; all-composition or cloth body with composition hands; dressed; all in good condition. Some heads incised "A.M.," "**341**" or "**351**"; some incised "ARRANBEE." See Armand Marseille infant on page 279 for prices.

Storybook Dolls: 1930s. All-composition with swivel neck, jointed arms and legs; molded and painted hair, painted eyes; all original storybook costumes; all in good condition. (For photograph see *10th Blue Book*, page 78.)
9-10in (23-25cm) **$160 - 185***

*Allow more for original box.

17in (43cm) *Nancy*, all original. *H & J Foulke, Inc.*

Nancy: 1930. All-composition, jointed at neck, shoulders and hips, molded hair, painted eyes and closed mouth; original clothes; all in good condition. (For photograph see *11th Blue Book*, page 62.)
Mark: "ARRANBEE" or "NANCY"

12in (31cm)	**$ 225 - 250**
16in (41cm) sleep eyes, wig, open mouth	**300 - 325**
12in (31cm) with trousseau in wardrobe trunk	**475**

Debu' Teen and Nancy Lee: 1938-on. All-composition or composition swivel shoulder head and limbs on cloth torso; mohair or human hair wig, sleep eyes, closed mouth, original clothes; all in good condition.

11in (28cm)	**$ 175 - 195**
14in (36cm)	**250 - 275**
21in (53cm)	**325 - 350**

Skating Doll. 18in (46cm) **300 - 350**
Brother. 14in (36cm) **325 - 350**

Little Angel Baby: 1940s. Composition head and lower limbs, cloth torso, molded hair, sleep eyes, closed mouth; original clothes; all in good condition.

16-18in (41-46cm)	**$ 250 - 300**
Hard plastic, 18in (46cm)	**300**

Nanette and Nancy Lee: 1950s. All-hard plastic, jointed at neck, shoulders and hips; synthetic wig, sleep eyes, closed mouth; original clothes; all in excellent condition.

14in (36cm)	**$ 225 - 250**
17in (43cm)	**300 - 325**

18in (46cm) *Little Angel Baby,* all original. *H & J Foulke, Inc.*

14in (36cm) *Nanette,* hard plastic, all original. *H & J Foulke, Inc.*

62

ARTIST DOLLS

Modern Artist Dolls: 1930s-on.
Original dolls which were created as
works of art and decorative objects, not
intended as playthings.

Armstrong-Hand, Martha, porcelain
babies and children. $ 1200 up
Barrie, Mirren, cloth
Historical children   95
Beckett, Bob & June, carved wood
children.   300 - 450
Blakeley, Halle, high-fired clay lady dolls.
                                  550 - 750
Brandon, Elizabeth, porcelain children.
Theola, Joshua, Joi Lin, Jael
                                  300 - 500
Bringloe, Frances, carved wood.
American Pioneer Children,
6-1/4in (16cm) pair   600
Bullard, Helen, carved wood.
Holly   100 - 125
Hitty   175 - 195
American Family Series
(16 dolls)   225 - 250 each
Campbell, Astry, porcelain.
Ricky & Becky   850 pair
Clear, Emma, porcelain, china and bisque
shoulder head dolls.   350 - 500
Danny   450
DeNunez, Marianne,
10in (25cm) Bru Jne.   300
Florian, Gertrude, ceramic composition
dressed ladies.   300
Goodnow, June, bisque Indians.
16-17in (41-43cm)   550 - 650
Heiser, Dorothy, cloth sculpture.
Early dolls   400 - 500
Queens 10-13in (25-33cm)   1100 - 1500

Kane, Maggie Head, porcelain.
Gypsy Mother   400 - 450
Oldenburg, Mary Ann,
porcelain children.   200 - 250
Park, Irma, wax-over-porcelain minia-
tures, depending upon detail.   125 up
Parker, Ann
Historical Characters $ 150 - 200
Redmond, Kathy, elaborately modeled
porcelain ladies.   400 - 450
Roche, Lynn & Michael, porcelain.
17in (43cm) children   1100 - 1500
Sandreuter, Regina, carved wood.
17in (43cm)   550 - 650
Smith, Sherman, carved wood.
5-6in (13-15cm).   235
Sorensen, Lewis, wax.
Father Christmas   1200
Toymaker   800
Sweet, Elizabeth, 18in (46cm)
Amy, 1970.   250

18in (46cm) Emma Clear *Grape Lady*,
1948. *H & J Foulke, Inc.*

Thompson, Martha, porcelain.

Princess Caroline, Prince Charles, Princess Ann	$ 900 each
Little Women	800 - 900 each
Betsy	900
McKim Child (not bisque)	800
Princess Margaret Rose, Princess Grace	1500 - 2000
Young Victoria	2300
Queen Anne	2300

Thorp, Ellery, porcelain

children.	300 - 500

Tuttle, Eunice, miniature porcelain

children.	700 - 800
Angel Baby	400 - 425

Walters, Beverly, porcelain, miniature

fashions.	500 up

Wright, John, cloth.

7-1/2in (18cm) Elfin girl	800
Adult characters	1500
Children	900 - 1300
Christopher Robin with Winnie the Pooh	1600 - 2000

Winnie the Pooh, 1987.

18in (46cm)	950
14in (36cm) with Honeypot	500 - 550

Wyffels, Berdine, porcelain.

6in (15cm) girl, glass eyes	195

Zeller, Fawn, porcelain.

One of a Kind Dolls	2000 up
Angela	800 - 900
Polly Piedmont, 1965. (For photograph see page 64.)	800 - 900
Holly, U.S. Historical Society	500 - 600
Polly II, U.S. Historical Society	200 - 225

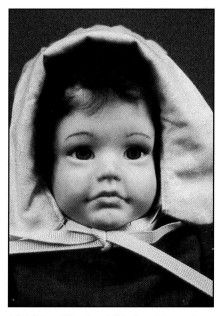

12-1/2in (32cm) child by Mary Ann Oldenburg, 1983. *H & J Foulke, Inc.*

17-1/2in (44cm) *Amy* from *Little Women* by Martha Thompson. *H & J Foulke, Inc.*

14in (36cm) *Polly Piedmont* by Fawn Zeller. *H & J Foulke, Inc.* (For further information see page 63.)

Crystal Faerie by Kazue Moroi and Lita Wilson. *H & J Foulke, Inc.*

U.F.D.C. National & Regional Souvenir Dolls: Created by doll artists in limited editions and distributed to convention attendees as souvenirs. Before 1982, most dolls were given as kits; after 1982, most dolls were fully made up and dressed. Except as noted, dolls have porcelain heads, arms and legs; cloth bodies. A few are all porcelain.

Alice in Wonderland: Yolanda Bello, 1990 Ohio Regional. Complete doll. $ **165**
Alice Roosevelt: Kathy Redmond, 1990 National. Complete doll.   **125**
Crystal Faerie: Kazue Moroi and Lita Wilson, 1983 Midwest Regional. Complete.   **85**
Father Christmas: (Kit) Beverly Walters, 1980 National. Fully made up. **400 - 500**
Janette: Fawn Zeller, 1991 National. Complete doll and pattern portfolio.   **350**
Kate: All cloth by Anili, 1986 National. With original box.   **165 - 185**
Li'l Apple: Faith Wick, 1979 National. Fully made up with romper suit.   **50**
Ken-Tuck: (Kit) Janet Masteller, 1972 Regional. Fully made up.   **65 - 75**
Little Miss Sunshine: (Kit) 1974 Florida Regional. Fully made up.   **65 - 75**
Mary: Linda Steele, 1987 National. Fully made up.   **100**
Miami Miss: (Kit) Fawn Zeller, 1961 National.
Fully made up.   **200 - 250**
Dressed.   **300 - 350**

Nellie Bly: Muriel Kramer, 1985 Pittsburgh Regional. Complete doll.   **85 - 95**
Pinky: Linda Cheek, California Regional. Complete doll.   **300**
Portrait of a Young Girl: Jeanne Singer, 1986 Rochester Regional. Complete doll.   **300**
Princess Kimimi: (Kit) 1977 Ohio Regional. Fully made up.   **85 - 95**
Rose O'Neill: Lita Wilson, 1982 National. Complete doll.   **165 - 200**
Sunshine: Lucille Gerrard, 1983 National. Complete doll.   **100**
Tammy: Jeanne Singer. 1989 Western N.Y. Doll Club. Complete doll.   **85**
Emma: Rappahannock Rags. Cloth. 1993 National.   **95**
Scarlett: Lita Wilson and Muriel Kramer, 1989 Florida Regional. Half doll fully-made up.   **100 - 125**

9in (23cm) *Alice Roosevelt* by Kathy Redmond. *H & J Foulke, Inc.*

GEORGENE AVERILL (MADAME HENDREN)

Tagged Mme. Hendren Character: Ca. 1915 - on. Composition character face, usually with painted features, molded hair or wig (sometimes yarn); hard-stuffed cloth body with composition hands; original clothes often of felt; included Dutch children, Indians, sailors, cowboys, blacks; all in good condition. (For photograph see *10th Blue Book*, page 80.)

Cloth Label:

Madame Hendren
CHARACTER   DOLL
COSTUME PAT   MAY 9TH 1916

10-14in (25-36cm)	**$ 125 - 150**
18in (46cm)	**325 - 350**

Mama & Baby Dolls: Ca. 1918 - on. Composition shoulder head, lower arms and legs, cloth torso with cry box; mohair wig or molded hair, sleep eyes, open mouth with teeth or closed mouth; appropriately dressed; all in good condition. Names such as **Baby Hendren, Baby Georgene** and others.

15-18in (38-46cm)	**$ 250 - 300**
22-24in (56-61cm)	**400 - 450**

Dolly Reckord: 1922. Record playing mechanism in torso. Good condition with records. (For photograph see *11th Blue Book*, page 68.)

26in (66cm)	**$ 550 - 650**

FACTS

Averill Mfg. Co. and Georgene Novelties, Inc., New York, N.Y., U.S.A. 1915-on. **Designer:** Georgene Averill. **Trademarks:** Madame Hendren, Georgene Novelties.

16in (41cm) Mme. Hendren Baby, all original. *H & J Foulke, Inc.*

Whistling Doll: 1925-1929. Composition head with molded hair, side-glancing eyes, mouth pursed to whistle through round opening; composition arms, cloth torso; legs are coiled spring bellows covered with cloth; when head is pushed down or feet are pushed up, the doll whistles. Original or appropriate clothes; all in good condition. (For photographs see *7th Blue Book*, page 198, and *9th Blue Book*, page 84.)
Mark: None.
Original Cardboard Tag:
"I whistle when you dance me on one foot
    and then the other.
    Patented Feb. 2, 1926
    Genuine Madame Hendren Doll."

14-15in (36-38cm) sailor, cowboy,		
(Dan)	$	**250 - 275**
Black **Rufus** or **Dolly Dingle**		**400 - 450**

Bonnie Babe: 1926. Bisque heads by Alt, Beck & Gottschalck; cloth bodies by K & K Toy Co.; distributed by George Borgfeldt, New York. Perfect bisque head with smiling face, molded hair, glass sleep eyes, open mouth with two lower teeth; cloth body with composition arms (sometimes celluloid) and legs often of poor quality; all in good condition. Mold #1386 or 1402
Mark:

*Copr. by
Georgene Averill
Germany
1005/3652
1386*

Length:

12-13in (31-33cm)	$	**1000 - 1100**
16-18in (41-46cm)		**1400 - 1600**
22-23in (56-58cm)		**1800 - 1900**
Composition body,		
8in (20cm) tall		**1250****
Celluloid head:		
16in (41cm) tall		**550 - 650****

All-Bisque Bonnie Babe: 1926. Jointed at neck, shoulders and hips; pink or blue molded slippers. Unmarked except for round paper label on stomach. (For photograph see *11th Blue Book*, page 69.)

5in (13cm)	$	**750 - 850**
7in (18cm)		**1050 - 1150**

****Not enough price samples to compute a reliable range.

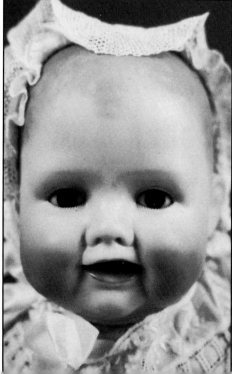

15-1/2in (40cm) *Bonnie Babe.*
H & J Foulke, Inc.

14-1/2in (37cm)
Dimmie. *H & J Foulke, Inc.*

16in (41cm)
Sunny Girl, all
original. *H & J
Foulke, Inc.*

All-Bisque Sonny: Jointed at neck, shoulders and hips; glass eyes; bare feet.

6-1/2in (16cm) **$ 3250****

Rag and Tag: All bisque dog and cat; swivel neck, jointed shoulders and hips, glass eyes; fully marked on back. Rag (890), Tag (891). (For photograph of Rag, see *5th Blue Book*, page 52; for photograph of Tag see *11th Blue Book*, page 72.)

5in (13cm) **$ 3000****

Body Twists: 1927. All-composition, jointed at neck, shoulders and hips, with a large round ball joint at waist; molded and painted hair, painted eyes, closed mouth; dressed; all in good condition. Advertised as Dimmie and Jimmie.

14-1/2in (37cm) **$ 425 - 475**

Sunny Boy and Girl: Ca. 1927. Celluloid "turtle" mark head with molded hair and glass eyes; stuffed body with composition arms and legs; appropriate or original clothes; all in good condition.

15in (38cm) **$ 350 - 400**
19in (48cm) all original and mint,
at auction. **550**

**Not enough price samples to compute a reliable range.

20in (51cm) *Nurse Jane. H & J Foulke, Inc.* (For further information see page 70.)

13in (33cm) Georgene girl, all original. *H & J Foulke, Inc.*

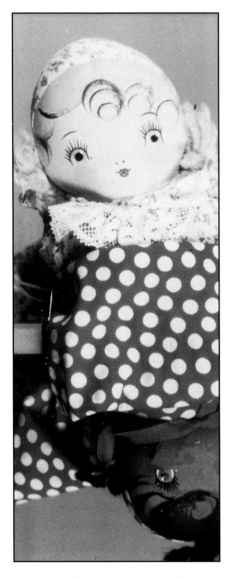

10in (25cm) *Topsy & Eva. H & J Foulke, Inc.*

Composition Dolls: Original clothes; all in good condition.
Snookums, 1927. (For photograph see *5th Blue Book*, page 169.)
14in (36cm) $ 325 - 375

Patsy-Type Girl, 1928. (For photograph see *9th Blue Book*, page 86.)
14in (36cm)   250 - 300
17-18in (43-46cm)   325 - 350

Harriet Flanders, 1937. Little Cherub. (For photograph see *7th Blue Book*, page 167.)
16in (41cm)   275 - 300
Painted eyes, 12in (31cm)   160 - 175

Cloth Dolls: Ca. 1930s - on. Mask face with painted features, yarn hair, painted and/or real eyelashes; cloth body with movable arms and legs; attractive original clothes; all in excellent condition, clean with bright color.

Children or Babies:
12in (31cm) $ 125 - 150
24-26in (61-66cm)   225 - 275

International and Costume Dolls:
12in (31cm)   90 - 100
Mint in box with wrist tag   115 - 135

Uncle Wiggily or Nurse Jane (For photograph see page 69.),
18-20in (46-51cm)   500 - 550
Characters, 14in (36cm):
Little Lulu, Nancy, Sluggo, 1944.
                                      400 - 500

Flat Painted Faces:
14in (36cm) girls   150 - 185

Topsy & Eva
10in (25cm)   150- 175

Maud Tousey Fangel, 1938. Snooks, Sweets, Peggy-Ann. Marked "M.T.F." (For photographs see *11th Blue Book*, page 73 and *8th Blue Book*, page 168.)
12 - 14in (31 - 36cm)   600 - 650
17in (43cm)   800 - 850
22in (56cm)   1100

BABY BO KAYE

Baby Bo Kaye: Perfect bisque head with flange neck marked as at right, molded hair, glass eyes, open mouth with two lower teeth; cloth torso with composition limbs; dressed; all in good condition. (For photograph see *11th Blue Book*, page 74.)

16-19in (41-48cm)	**$ 2400 - 2800**
#1407 (ABG) bisque head, composition body	
7-1/2in (19cm)	**1300 - 1400**
Celluloid head, 16in (41cm)	**750**

All-Bisque Baby Bo Kaye: Molded hair, glass sleep eyes, open mouth with two teeth; swivel neck, jointed shoulders and hips; molded pink or blue shoes and socks; unmarked but may have sticker on torso:

5in (13cm)	**$ 1350 - 1400**
6in (15cm)	**1700 - 1800**

FACTS

Composition heads by Cameo Doll Company; bisque heads made in Germany by Alt, Beck & Gottschalck; bodies by K & K Toy Co., New York, N.Y., U.S.A. 1925.
Designer: J.L. Kallus.
Distributor:
George Borgfeldt Co., N.Y.
Mark: "Copr. by
J.L. Kallus
Germany
1394/30"

5in (13cm) all-bisque *Baby Bo Kaye.*
H & J Foulke, Inc.

BABYLAND RAG

Babyland Rag: Cloth face with hand-painted features, sometimes mohair wig; cloth body jointed at shoulders and hips; original clothes.

Early face:

13-15in (33-38cm)

very good	$	750 - 850*
fair		400 - 500

22in (56cm)

very good	900 - 1000*
fair	550 - 600
30in (76cm) very good	2000 - 2200**

Topsy Turvy.

13-15in (33-38cm) very good

700 - 800*

Black,

15in (38cm) fair	650 - 700*
20-22in (51-56cm) very good	
	1100 - 1300*

*Allow more for mint condition doll.

**Not enough price samples to compute a reliable average.

FACTS

E. I. Horsman, New York, N.Y., U.S.A. Some dolls made for Horsman by Albert Brückner. 1901-on.
Mark: None.

Mammy with early brown face, all original. *Nancy A. Smith Collection.*

15in (38cm) boy with "Life-like" face, replaced sweater. *H & J Foulke, Inc.*

Life-like face (printed features)**:**
  13-15in (33-38cm)
  very good   **600 - 650***
Babyland Rag-type (lesser quality):
  White, 14in (36cm) good   **375 - 475**
Topsy Turvy,
  14in (36cm) good   **450 - 550**

Brückner Rag Doll:
Mark:

  PAT'D. JULY 8ᵀᴴ 1901

Stiffened mask face, cloth body, flexible shoulders and hips; appropriate clothes; all in good condition. (For photograph see *8th Blue Book*, page 105.)
12-14in (31-36cm)
  White   **$ 210 - 235**
  Black   **275 - 300**
  Topsy Turvy   **500 - 550**
  Dollypop   **250****

*Allow more for mint condition doll.
** Not enough price samples to compute a reliable range.

BÄHR & PRÖSCHILD

Marked Belton-type Child Doll: Ca. 1880. Perfect bisque head, solid dome with flat top having two or three small holes, paperweight eyes, closed mouth with pierced ears; wood and composition jointed body with straight wrists; dressed; all in good condition. Mold numbers in 200 series.

Mark: 204

12-14in (30-36cm)	$ 1750 - 2000
18-20in (46-51cm)	2500 - 3000
24in (61cm)	3600 - 3800

FACTS

Bähr & Pröschild, porcelain factory, Ohrdruf, Thüringia, Germany. Made heads for Bruno Schmidt, Heinrich Stier, Kley & Hahn and others. 1871- on. Bisque heads for use on composition or kid bodies, all-bisque dolls.

16in (41cm) 213 girl. *H & J Foulke, Inc.*

BÄHR & PRÖSCHILD *continued*

Marked Child Doll: 1888-on. Perfect bisque shoulder or socket head, set or sleeping eyes, open mouth with four or six upper teeth, good human hair or mohair wig; gusseted kid or jointed composition body (many of French-type); dressed; all in good condition. Mold numbers in 200 and 300 series.

Mark: 224
    dep

#224, 239, 273, 275, 277, 289, 297, 325, 340, 379, 394 and other socket heads:

8in (20cm), 5-piece body	$	400 - 425
12-13in (30-33cm)		550 - 650
16-18in (41-46cm)		750 - 800
22-24in (56-61cm)		1000 - 1100

#224 (dimples):

14-16in (36-41cm)	$	875 - 925
22-24in (56-61cm)		1250 - 1500

#246, 309 and other shoulder heads:

16-18in (41-46cm)	$	475 - 525
22-24in (56-61cm)		650 - 700

#302, swivel neck, kid body:

20in (51cm)	$	750 - 800

All-Bisque Girl, yellow stockings (Heart mark)

5in (13cm)	325 - 350
7in (18cm)	450

#513, possibly by B.P.:

22-26in (56-66cm)	$	850 - 900

13in (33cm) 297 dep girl.
H & J Foulke, Inc.

26in (66cm) 513, possibly by B.P.
H & J Foulke, Inc.

BÄHR & PRÖSCHILD *continued*

Marked B.P. Character Baby: Ca. 1910-
on. Perfect bisque socket head, solid dome
or good wig, sleep eyes, open mouth; composition bent-limb baby body; dressed; all in
good condition. Mold #585, 604, 624, 678,
619, 620 and 587.

Mark:

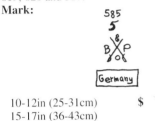

10-12in (25-31cm)	$ 400 - 500
15-17in (36-43cm)	600 - 700
20-21in (51-53cm)	800 - 900
24-25in (61-64cm)	1100 - 1200

Toddler:

10-12in (25-31cm)	$	675 - 750
17-19in (43-48cm)		1000 - 1200
28in (71cm)		2600 - 2700

#425. All-bisque baby (For photograph see
10th Blue Book, page 88.)

5-1/2–6in (13-15cm)	$	250 - 300

#563 Schneeglockchen:

11in (28cm) at auction	$	3900**

#641.

15in (38cm) toddler	$	1500**
12in (30cm) baby		765**

**Not enough price samples to compute
a reliable average.

14in (36cm) 620 toddler made for George Borgfeldt. *Rhoda Shoemaker Collection.*

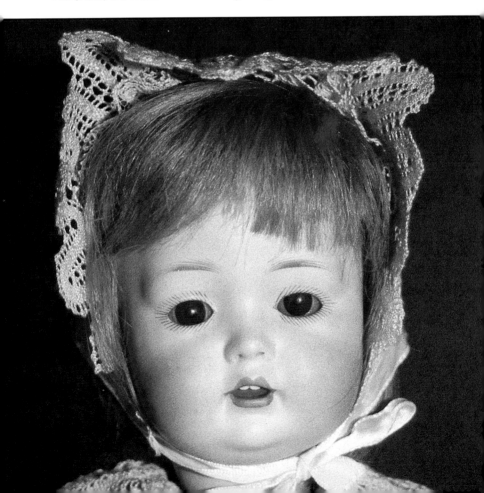

BARBIE®

FACTS

Mattel, Inc., Hawthorne, Calif., U.S.A. 1959 to present. Hard plastic and vinyl.
11-1/2–12in (29-31cm).
Mark: 1959-1962: BARBIE TM/Pats. Pend./© MCMLVIII/by/Mattel, Inc.
1963-1968: Midge TM/© 1962/BARBIE®/© 1958/by/Mattel, Inc.
1964-1966: © 1958/Mattel, Inc./U.S. Patented/U.S. Pat. Pend.
1966-1969: © 1966/Mattel, Inc./U.S. Patented/U.S. Pat.
Pend./Made in Japan.

#4, 2 and *3 Ponytail BARBIES*® wearing first three outfits produced for BARBIE®: *Gay Parisienne #964, Easter Parade #971,* and *Roman Holiday #968. Courtesy of McMasters Doll Auctions.* (For further information see pages 78 and 79.)

First BARBIE®: 1959. Vinyl, solid body; very light complexion, white irises, pointed eyebrows, ponytail, black and white striped bathing suit, holes in feet to fit stand, gold hoop earrings; mint condition.
11-1/2in (29cm) boxed $ 3400 - 3800
Doll only, no box or accessories

Mint	2800
Very good	2300
Stand	350
Shoes	20
Hoop earrings	65

Second BARBIE®: 1959-1960. Vinyl, solid body; very light complexion, same as above, but no holes in feet, some wore pearl earrings; mint condition. Made 3 months only.
11-1/2in (29cm) boxed $ 3200 - 3500*
Doll only, no box or accessories, very
good   2600

*Brunette harder to find than blonde.

BARBIE® is a registered
trademark of Mattel, Inc.

Third BARBIE®: 1960. Vinyl, solid body; very light complexion, same as above, but with blue irises and curved eyebrows; no holes in feet; mint condition.
11-1/2in (29cm) boxed $ 700 - 800
Doll only, mint   450 - 550

Fourth BARBIE®: 1960. Vinyl; same as #3; but with solid body of flesh-toned vinyl; mint condition.
11-1/2in (29cm) boxed $ 500 - 550
Doll only, mint   250 - 300

Fifth BARBIE®: 1961. Vinyl; same as #4; ponytail hairdo of firm Saran; mint condition.
11-1/2in (29cm) boxed $ 375 - 425
Doll only, mint   250 - 300

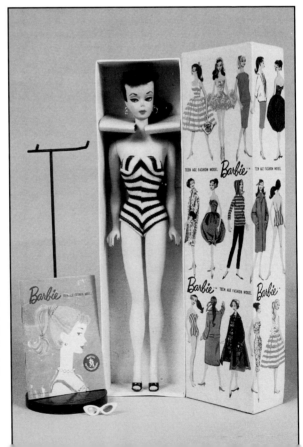

#2 Ponytail BARBIE® with box, original swimsuit, earrings, shoes and pedestal stand. Sold for $5100 in November 1994. *Courtesy of McMasters Doll Auctions.*

Bubble Cut BARBIE®, 1961 on.
Mint-in-box $ 225 - 250
Doll only, mint   100 - 125

Fashion Queen BARBIE®, 1963.
Mint-in-box   300 up

Miss BARBIE®, 1964.
Mint-in-box   900 - 1100

Swirl Ponytail BARBIE®, 1964. (See photograph on page 80.)
Mint-in-box   400 - 450
Doll only, mint   225

Bendable Leg BARBIE®, 1965 & 1966.
American girl, center part,
mint-in-box   800 - 1200
Side-part, mint-in-box   3500 - 4500

Color Magic BARBIE®, 1966.
Mint-in-box, black   1400
        blonde   850 - 950
Doll only, mint, black   1100
        blonde   650
Twist & Turn BARBIE®, 1967.
Mint-in-box   300 - 350

Talking BARBIE®, 1970.
Mint-in-box   225 - 250

Living BARBIE®, 1970.
Mint-in-box   200

Hair Happenin's BARBIE®, 1971.
Mint-in-box   750

Montgomery Ward BARBIE®, 1972.
Mint doll   225 - 275

Gift Sets   550 - 800 up

Outfits, all mint-in-package:
Roman Holiday $ 2000 up
Gay Parisienne   1700 up
Easter Parade   2200 up
Shimmering Magic   750 up
Here Comes the Bride   600 up
Pan Am Stewardess   2000 up
BARBIE® Baby Sits   200 up
Dogs & Duds   200 up
Enchanted Evening   275 up
1600 Series and Jacqueline
  Kennedy-style outfits   295 up

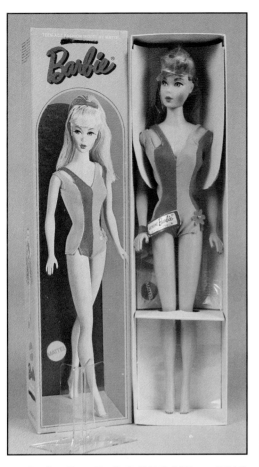

Previous Page: **Top Left:**1964 *Swirl Ponytail BAR-BIE®,* all original in box with stand and accessories. *Courtesy of McMasters Doll Auctions.* (For further information see page 79.) **Top Right:** *Black Francie,* 1967, twist waist, bendable knees, rooted eyelashes, medium brown skin. *Courtesy of McMasters Doll Auctions.* (For further information see page 82.) **Bottom:** *BARBIE® Round the Clock Gift Set,* box dated, 1963 includes *Bubble Cut BAR-BIE®* with various outfits and accessories. Sold for $4300 in November 1994. *Courtesy of McMasters Doll Auctions.*

Top Left: *Standard BARBIE®,* 1970 Doll has painted eyelashes; however the boxes read "real eyelashes." Most were crossed through as in this box. All original. Sold in November 1994 for $550. *Courtesy of McMasters Doll Auctions.* **Top Right:** *Twist Francie,* 1971, referred to as a *"No Bangs" Francie,* twist waist, bendable knees, rooted eye lashes. *Courtesy of McMasters Doll Auctions.* **Right:** *Bob Mackie Gold BARBIE®,* first in series, 1990. *Courtesy of McMasters Doll Auctions.* (For further information see page 82.)

82

BARBIE® *continued*

Other Dolls:

Ken #1, 1961, mint-in-box **$ 175**	
Bendable legs, mint-in-box	**300**

Midge, 1963, mint-in-box **180**
1966 bendable legs, mint-in-box **385**

Allen, 1964-1966:
Mint-in-box, bendable legs **350**
straight legs **150**

Francie, 1966-1967:
Doll only, mint bendable legs **165**
straight legs **185**
Twist 'n Turn **235**
Black, 1967, mint-in-package. (For photograph see page 80.)
Doll only, mint **600**
"No Bangs", 1970. (For photograph see page 81.)
Mint-in-box **1200**
Doll only, mint **700 up**
Hair Happenin's, 1970, mint-in-box **275**

Twiggy, 1967.
Mint-in-box **250**
Truly Scrumptious, 1969:
Mint-in-box **475**
Doll only, mint **250 up**

Julia, 1969:
Mint-in-box one-piece uniform **95 - 110**
Mint-in-box two-piece uniform **125 - 135**
Talking, mint-in-box **125**

Tutti, 1967-1970, mint-in-box **135**

Chris, 1967-1970, mint-in-box **170**

Todd, 1967-1970, mint-in-box **150**
Bob Mackie BARBIES®:
1990 Gold (For photograph see page 81.) **$ 550 up**
1991 Platinum **450 up**
1991 Starlight Splendor (black) **475 up**
1992 Empress Bride **475 up**
1992 Neptune Fantasy **495 up**
1993 Masquerade Ball **395 up**
1994 Queen of Hearts **175**

Christmas BARBIES®:
1988 English Language Box **$ 575 up**
4 Language Box **425 up**
1989 **125**
1990 **85**
1991 **110**
1992 **125**
1993 **125**
1994 **125**

Special BARBIES®:
1994 Bloomingdales **$ 100**
1994 Hallmark **100**
1994 Golden Jubilee **1200**

E. BARROIS

FACTS

E. Barrois, doll factory, Paris, France.
1844-1877.

Mark:

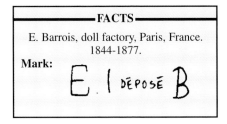

E.B. Poupée: Perfect bisque shoulder head (may have a swivel neck), glass eyes (may be painted with long painted eyelashes), closed mouth; appropriate wig; adult kid body, some with jointed wood arms or wood and bisque arms; appropriate clothing. All in good condition.

14-16in (36-41cm)	$ 2500 - 3000
20-22in (51-56cm)	3200 - 3500
35in (89cm)	5500 - 6500

19in (48cm) Black fashion with rare swivel neck. (For photograph see *11th Blue Book*, page 84.) **$30,000 up**

**Not enough price samples to compute a reliable range.

15-1/2in (39cm) *poupée* in the Barrois style. *Private Collection.*

BELTON-TYPE (So-called)

Belton-type Child Doll: Perfect bisque socket head, solid but flat on top with two or three small holes for stringing; paperweight eyes, closed mouth, pierced ears; wood and composition ball-jointed body with straight wrists; dressed; all in good condition.

TR 809:

12-1/2in (32cm)	**$ 1250 - 1450**

Bru-type face:

12in (30cm)	**2500 - 2700**

Fine early quality, French-type face (some mold #137 or #125)

13-15in (33-38cm)	**$ 2400 - 2700**
18-20in (46-51cm)	**3100 - 3400**
22-24in (56-61cm)	**3600 - 4000**

Good quality, German-type face:

12in (31cm)	**1250 - 1450**
15-17in (38-43cm)	**1600 - 1800**
20in (51cm)	**2200 - 2400**

Tiny with five-piece body (pretty):

8-9in (20-23cm)	**850 - 950**

#200 Series, see Bähr & Pröschild, page 74.

FACTS

Various German firms, such as Bähr & Pröschild. 1875-on. Bisque socket head, ball-jointed wood and composition body with straight wrists.

Mark:

None, except sometimes numbers.

BELOW: **Left:** 12-1/2in (32cm) TR 809 Belton-type girl. *H & J Foulke, Inc.* **Right:** 20in (51cm) Belton-type girl incised "11," French-type face. *H & J Foulke, Inc.*

C. M. BERGMANN

Bergmann Child Doll: Ca. 1889-on. Marked bisque head, composition ball-jointed body, good wig, sleep or set eyes, open mouth; dressed; all in nice condition.

Heads by **A.M.** and unknown makers:

10in (25cm)	$	400
14-16in (36-41cm)		375 - 425
20in (51cm)		475 - 525
23-24in (58-61cm)		550
28-29in (71-74cm)		700 - 800
32-33in (81-84cm)		1100 - 1200
35-36in (89-91cm)		1400 - 1600
39-42in (99-111cm)		2200 - 2600

Heads by **Simon & Halbig**:

10in (25cm)	$	450 - 500
13-15in (33-38cm)		400 - 450
18-20in (46-51cm)		525 - 575
23-24in (58-61cm)		600 - 650
29-30in (74-76cm)		1000 - 1100
35-36in (81-91cm)		1600 - 1800
39in (99cm)		2500
Eleonore, 25in (64cm)		800 - 900

#612 Character Baby, open closed mouth:

14-16in (36-41cm)	$ 1500 - 1800**

**Not enough price samples to compute a reliable average.

┌─────────── FACTS ───────────┐

C. M. Bergmann doll factory of Waltershausen, Thüringia, Germany; heads manufactured for this company by Armand Marseille, Simon & Halbig, Alt, Beck & Gottschalck and perhaps others. 1888-on.

Distributor: Louis Wolfe & Co., New York, N.Y., U.S.A.

Trademarks: Cinderella Baby (1897), Columbia (1904), My Gold Star (1926).

Mark:

CM BERGMANN
A - H 1/2 - M:
Made in Germany

C. M. Bergmann
Waftershausen
Germany
1916
6 1/2 a

22in (56cm) CMB//S&H child. *H & J Foulke, Inc.*

BISQUE, FRENCH

(Unmarked or Unidentified Marks and Unlisted Small Factories)

Marked H Bébé: Ca. late 1870s. Possibly by A. Halopeau. Perfect pressed bisque socket head of fine quality, paperweight eyes, pierced ears, closed mouth, cork pate, good wig; French wood and composition jointed body with straight wrists; appropriate clothing; all in excellent copndition. (For photograph see *10th Blue Book*, page 195.)
Mark:

2 • H

Size 0 = 16-1/2in (42cm)
2 = 19in (48cm)
3 = 21in (56cm)
4 = 24in (61cm)

21-24in (53-61cm)   **$75,000**

Marked J.M. Bébé: Ca. 1880s. Perfect pressed bisque socket head, paperweight eyes, closed mouth, pierced ears, good wig; French composition and wood body; appropriate clothing; all in good condition. (For photograph see *11th Blue Book,* page 168.)
Mark:

19-21in (48-53cm)   **$20,000****

Marked M. Bébé: Mid 1890s. Perfect bisque socket head, closed mouth, paperweight eyes, pierced ears, good wig; French jointed composition and wood body; appropriate clothing; all in good condition. Some dolls with this mark may be **Bébé Mascottes**. (For photograph see *10th Blue Book*, page 196.)
Mark:

M
4

13in (33cm)   **$2500**
18-21in (46-53cm)   **3200-3800**

Marked PAN Bébé: Ca. 1887. Henri Delcroix, Paris and Montreuil-sous-Bois (porcelain fatory). Perfect bisque socket head, paperweight eyes, closed mouth, pierced ears, good wig; French composition and wood body; appropriate clothes; all in good condition. (For additional photograph see *9th Blue Book*, page 140.)
Mark:

PAN
2

Size 2 = 12in (31cm)
10 = 27in (68cm)
11 = 28-1/2in (72cm)

11in (28cm)   **$5000****

** Not enough price
samples to compute
a reliable average.

11in (28cm) Unmarked
Pan-type Bébé. *Kay &
Wayne Jensen Collection.*

Unmarked Adult Character Head: Perfect bisque socket head, inset glass eyes, closed mouth, slender face, appropriate wig; jointed composition bodfy (not original); dressed; all in good condition.

22in (56cm)   **$5000***

Marked P.G. Bébé: Ca. 1880-1899. Pintel & Godchaux, Montreuil, France. Perfect bisque socket head, paperweight eyes, closed mouth, good wig; jointed French composition and wood body; appropriate clothing; all in good condition. (For photo-graph see *11th Blue Book,* page 298.)

Trademark: Bébé Charmant
Mark:

B	A
P9G	P7G

20-22in (51-56cm)   **$2500-3000**
Open mouth, 18-20in (46-51cm)
     1600-1800

** Not enough price samples to compute a reliable average.

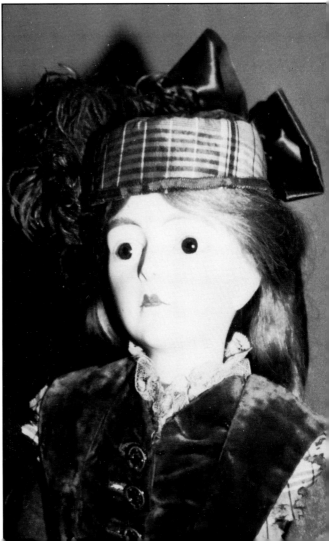

22in (56cm) Unmarked French character lady. *Private Collection.*

BISQUE, German

(Unmarked or Unidentified Marks and Unlisted Small Factories)

Molded Hair Doll: Ca. 1880. Tinted bisque shoulder head with beautifully molded hair (usually blonde), painted eyes, closed mouth; original kid or cloth body; bisque lower arms; appropriate clothes; all in good condition.

Painted eyes:

7-8in (18-20cm)	$	150 - 175*
11-13in (28-33cm)		250 - 300*
15-17in (38-43cm)		375 - 425*
22-23in (56-58cm)		525 - 575*
25-26in (64-66cm)		650 - 700*

Glass eyes:

14-16in (36-41cm)	600 - 700*
20-22in (51-56cm)	900 - 1100*

Unusual hairdo:

18-22in (46-56cm)	700 up
With glass eyes	1000 up
With glass eyes and decorated bodice	1200 up

Early Untinted Bisque Child: Cobalt blue glass eyes, blonde molded-hair.

8in (20cm)	$	500
12in (30cm)		750 - 850
17in (43cm)		1200 - 1300

American Schoolboy: Cloth or kid body,

10-12in (25-31cm)	$	450 - 550
15-17in (38-43cm)		650 - 750
20in (51cm)		850 - 950
Composition body,		
9-11in (23-28cm)		500 - 600

*Allow extra for a fancy hairdo.

FACTS

Various German firms. 1860s-on.
Mark: Some numbered, some "Germany," some both.

16in (41cm) so-called *American School Boy*. *H & J Foulke, Inc.*

Hatted or Bonnet Doll: Ca. 1880-1920. Bisque shoulder head with painted molded hair and molded fancy bonnet with bows, ribbons, flowers, feathers, and so forth; painted eyes and facial features; original cloth body with bisque arms and legs; good old clothes or nicely dressed; all in good condition.

Standard quality:

8-9in (20-23cm)	$	185 - 225*
12-15in (31-38cm)		250 - 300*

Fine quality:

18-22in (46-56cm)	1000 up*
All bisque, 4-1/2in (12cm)	175 - 195*
7in (18cm)	250 - 300*

Doll House Doll: 1890-1920. Man or lady bisque shoulder head with molded hair, painted eyes; cloth body, bisque lower limbs; original clothes or suitably dressed; all in nice condition.

4-1/2-7in (12-18cm)

Victorian man with mustache $	175 - 225
Victorian lady, all original	200
Lady with glass eyes and wig	350 - 400
Man with mustache, original military uniform	700 - 750
Molded hair, glass eyes, Ca. 1870	450 - 500
Girl with bangs, Ca. 1880	150 - 165
Molded hair, painted eyes, Ca. 1870	250 - 275
Chauffeur with molded cap	250 - 300
Black man	550 - 650
Soldier, molded hat, goatee and mustache	1250
1920s man or lady	100 - 125

*Allow extra for unusual style.

Bisque bonnet head doll. *H & J Foulke, Inc.*

16in (41cm) German fashion, all original. *Doelman Collection. Courtesy of Richard W. Withington, Inc.*

Child Doll with closed mouth: Ca. 1880-1890. Perfect bisque head; kid or cloth body, gusseted at hips and knees with good bisque hands or jointed composition body; good wig; nicely dressed; all in good condition.

Kid or cloth body:

12-13in (31-33cm)	$	675 - 775*
15-17in (38-43cm)		800 - 900*
21-23in (53-58cm)		1200 - 1300*
25-26in (64-66cm)		1500 - 1600*

#50:

5in (13cm) head only	$	650
18-20in (46-51cm)		1500 - 1600

#132 Bru-type face:

19-21in (48-53cm)	2800 - 3000

#51:

13-15in (33-38cm)	1550 - 1750

* All 30% extra for swivel neck fashion-type model.

13in (33cm) *136* child. H & J Foulke, Inc.

Composition body:

11-13in (28-33cm)	$	1450 - 1650
16-19in (41-48cm)		1950 - 2250
22-23in (56-58cm)		2700 - 3000
#136:		
12-15in (31-38cm)	$	2200 - 2400
19-21in (48-53cm)		2800 - 3200

Child Doll with open mouth "Dolly Face": 1888-on. Perfect bisque head, ball-jointed composition body or kid body with bisque lower arms; good wig, glass eyes, open mouth; dressed; all in good condition. Including dolls marked "G.B.," and "K," inside "H." "L.H.K.," and P.Sch.

Very good quality:

12-14in (31-35cm)	$	400 - 450
18-20in (46-51cm)		600 - 700
23-25in (58-64cm)		800 - 900
30-32in (76-81cm)		1300 - 1500
#444:		
23-25in (58-64cm)	$	900 - 1000
35in (81cm)		2000 - 2200

Standard quality; including name dolls, Princess, My Girlie, My Dearie and Pansy and G & S, MOA, S & Q and A.W.:

14-16in (35-41cm)	$	350 - 400
20-23in (51-58cm)		525 - 550
30-32in (76-81cm)		1000 - 1100
35-36in (89-91cm)		1400 - 1600

Tiny child doll: 1890 to World War I. Perfect bisque socket head of good quality, 5-piece composition body of good quality with molded and painted shoes and stockings; good wig, set or sleep eyes, open mouth; cute clothes; all in good condition. Very good quality (Simon & Halbig type):

5-6in (13-15cm)	$	275 - 325
8-10in (20-25cm)		375 - 425
Fully-jointed body,		
7-8in (18-20cm)		450 - 500
Closed mouth:		
4-1/2–5-1/2in (12-14cm)		325 - 375
8in (20cm)		700 - 800

Standard quality:

5-6in (13-15cm)		100 - 125
8-10in (20-25cm)		150 - 175

#39-13, 5-piece mediocre body, glass eyes, original clothes:

5in (13cm)	$	200 - 225
painted eyes		90 - 100

Character Baby: 1910-on. Perfect bisque head, good wig or solid dome with painted hair, sleep eyes, open mouth; composition bent-limb baby body; suitably dressed; all in good condition.

9-10in (23-25cm)	$	300 - 350
14-16in (35-41cm)		500 - 550
19-21in (48-53cm)		600 - 700
23-24in (58-61cm)		800 - 900
Toddler,		
12-14in (31-35cm)		650 - 850
Painted eyes:		
7-8in (18-20cm)	$	225 - 275*
12in (31cm)		425 - 475*
16in (41cm)		600 - 650*

* Allow more for open/closed mouth, closed mouth or unusual face.

Character Child: 1910-on. Bisque head with good wig or solid dome head with painted hair, sleep or painted eyes, open or closed mouth, expressive character face; jointed composition body; dressed; all in good condition.

15-19in (38-48cm)	$	1000 up*

*Depending upon individual face.

#111, 18-20in (45-51cm)	$	15,000
#128, 18-20in (45-51cm)		17,500

Infant, unmarked or unidentified maker: 1924-on. Perfect bisque head with molded and painted hair, glass sleep eyes; cloth body, celluloid or composition hands; dressed; all in good condition.

10-12in (25-31cm) long	$	325 - 375*
15-18in (38-46cm) long		525 - 625*

*More depending upon appeal and rarity of face.

HvB:

15in (38cm) long	$	450

See photographs on following pages.

16in (41cm) *1007X* child. *H & J Foulke, Inc.*

See preceding pages for further information on German Bisque Dolls.

BOTTOM: *Left:* 18in (46cm) *50* child. *H & J Foulke, Inc.* **Right:** 23in (58cm) *Princess. H & J Foulke, Inc.*

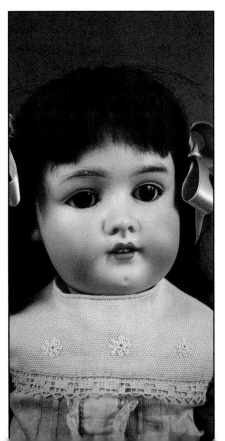

128 character girl. *Richard Wright Collection.*

BOTTOM: *Left:* 12in (31cm) **B4** Toddler. *H & J Foulke, Inc.* **Right:** 15in (38cm) long **HvB** (Hermann von Berg) baby. *H & J Foulke, Inc.*

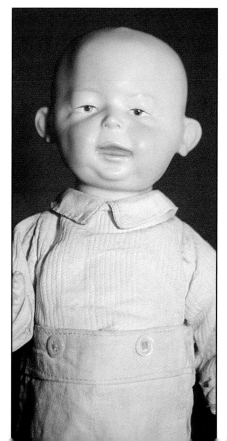

BISQUE JAPANESE (CAUCASIAN DOLLS)

Character Baby: Perfect bisque socket head with solid dome or wig, glass eyes, open mouth with teeth, dimples; composition bent-limb baby body; dressed; all in good condition.

9-10in (23-25cm) $ **175 - 200***
13-15in (33-38cm)   **275 - 325***
19-21in (48-53cm)   **450 - 500***
24in (61cm)   **600 - 650***

Hilda look-alike, 19in (48cm)   **750 - 850***

Child Doll: Perfect bisque head, mohair wig, glass sleep eyes, open mouth; jointed composition or kid body; dressed; all in good condition.

14-16in (36-41cm) $ **250 - 300***
20-22in (51-56cm)   **350 - 400***

*Do not pay as much for doll with inferior bisque head.

FACTS

Various Japanese firms; heads were imported by New York distributors, such as Morimura Brothers, Yamato Importing Co. and others. 1915-on.
Mark: Morimura Brothers.
Various other marks with Japan or Nippon, such as J.W., F.Y., and others

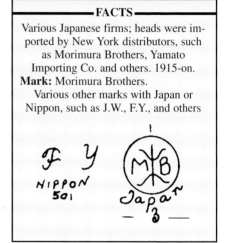

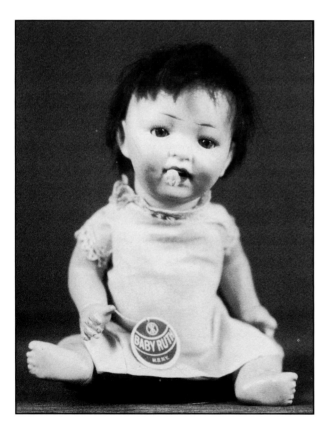

9in (23cm) Baby Ruth.
H & J Foulke, Inc.

BLACK DOLLS*

*Also see entry for specific maker of doll or for material of doll.

Black Bisque Doll: Ca. 1880-on. Various French and German manufacturers from their regular molds or specially designed ones with Negroid features. Perfect bisque socket head either painted dark or with dark coloring mixed in the slip, running from light brown to very dark; composition or sometimes kid body in a matching color; cloth bodies on some baby dolls; appropriate clothing; all in good condition.

French Makers:

Bru, Circle Dot, 17in (43cm).	$30,000
E.D., open mouth, 16in (41cm).	2200
Jumeau	
Poupée, 15in (38cm).	5000
Bébé, open mouth, 15in (38cm)	2600 - 2800
Paris Bébé, closed mouth,	
15-1/2in (39cm)	4800 - 5000
Poupée Shoulder Head, jointed wood	
body, original ethnic clothes	13,000
Steiner, Figure A, open mouth,	
27-1/2in (69cm) at auction	6325
Van Rozen, 15in (38cm), all original,	
at auction	17,000

German Makers:

Belton-type, Bru-style face,		
14in (36cm) Mulatto	$	2500
Gebr. Heubach #7671,		
18in (46cm)		3500
H. Handwerck, 18in (46cm)		1600 - 1800
E. Heubach		
#399, 414, 452 (For photograph see		
page 96.)		
7-1/2in (19cm) toddler		425 - 450
10-12in (25-30cm) baby		500 - 550
#444, 13in (33cm)		650
#463, 12in (30cm)		700
Kämmer & Reinhardt		
Child, 16in (41cm)		1800 - 2000
#100 Baby, 14in (36cm) (For		
photograph see page 96.)		1000 - 1100
#101, 11in (28cm)		3500 - 3600

J. D. Kestner

Child, 12in (30cm)	1300
A. T.-type,	
17in (43cm) damaged ear lobes,	
naked, no wig, at auction	5175
Hilda, 10in (25cm)	3800 - 4200
Kuhnlenz #34	
7-8in (18-20cm) fully jointed	500 - 600
8-1/2in (21cm) 5-piece body all	
original Mammy with baby	700
21in (53cm)	5500 -6500
Armand Marseille	
#341, cloth body,	
10-12in (25-31cm)	400 - 425
#351, composition body,	
8-12in (20-31cm)	500 - 525
14-16in (38-41cm)	650 - 750
#362, composition body,	
12in (31cm)	600
S PB H Hanna,	
7-8in (18-20cm)	375 - 425
Simon & Halbig	
#739, 15-17in (38-43cm)	2600 - 2900
#949, open mouth,	
16in (41cm)	2600 - 2900
#970, 16-1/2in (42cm)	1600 - 1700
#1009, 18in (46cm)	2100 - 2200
#1249, 20in (51cm)	1900 - 2100
#1294, 20in (51cm) wig pulls,	
at auction	920
#1358, 22in (56cm)	10,350
Franz Schmidt 1272,	
22-1/2in (57cm)	2600
Unmarked Child	
10-13in (25-33cm)	
jointed body	400 - 500
8-9in (20-23cm) 5-piece body	300 - 350
4-5in (10-14cm) closed mouth,	
S & H quality	450 - 500
All-Bisque	
5in (14cm) glass eyes	450 - 500
6in (15cm) Kestner, swivel neck,	
bare feet	1500

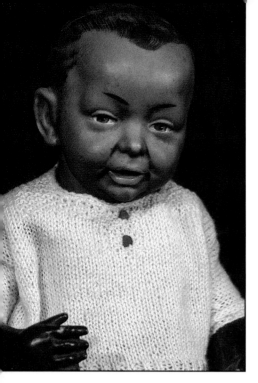

14in (36cm) K & R #100 Baby. *Richard Wright Antiques.* (For further information see page 95.)

BELOW: *Left:* 8-1/2in (21cm) E. Heubach 452 toddler. *H & J Foulke, Inc.* (For further information see page 95.) *Right:* 16-1/2in (42cm) 1907 Jumeau. *Keifer Collection.*

15-1/2in (39cm) S & H 1039. *Carol Green Collection.*

BELOW: *Left:* 19in (49cm) primitive black cloth doll. *H & J Foulke, Inc.* *Right:* 16in (41cm) 1930s black cloth "Mammy." *H & J Foulke, Inc.* (For further information see page 98.)

BLACK DOLLS *continued*

Cloth Black Doll*: 1880s-on. American-made cloth doll with black face, painted, printed or embroidered features; jointed arms and legs; original clothes; all in good condition.

Primitive, painted or embroidered
face   **$ 1000 - 2000+**

Stockinette (so-called Beecher-type). (For photograph see *8th Blue Book*, page 98.)
20in (51cm)   **2000 - 2500**

1930s Mammy. (See photograph on page 97.)
18-20in (46-51cm)   **250 - 350+**

WPA, molded cloth face. (For photograph see *7th Blue Book*, page 83.)
22in (56cm)   **$ 1400 - 1500**
Alabama-type, 24in (61cm)   **3500**
Chase Mammy, 26in (66cm)   **10,000**

Black Papier-Mâché Doll: Ca. 1890. By various German manufacturers. Papier-mâché character face, arms and legs, cloth body; glass eyes; original or appropriate clothes; all in good condition.
12-14in (31-36cm)   **$ 350 -450**
18-20in (46-51cm) character with broad
smile   **900 - 1000**
Wax over shoulder head peddlar
at auction   **1265**

*Also check under manufacturer if known.

+Greatly depending upon appeal.

Black Low-Fired Pottery: Ca. 1930. English and German. 16in (41cm) molded curly hair.   **$ 850**

Black Composition Doll: Ca. 1920-on. German made character doll, all-composition, jointed at neck, shoulders and hips; molded hair or wig, glass eyes (sometimes flirty); appropriate clothes; all in good condition.
11in (28cm)   **$ 350**
16-18in (41-46cm)   **650 - 750***

Black Composition Doll: Ca. 1930. American-made bent-limb baby or mama-type body, jointed at hips, shoulders and perhaps neck; molded hair, painted or sleep eyes; original or appropriate clothes; some have three yarn tufts of hair on either side and on top of the head; all in good condition.
"Topsy" Baby,
10-12in (25-31cm)   **$ 150 - 165**
Toddler,
15-16in (38-46cm)   **300 - 350**
Girl, 17in (43cm)   **350 - 400**
1910 character,
13-1/2in (34cm)   **300 - 350**
Patsy-type,
13-14in (33-36cm)   **300 - 350**

Black Hard Plastic Characters: Ca. 1950. English made by Pedigree and others. All hard plastic, swivel neck, jointed shoulders and hips, sleeping eyes, curly black wig sometimes over molded hair.
16in (41cm)   **$ 150 - 175**
21in (53cm)   **225 - 275**

*Allow $50-75 extra for flirty eyes.

OPPOSITE PAGE: 17in (43cm) brown composition girl. *H & J Foulke, Inc.*

BOUDOIR DOLLS

Boudoir Doll: Head of composition, cloth or other material, painted features, mohair wig, composition or cloth stuffed body, unusually long extremities, usually high-heeled shoes; original clothes elaborately designed and trimmed; all in excellent condition.

1920s Art Doll, exceptional quality, silk hair,
28-30in (71-76cm) $ **400 - 500**

Standard quality, dressed,
28-30in (71-76cm) **175 - 225**
undressed **90 - 110**

1940s composition head,
dressed **90 - 110**

Lenci, 24-28in (61-71cm) **2000 up**

Smoking Doll, 25in (64cm) **450 - 500**

Poured Wax, 22in (56cm) **600**

FACTS
Various French, U.S. and Italian firms.
Early 1920s into the 1940s. Many
24-36in (61-91cm); some smaller.
Mark: Mostly unmarked.

27in (68cm) boudoir doll, all original. *Private Collection.*

BRU

Poupée (Fashion Lady): 1873-on. Perfect bisque swivel head on shoulder plate, cork pate, appropriate old wig, closed smiling mouth, paperweight eyes, pierced ears; gusseted kid lady body; original or appropriate clothes; all in good condition. Incised with letters "A" through "O" in sizes 11in (28cm) to 36in (91cm) tall.

14-16in (35-41cm)	$	3200 - 3800*
20-21in (51-53cm)		5500 - 6000*
Wood arms,		
13-14in (33-35cm)		3800 - 4000*
Wood body, naked		
15-17in (38-43cm)		6000 - 6800*

*Allow extra for original clothes.

FACTS

Bru Jne. & Cie, Paris, and Montreuil-sous-Bois, France. 1866-1899.

17in (43cm) Bru *poupée*, kid body with bisque hands. *Private Collection.*

BRU *continued*

Poupée (Fashion Lady): 1866-on. Perfect bisque swivel head on shoulder plate, cork pate, old mohair wig, closed mouth, paperweight eyes, pierced ears; gusseted or straight kid lady body; appropriate clothes; all in good condition. Oval face, incised with numbers only. Shoulder plate sometimes marked "B. Jne & Cie."

12-13in (31-33cm)	$	**2500 - 2800***
15-17in (38-43cm)		**3200 - 3600***
20-21in (51-53cm)		**4200 - 4700***
Wood body, naked		
16in (41cm)		**5000 - 5200**

Marked Breveté Bébé: Ca. 1870s. Perfect bisque swivel head on shoulder plate, cork pate, skin wig, paperweight eyes with shading on upper lid, closed mouth with white space between lips, full cheeks, pierced ears; gusseted kid body pulled high on shoulder plate and straight cut with bisque lower arms (no rivet joints); original or appropriate old clothes; all in good condition. (For photograph see page 104.)

Mark: Size number only on head.
Oval sticker on body:

or rectangular sticker like Bébé Bru one, but with words "Bébé Breveté."

Size 5/0	= 10-1/2in (27cm)
Size 2/0	= 14in (36cm)
Size 1	= 16in (41cm)
Size 2	= 18in (46cm)
Size 3	= 19in (48cm)

14-16in (35-41cm)	$ **14,000 - 16,000**
19-22in (48-56cm)	**19,000 - 22,000**
12in (30cm) with trousseau	**15,000**

*Allow extra for original clothes.

18in (46cm) **Bébé Gourmand.** *Private Collection.* (For close-up photograph see page 1.)

17in (43cm) **Bébé Têteur.** *Private Collection.*

BRU *continued*

Marked Crescent or Circle Dot Bébé: Ca. late 1870s. Perfect bisque swivel head on a deep shoulder plate with molded breasts, cork pate, attractive wig, paperweight eyes, closed mouth with slightly parted lips, molded and painted teeth, plump cheeks, pierced ears; gusseted kid body with bisque lower arms (no rivet joints); original or appropriate old clothes; all in good condition. (For photographs see *11th Blue Book*, cover and page 104.)

Mark:

Sometimes with "BRU J^{ne}"

Approximate size chart:
0	= 11in	(28cm)
1	= 12in	(31cm)
2	= 13in	(33cm)
5	= 17in	(43cm)
8	= 22in	(56cm)
10	= 26in	(66cm)
12	= 30in	(76cm)
14	= 35in	(89cm)

10-1/2in (26cm)	$	**8000 - 9000**
13-14in (33-35cm)		**13,000 - 15,000**
18-19in (46-48cm)		**18,000 - 20,000**
24in (61cm)		**24,000 - 25,000**

Bébé Gourmand:
18in (46cm) **no prices available**

Marked Nursing Bru (Bébé Têteur): 1878-1898. Perfect bisque head, shoulder plate and lower arms, kid body; upper arms and upper legs of metal covered with kid, lower legs of carved wood, or jointed composition body; attractive wig, lovely glass eyes, open mouth with hole for nipple, mechanism in head sucks up liquid, operates by turning key; nicely clothed; all in good condition.
13-15in (33-38cm)
Early model	$	**8500 - 9500**
Later model		**5500 - 6500**

Marked Bru Jne Bébé: Ca. 1880s. Perfect bisque swivel head on deep shoulder plate with molded breasts, cork pate, attractive wig, paperweight eyes, closed mouth, pierced ears; gusseted kid body with scalloped edge at shoulder plate, bisque lower arms with lovely hands, kid over wood upper arms, hinged elbow, all kid or wood lower legs (sometimes on a jointed composition body); original or appropriate clothes; all in good condition. (For color photograph see page 105, for body photograph see *6th Blue Book*, page 79.))

Mark: "BRU J^{ne}"

Body Label:

12-13in (31-33cm)	$	**12,000 - 14,000***
15-17in (38-43cm)		**15,500 - 17,500***
23-24in (58-61cm)		**22,000***
27in (69cm)		**23,000 - 24,000***

Marked Bru Shoes: $ **500 - 600**

Marked Bru Jne R Bébé: Ca. Early 1890s. Perfect bisque head on a jointed composition body; attractive wig, paperweight eyes, closed mouth, pierced ears; dressed; all in good condition. (For photograph see *11th Blue Book*, page 105.)

Mark:

BRU J^{ne} R
11

Body Stamp: "Bebe Bru" with size number
11-13in (28-33cm)	$	**2200 - 2600**
19-21in (48-53cm)		**6000 - 7000**

Open mouth:
12in (31cm)	**1500 - 1800**
20-21in (51-53cm)	**3000 - 4000**

17in (43cm) **Bébé Breveté**. *H & J Foulke, Inc.*

See preceding pages for further information about Bru dolls.

23in (58cm) Circle dot **Bébé Bru**. *Kay & Wayne Jensen Colection.*

22in (56cm) **Bru Jne 8**. *Kay & Wayne Jensen Collection.*

BUCHERER

Bucherer Doll: Composition character head sometimes with molded hat; metal ball-jointed body with large composition hands and composition molded shoes; original clothes, often felt; all in good condition.
8in (20cm) average
Man and woman in provincial
   costumes   **$ 175 - 200 each**
Fireman, clown, black man, aviator,
   rabbit, baseball player. **Becassine**
   and others   **$ 225 - 275**

Comic characters: Mutt, Jeff, Maggie, Jiggs, Katzenjammers, Fanny Brice, Happy Hooligan and others. **$ 350 up**

FACTS
A. Bucherer, Amriswil,
Switzerland. 1921.
Mark:
"MADE IN
SWITZERLAND
PATENTS
APPLIED FOR"

Becassine, all original. *H & J Foulke, Inc.*

BYE-LO BABY

FACTS

Bisque heads — J.D. Kestner; Alt, Beck & Gottschalck; Kling & Co.; Hertel, Schwab & Co.; all of Thüringia, Germany.
Composition heads — Cameo Doll Company, New York, N.Y.
Celluloid heads — Karl Standfuss, Saxony, Germany.
Wooden heads (unauthorized) — Schoenhut of Philadelphia, Pa.
All-Bisque Baby — J.D. Kestner.
Cloth Bodies and Assembly — K & K Toy Co., New York, N.Y.
Composition Bodies — König & Wernicke. 1922-on.
Designer: Grace Storey Putnam.
Distributor: George Borgfeldt, New York, N.Y., U.S.A.

14in (36cm) *Bye-Lo Baby* with original gown. *H & J Foulke, Inc.*

Bisque Head Bye-Lo Baby: Ca. 1923. Perfect bisque head, cloth body with curved legs (sometimes with straight legs), composition or celluloid hands; sleep eyes; dressed. Made in seven sizes, 9-20in (23-51cm). (May have purple "Bye-Lo Baby" stamp on front of body.) Sometimes Mold **#1373** (ABG).

Mark:

© 1923 *by*
Grace S. Putnam
MADE IN GERMANY

Head circumference:

7-1/2–8in (19-20cm)	$	500 - 525*
9-10in (23-25cm)		475 - 500*
12-13in (31-33cm)		550 - 600*
15in (38cm)		900*
17in (43cm)		1100 - 1300*
18in (46cm)		1400 - 1600*

Tagged Bye-Lo gown		50
Bye-Lo pin		95
Bye-Lo type, incised "45," open mouth 12in (31cm) h.c.	$	800

* Allow extra for original tagged gown and button.

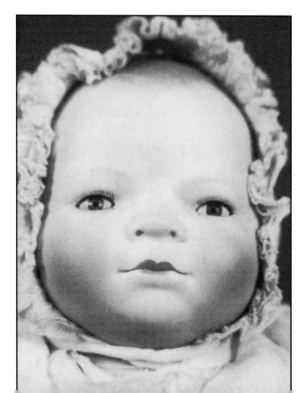

Mold #1369 (ABG) socket head on composition body, some marked "K&W."
12-13in (30-33cm) long   **$ 1200 - 1300**

Mold #1415, smiling with painted eyes (For photograph see *11th Blue Book*, page 108.)
13-1/2in (34cm) h.c.   **$ 4000****
Composition head, 1924.
12-13in (31-33cm) h.c.   **350 - 375**
Celluloid head,
10in (25cm) h.c.   **300 - 350****
Painted bisque head, late 1920s.
12-13in (31-33cm) h.c.   **325****
Wooden head, (Schoenhut), 1925.
1500 - 1600

Vinyl head, 1948.
16in (41cm)   **150 - 200**

Wax head, 1922.   **700 - 800**

Baby Aero or Fly-Lo Baby bisque head Mold #1418. (See *11th Blue Book*, page 107.)
11in (28cm)   **$ 3800 - 4200**
Composition head, original costume,
12in (31cm)   **800 - 900**

**Not enough price samples to compute a reliable range.

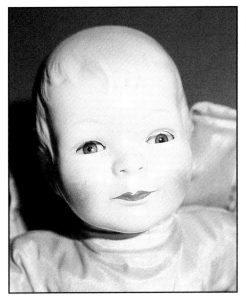

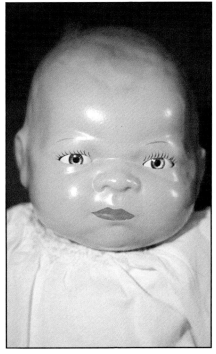

10in (25cm) long **Fly-Lo** with composition head, all original. *Doelman Collection. Courtesy of Richard W. Withington, Inc.*

17in (43cm) long composition head, **Bye-Lo Baby.** *H & J Foulke, Inc.*

BYE-LO BABY *continued*

Marked All-Bisque Bye-Lo Baby: 1925-on. Sizes 10cm (4in) to 20cm (8in).
Mark: Dark green paper label on front torso often missing; incised on back "20-12" (or other stock and size number).

> "Copr. by
> G.S. Putnam"

Solid head with molded hair and painted eyes, jointed shoulders and hips,

4-5in (10-13cm)	$	275 - 375
6in (15cm)		475 - 525
8in (20cm)		675 - 725

Solid head with swivel neck, glass eyes, jointed shoulders and hips,

4-5in (10-13cm)	$	550 - 625
6in (15cm)		725 - 825
8in (20cm)		1100 - 1200

Head with wig, glass eyes, jointed shoulders and hips,

4-5in (10-13cm)	650 - 750
6in (15cm)	850 - 950
8in (20cm)	1250 - 1450

Action Bye-Lo Baby, immobile in various positions, painted features,

3in (8cm)	$	400
Celluloid 4in (10cm)		250 - 300

6-1/2in (17cm) all-bisque ***Bye-Lo***. *H & J Foulke, Inc.*

CAMEO DOLL COMPANY

───── FACTS ─────

Cameo Doll Company, New York, N.Y., U.S.A., later Port Allegany, Pa., U.S.A. Original owner: Joseph L. Kallus. 1922-on.

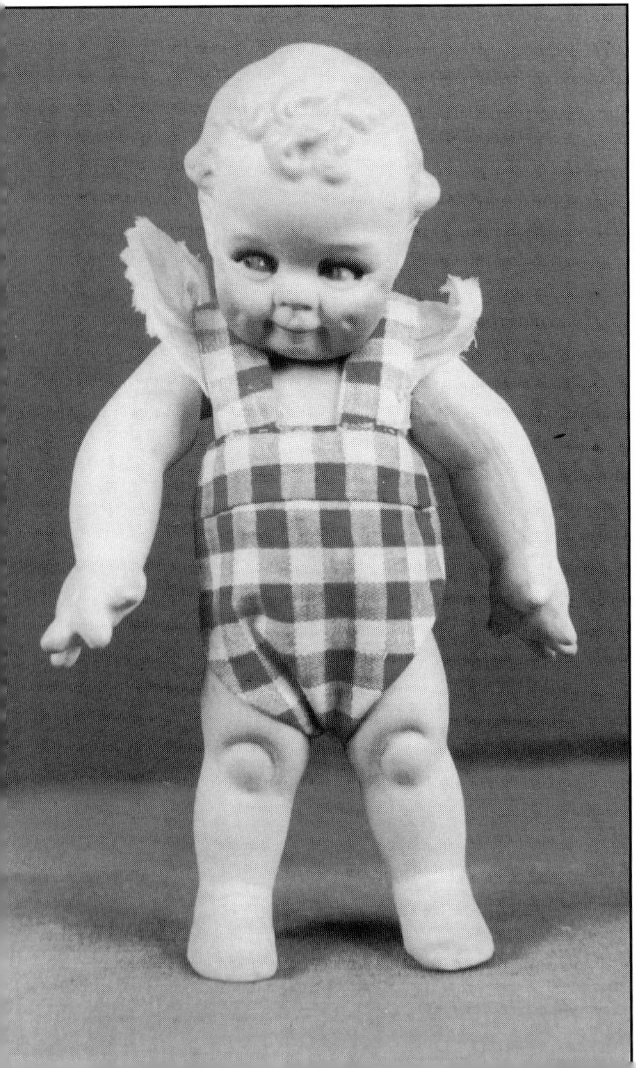

6-1/2in (17cm) all-bisque *Scootles*, signed on foot. *H & J Foulke, Inc.*

Baby Bo Kaye: 1925. (See page 71.)
Kewpie: 1913. (See page 244.)
Scootles: 1925. Designed by Rose O'Neill. All-composition, unmarked, jointed at neck, shoulders and hips; molded hair, blue or brown painted eyes looking to the side, closed smiling mouth; appropriate clothes; all in very good condition. (For photograph see page 9.)
Mark: Wrist tag only.

7in-8in (18-20cm)	$ 375 - 425**
12-13in (31-33cm)	500 - 525
15-16in (38-41cm)	650 - 700
20in (51cm)	800 - 900**

12in (30cm) sleep eyes,
at auction **1000**
Black,
13-14in (33-36cm)
750 - 850
All-bisque, marked on feet
5-6in (13-15cm)
Germany **650 - 750**
6-7in (15-18cm)
Japan **500 - 550**
Vinyl, 14in (36cm)
1973 Maxine's
Ltd. Ed. **125 - 150**

**Not enough price samples to compute a reliable range.

13in (33cm) black
composition
Scootles, original
sunsuit. *H & J
Foulke, Inc.*

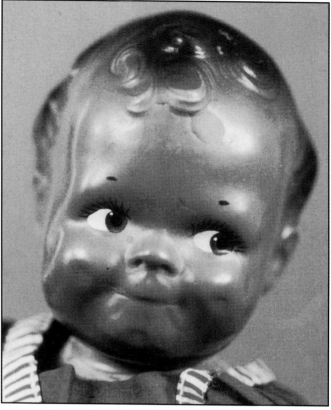

Wood Segmented Characters: Designed by
Joseph L. Kallus. Composition head, molded
hair, painted features; segmented wood
body; undressed; all in very good condition.
Mark: Label with name on chest.

Margie, 1929. 10in (25cm)	$	225 - 250
Pinkie, 1930. 10in (25cm)		275 - 325
Joy, 1932. 10in (5cm)		275 - 325
15in (38cm)		375 - 425
Betty Boop, 1932.		
12in (31cm)		550 - 650

With molded bathing suit and composition
legs; wearing a cotton print dress,

		650 - 700
Pop-Eye, 1935		300**
Hotpoint Man, 16in (41cm)		800**
RCA Radiotron, 16in (41cm)		800**

Giggles: 1946. Designed by Rose O'Neill.
All-composition, unmarked, jointed at neck,
shoulders and hips, molded hair with bun in
back, large painted side-glancing eyes,
closed mouth; original romper; all in very
good condition. (For photograph see *11th
Blue Book*, page 111.)
Mark: Paper wrist tag only.

14in (36cm)	$	650 - 750**

Little Annie Rooney: 1925. Designed by
Jack Collins. Composition, painted eyes,
yarn wig, all original.

16in (41cm)	$	700**

Baby Blossom: 1927. Composition and
cloth, 19-20in (48-51cm), all original with
label, excellent, at auction $ **1100**

Champ: 1942. Composition, molded hair,
freckles, all original.

16in (41cm)	$	500 - 600**

**Not enough price samples to compute a
reliable range.

CAMEO DOLL COMPANY *continued*

Vinyl Dolls:

Miss Peep, 1957, all original.
16-18in (41-46cm) boxed $	**195**
Black	**195**

Baby Mine, 1961, all original.
20in (51cm) boxed	**175**

Margie, 1958, all original.
17in (43cm) boxed	**150 - 175****

Scootles, 1964, all original.
14in (36cm)	**165 - 185**

**Not enough price samples to compute a reliable range.

10in (25cm) ***Margi****e. H & J Foulke, Inc.*

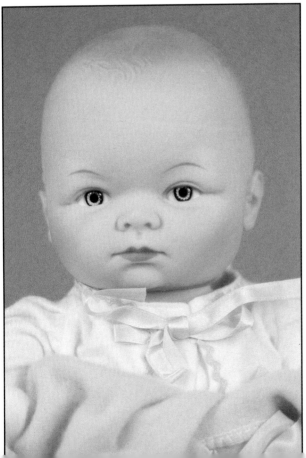

Miss Peep*, all original. H & J Foulke, Inc.*

CATTERFELDER PUPPENFABRIK

C.P. Child Doll: Ca. 1902-on. Perfect bisque head, good wig, sleep eyes, open mouth with teeth; composition jointed body; dressed; all in good condition. (For photograph see *11th Blue Book*, page 112.)

#264 (made by Kestner):

17-19in (43-48cm)	$	**800 - 850**
22-24in (56-61cm)		**950 - 1000**
35-36in (89-91cm)		**2000 - 2500****

C.P. Character Child: Ca. 1910-on. Perfect bisque character face with wig, painted eyes; composition jointed body; dressed; all in good condition. Sometimes mold #207 or #219.

15-16in (38-41cm)	$	**3000 - 4000****
#217, 18in (46cm)		**9750****
#220, 14in (36cm) glass eyes,		**7500****

C.P. Character Baby: Ca. 1910-on. Perfect bisque character face with wig or molded hair, painted or glass eyes; jointed baby body; dressed; all in good condition.

#200, 201:

13-15in (33-38cm)	$	**500 - 600**
18-19in (46-48cm)		**800 - 900**

#201, toddler, 10in (25cm)	$	**700 - 900****

#262, 263, (made by Kestner)

15-17in (38-43cm)	$	**525 - 625**
20-22in (51-56cm)		**800 - 900**

#262, toddler, 5-piece body

16-1/2in (42cm)	$	**1000 - 1100**

#208,

15-17in (38-43cm)	$	**525 - 575**
22-24in (56-61cm)	$	**800 - 900**

**Not enough price samples to compute a reliable range.

FACTS

Catterfelder Puppenfabrik, Catterfield, Thüringia, Germany. Heads by J.D. Kestner and other porcelain makers. 1902-on. Bisque head; composition body. **Trademark:** My Sunshine.

Mark:

C. P.
208
45
N

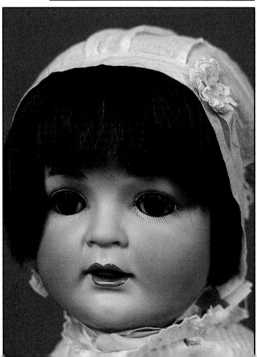

22in (56cm) 262 character baby. *H & J Foulke, Inc.*

CELLULOID DOLLS

FACTS

Germany: Rheinische Gummi und Celluloid Fabrik Co. (Turtle symbol); Buschow & Beck, *Minerva* trademark (Helmet symbol); E. Maar & Sohn, *Emasco* trademark (3 M symbol); Cellba (Mermaid symbol). **Poland:** P.R. Zask (ASK in triangle). **France:** Petitcolin (Eagle symbol); Société Nobel Francaise (SNF in diamond); Neumann & Marx (Dragon symbol); Société Industrielle de Celluloid (Sicoine). **United States:** Parsons-Jackson Co., Cleveland, Ohio, and other companies. **England:** Cascelloid Ltd. (Palitoy). 1895-1940s.

Marks: Various as indicated above: sometimes also in combination with the marks of J. D. Kestner, Kämmer & Reinhardt, Bruno Schmidt, Käthe Kruse and König & Wernicke.

Celluloid Shoulder Head Child Doll: Ca. 1900-on. Molded hair or wig, painted or glass eyes, open or closed mouth; cloth or kid body, celluloid or composition arms; dressed; all in good condition.

Painted eyes:
13-15in (33-38cm)	**$ 135 - 160**

Glass eyes:
19-22in (48-56cm) child	**225 - 250**
12-14in (30-36cm) original provincial costume	**200 - 225**

All-Celluloid Child Doll: Ca. 1900-on. Jointed at neck, shoulders, and hips; molded hair or wig, painted eyes; dressed; all in good condition. (For additional photograph see page 9.)

5in (12cm) googly	**$ 125 - 135***
4in (10cm)	**45 - 60***
7-8in (18-20cm)	**75 - 85***
10-12in (25-31cm)	**110 - 135***
14-15in (36-38cm)	**160 - 185***

*Allow extra for unusual dolls.

6-3/4in (18cm) German turtle mark character. *H & J Foulke, Inc.*

14in (36cm) German turtle mark boy, all original. *H & J Foulke, Inc.*

SNF pair with molded provincial costumes,
9in (23cm) **200 - 225**
Tommy Tucker-type character:
12-14in (31-36cm) **$ 185 - 210**

Glass Eyes:
12-13in (31-33cm) **175 - 200***
15-16in (38-41cm) **250 - 275***
18in (46cm) **350 - 400***

*Allow extra for unusual dolls.

K★R 717 or 728:
14-16in (36-41cm) **$ 550 - 650**
14in (36cm) cloth body **375**

All-Celluloid Baby: Ca. 1910-on. Bent-limb baby, molded hair, painted eyes, closed mouth; jointed arms and/or legs; no clothes; all in good condition.
6-8in (15-20cm) **$ 65 - 85**
10-12in (25-31cm) **110 - 135***
15in (38cm) **175 - 200***
21in (53cm) **250 - 300***

SNF black with African features
10in (25cm) **450**

French Oriental
8in (20cm) **475**
11in (28cm) **650**

*Allow $25-35 extra for glass eyes.

All-Celluloid, Made in Japan: Ca. 1920s.
Molded clothes,
4-5in (10-12cm) **$ 60 - 80**
8-9in (20-23cm) **150 - 175**
Baby, 13in (33cm) **175**
24in (61cm) **350 - 400**

Parsons-Jackson, Stork Mark:
11-1/2in (29cm) baby **$ 165 - 185***
14in (36cm) toddler **275 - 325***

*Allow extra for molded shoes and socks.

Celluloid Head Infant: Ca. 1920s-on. Celluloid baby head with glass eyes, painted hair, open or closed mouth; cloth body, sometimes with celluloid hands; appropriate clothes; all in good condition.
12-15in (31-38cm) **$ 150 - 200**

Celluloid Socket Head Doll: Ca. 1910-on. Wig, glass eyes, sometimes flirty, open mouth with teeth; ball-jointed or bent-limb composition body; dressed; all in good condition.

K★R 701, child,
12-13in (31-33cm) **$ 900 - 1100****
K★R 717 child,
12in (31cm) **300 - 350**
16-18in (41-46cm) **600 - 650**
K★R 700, baby,
14-15in (36-38cm) **325 - 375**
K★R 728,
12-13in (31-33cm) baby **325 - 375**
20in (51cm) **550**
18in (46cm) flapper **850**
F.S. & Co. 1276,
20in (51cm) baby **550**

**Not enough price samples to compute a reliable range.

10in (25cm) Plawo Holland girl. *H & J Foulke, Inc.*

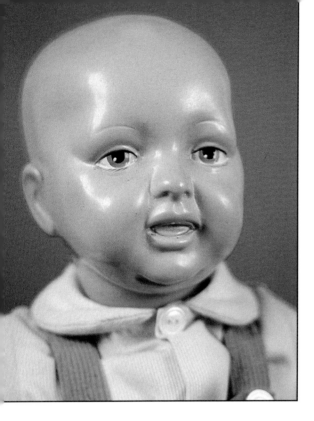

14in (36cm) Parsons - Jackson baby with molded blue shoes and socks. *H & J Foulke, Inc.*

20in (51cm) K & R 728 character baby. *H & J Foulke, Inc.*

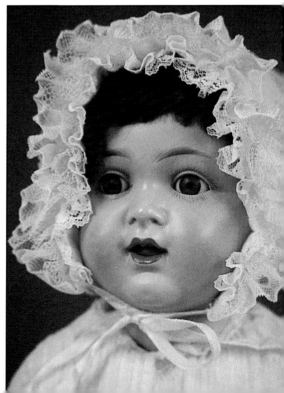

CENTURY DOLL CO.

FACTS

Century Doll Co., New York, N.Y.,
U.S.A.; bisque heads by J.D. Kestner,
Germany. 1909-on.

Mark:

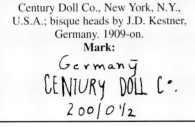

Germany
CENTURY DOLL Cº.
200/0½

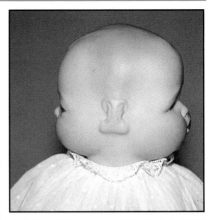

Marked Century Infant: Ca. 1925. Perfect bisque solid-dome head, molded and painted hair, sleep eyes, open/closed mouth; cloth body, composition hands or limbs; dressed; all in good condition. Some with smiling face are mold **#277**.

Head circumference:

10-11in (25-28cm)	$	**500 - 550**
13-14in (33-36cm)		**700 - 800**
Double-face		**2500****

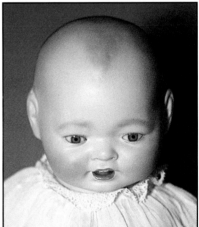

Mama doll, bisque shoulder head #281. (For photograph see *Kestner, King of Dollmakers*, page 194.)

21in (53cm)	$	**650 - 750****

Child with molded hair #200. (For photograph see *10th Blue Book*, page 132.)

12in (31cm)	$	**350****

Marked "Mama" Doll: Ca. 1920s. Composition shoulder head with character face, molded hair, smiling open mouth with two teeth, dimples, tin sleep eyes. Cloth torso with cryer, composition arms and legs; appropriate clothing. All in good condition.

16in (41cm)	$	**225 - 250**
23in (58cm)		**375 - 425**

** Not enough price samples to compute a reliable range.

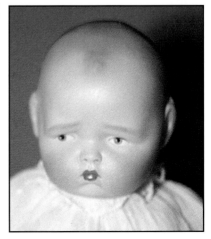

Three views of double-face Century infant.
Barbara Manhart Collection.

CHAD VALLEY

Chad Valley Doll: All-cloth, usually felt face and velvet body, jointed neck, shoulders and hips; mohair wig, glass or painted eyes; original clothes; all in excellent condition.

Characters, painted eyes,
10-12in (25-31cm)	$	85 - 115

Children, painted eyes,
9in (23cm)	135 - 150
13-14in (33-36cm)	375 - 475
16-18in (41-46cm)	550 - 650

Characters, glass eyes,
17-20in (43-51cm)	1000 - 2000*

Children, glass eyes,
16-18in (41-46cm)	700 - 775

Royal Children, glass eyes,
16-18in (41-46cm)	1450 - 1650

Mabel Lucie Attwell, glass inset side-glancing eyes, smiling watermelon mouth.
15-17in (38-43cm)	$	750 - 800

Dwarfs (Snow White Set),
10in (25cm)	250 - 275 each

*Depending upon rarity.

FACTS

Chad Valley Co. (formerly Johnson Bros., Ltd.), Birmingham, England. 1917-on.
Mark: Cloth label usually on foot:
"HYGIENIC TOYS
Made in England by
CHAD VALLEY CO. LTD."

17in (43cm) *Bambino* by Mabel Lucie Attwell, original print dress with Attwell design. *H & J Foulke, Inc.*

MARTHA CHASE

Martha Jenks Chase, Pawtucket, R.I., U.S.A. 1889-on. Stockinette and cloth, painted in oils; some fully painted washable models; some designed for hospital training use. 9in (23cm) to life-size. **Designer:** Martha Jenks Chase. **Mark:** "Chase Stockinet Doll" stamp on left leg or under left arm, paper label on back (usually gone).

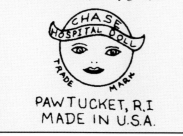

20in (51cm) Hospital baby with fully washable body. *H & J Foulke, Inc.*

Chase Doll: Head and limbs of stockinette, treated and painted with oils, large painted eyes with thick upper lashes, rough-stroked hair to provide texture, cloth bodies jointed at shoulders, hips, elbows and knees, later ones only at shoulders and hips; some bodies completely treated; appropriate clothing; showing wear, but no repaint.

Baby

9in (23cm)	$ 3000**
13-15in (33-38cm)	575 - 675*
17-20in (43-51cm)	750*
24-26in (61-66cm)	850*

Child, molded bobbed hair, (For photograph see page 12.)

12-15in (31-38cm)	1200 - 1600
20in (51cm)	2000

Lady,

13-15in (33-38cm)	1500 - 1600

*Allow extra for a doll in excellent condition or with original clothes.
**Very rare. Not enough price samples to compute a reliable average.

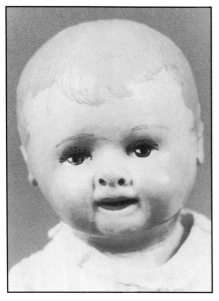

15-1/2in (39cm) lady. *Nancy A. Smith Collection.*

Man,
   15-16in (38-41cm)   **$**   **3000**
   Older with bald head, at auction   **6000**

Black, Mammy or child
                 $ 10,000 - 11,000
Boy with side part and side curl
   15-16in (38-41cm)   **3000**

16in (41cm) Black child. *Courtesy of Richard W. Withington, Inc.*

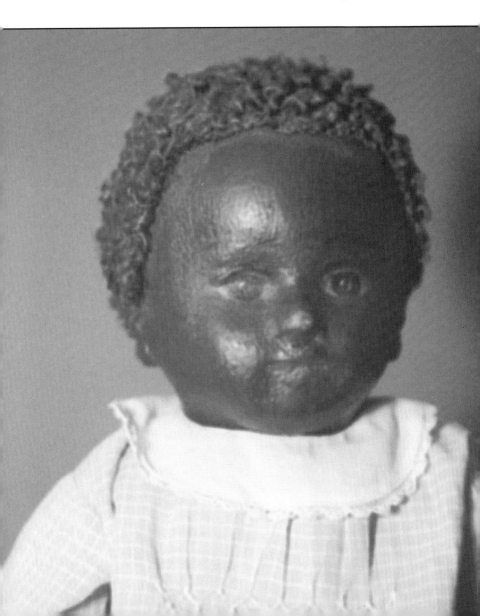

CHINA HEADS

(French*)

—— FACTS ——
Various French doll firms; some heads sold through French firms may have been made in Germany. 1850s.
Mark: None.

French China Head Doll: China shoulder head, glass or beautifully painted eyes, painted eyelashes, feathered eyebrows, closed mouth, open crown, cork pate, good wig; shapely kid fashion body (may have china arms curved to above elbow); appropriately dressed; all in good condition.

16-17in (41-43cm) $ 3200 - 3700
14in (36cm) with trunk and nice
    wardrobe, at auction   5830
16in (41cm) hairline   1200
Painted short black hair, pink kid body
12in (30cm)   1000 - 1200
17in (43cm)   1600 - 1800

* For dolls marked "Huret" or "Rohmer," see appropriate entry under those names.

(Attributed to England)

—— FACTS ——
Unidentified English firm, possibly Rockingham area. Ca. 1840-1860.
Mark: None.

English China Doll: Flesh-tinted shoulder head with bald head (some with molded slit for inserting wig), painted features, closed mouth; human hair wig. Cloth torso and upper arms and legs, china lower limbs with holes to attach them to cloth, bare feet. Appropriately dressed; all in good condition. (For photographs see *11th Blue Book*, page 120.)

19-22in (48-56cm) $ 2000 - 3000
without china limbs   1200

15in (38cm) French china. *Doelman Collection. Courtesy of Richard W. Withington, Inc.*

CHINA HEADS (German)

1840s Hairstyles: China shoulder head with black molded hair; may have pink tint complexion; old cloth body; (may have china arms); appropriate old clothes; all in good condition.

Hair swept back into bun,

13-15in (33-38cm)	$	**2000 - 2600**
18-21in (46-53cm)		**3000 - 5500**

Fancy braided bun,

22-24in (56-61cm)	**5000 - 6000**

20in (51cm) two hairlines on shoulder

2100

K.P.M., (For photographs see *11th Blue Book*, page 121.)

Brown hair with bun,

16-18in (41-46cm)	$	**4000 up***

Young Man, brown hair,

16-18in (41-46cm)	**3500 up**

Kinderkopf (child head),

15-16in (38-41cm)	**1000 - 1200**

13in (33cm) Royal Copenhagen china with bun. *Doelman Collection. Courtesy of Richard W. Withington, Inc.*

*Depending upon quality, hairdo and rarity.

FACTS

Some early dolls by K.P.M., Meissen and Royal Copenhagen (Denmark), but most by unidentified makers. Later dolls by firms such as Kling & Co., Alt, Beck & Gottschalck, Kestner & Co., Hertwig & Co., and others.
Mark: K.P.M., Meissen and Royal Copenhagen usually marked inside the shoulders; later dolls by Kling & Co. and A.B.G. are identifiable by their mold numbers. Most are unmarked.

13in (33cm) rare china with molded bonnet. *Doelman Collection. Courtesy of Richard W. Withington, Inc.*

Wood Body, china lower limbs,

5-6in (13-15cm)	$	1600 - 1800
11in (28cm)		3500 - 4000

1850s Hairstyles: China shoulder head (some with pink tint), molded black hair (except bald), painted eyes; old cloth body with leather or china arms; appropriate old clothes; all in good condition.

Bald head, some with black areas on top, proper wig. Allow extra for original human hair wig in fancy style.
Fine quality:

15-17in (38-43cm)	$	900 - 1000
22-24in (56-61cm)		1400 - 1600
15in (38cm) all original provincial costume, at auction		1155

Standard quality:

8-10in (20-25cm)	$	325 - 375
15-17in (38-43cm)		650 - 750
20-22in (51-56cm)		850 - 900

Covered Wagon:

9-10in (23-25cm)	$	400 - 450
15-17in (38-43cm)		650 - 750
21-23in (53-58cm)		1000 - 1100

With brown eyes,

6in (15cm) head only	750
20-22in (51-56cm)	1100 - 1200

Greiner-style, with brown eyes,

14-15in (36-38cm)	900 - 1000
19-22in (48-56cm)	1600 - 1800

With glass eyes,

15-16in (38-41cm)	3850**
22in (56cm)	4800**

** Not enough price samples to compute a reliable range.

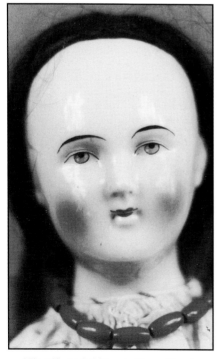

17in (43cm) bald head china with wig.
H & J Foulke, Inc.

15in (38cm) Greiner-style china with glass eyes. *Doelman Collection. Courtesy of Richard W. Withington, Inc.*

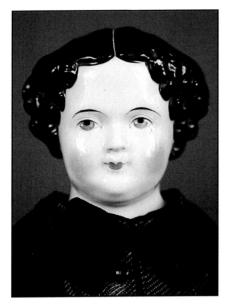

24in (61cm) china with rounded flat top hairdo. *H & J Foulke, Inc.*

17in (43cm) china with braided bun. *H & J Foulke, Inc.*

Waves framing face, brown eyes. (For photograph see *7th Blue Book*, page 114.)
20-21in (51-53cm) $ 1150 - 1350
With glass eyes,
18in (46cm)   2100
Child or Baby, flange swivel neck; china or papier-mâché shoulder plate and hips, china lower limbs; cloth midsection (may have voice box) and upper limbs. (For photograph see *9th Blue Book*, page 76.)
10in (25cm)   3000 - 3500**
Alice Hairstyle. (For photograph see *10th Blue Book*, page 99.)
8-11in (20-28cm)   4000**

1860s and 1870s Hairstyles: China shoulder head with black molded hair (a few blondes), painted eyes, closed mouth; old cloth body may have leather arms or china lower arms and legs with molded boots; appropriate old clothes; all in good condition.
Plain style with center part (so-called flat top and high brow):
6-7 in (15-18cm) $ 110 - 115

14-16in (36-41cm)	**265 - 295**
19-22in (48-56cm)	**350 - 385**
24-26in (61-66cm)	**425 - 525**
28in (71cm)	**625**
34-35in (86-89cm)	**800**
Molded necklace,	
22-24in (56-61cm)	**600 - 700**
Blonde hair,	
18in (46cm)	**400 - 500**
Brown eyes,	
20-22in (51-56cm)	**600 - 700**
Swivel neck,	
15-1/2in (40cm)	**1200****

Mary Todd Lincoln with snood. (For photograph see *8th Blue Book*, page 130.)
18-21in (46-53cm) $ 800 - 900
Brown hair,
14in (36cm)   1000

**Not enough price samples to compute a reliable range.

OPPOSITE PAGE: 16-1/2in (42cm) china with high forehead. *H & J Foulke, Inc.*

Dolley Madison with molded bow,
14-16in (36-41cm) $ **400 - 450**
21-24in (53-61cm)   **600 - 650**

Adelina Patti (For photograph see *11th Blue Book*, page 124.)
13-15in (33-38cm) $ **400 - 450**
19-22in (48-56cm)   **600 - 650**

Fancy style (only a sampling can be covered because of the wide variety):
Jenny Lind (For photograph see *Doll Classics*, page 130.)
21-24in (53-61cm) $ **1400 - 1500**
Curly Top (For photograph see *7th Blue Book*, page 115.)
14in (36cm) black hair   **600**
19in (48cm) tan hair   **900**
Grape Lady (For photograph see *8th Blue Book*, page 130.)
18in (46cm) $ **2200 - 2500**
Spill Curl (For photograph see *5th Blue Book*, page 98.)
19-22in (48-56cm)   **900 - 1100**
Morning Glory (For photograph see *11th Blue Book*, page 124.)
21in (53cm)   **5500 - 6500****

Slender face, brushed back into poufs and curls and roll, brush strokes around face,
17in (43cm) $ **1150**
Blonde hair, waves around face, falling onto neck and caught up into a black snood,
18in (46cm)   **6600**
Double-braided bun with braid across crown,
25in (63cm)   **3800**
Blonde hair curls cascading down back, blue hair band, pierced ears,
16in (41cm)   **2600**

Man or boy. (For photograph see *10th Blue Book*, page 100.)
Fine quality,
15-16in (38-41cm) $ **1100 - 1200**
Standard quality,
16in (41cm)   **500 - 550**
With jester cap,
16in (41cm)   **1100**
With molded black cap,
15in (38cm) at auction   **900**

**Not enough price samples to compute a reliable range.

9-1/2in (24cm) brown haired china with gold snood. *Richard Wright Antiques.*

24in (61cm) fancy hairdo china. *H & J Foulke, Inc.*

28in (71cm) china head wih 1880s hairdo. *H & J Foulke, Inc.*

1880s Hairstyles: China shoulder head with black or blonde molded hair, blue painted eyes, closed mouth; cloth body with china arms and legs or kid body; appropriate old clothes; all in good condition. Many made by Alt, Beck & Gottschalck (see page 48 for mold numbers) or Kling & Co. (see page 252 for mold numbers).

14-16in (36-41cm)	$	**300 - 350**
21-23in (53-58cm)		**450 - 500**
28in (71cm)		**550 - 600**

Dressel & Kister: 1890-1920. China shoulder head with varying hairdos and brush stroked hair, delicately painted features; cloth body with china arms having beautifully molded fingers. Often used as ornamental dolls in only half form as for a boudoir lamp or candy box. (For 14 different examples from Margaret Hartshorn Collection see January/February 1995 *Antique Doll World*, pages 50-56.)

13in (33cm) tall	$	**1500 up****

1890s Hairstyles: China shoulder head with black or blonde molded wavy hair, blue painted eyes, closed mouth; old cloth or kid body with stub, leather, bisque or china limbs; appropriate clothes; all in good condition.

8-10in (20-25cm)	$	**90 - 110**
13-15in (33-38cm)		**150 - 195**
19-21in (48-53cm)		**235 - 285**
24in (61cm)		**350**

Molded bonnet,		
8in (20cm)		**150 - 165**
Molded "Jewel" necklace,		
22in (56cm)		**400**

Pet Name: Ca. 1905. Made by Hertwig & Co. for Butler Bros., N.Y. China shoulder head, molded yoke with name in gold; black or blonde painted hair (one-third were blonde), blue painted eyes; old cloth body (some with alphabet or other figures printed on cotton material), china limbs; properly dressed; all in good condition. Used names such as **Agnes, Bertha, Daisy, Dorothy, Edith, Esther, Ethel, Florence, Helen, Mabel, Marion** and **Pauline.**

12-14in (30-36cm)	$	**200 - 250**
18-21in (46-53cm)	$	**350 - 400**
24in (61cm)		**450**

** Not enough price samples to compute a reliable average.

8in (20cm) china head with 1890s hairdo. *H & J Foulke, Inc.*

13in (33cm) D & K china head. *Doelman Collection. Courtesy of Richard W. Withington, Inc.*

CLOTH, PRINTED

FACTS

Various American companies, such as Cocheco Mfg. Co., Lawrence & Co., Arnold Print Works, Art Fabric Mills and Selchow & Righter and Dean's Rag Book Company in England. 1896-on.

Mark: Mark could be found on fabric part, which was discarded after cutting.

Cloth, Printed Doll: Face, hair, underclothes, shoes and socks printed on cloth; all in good condition, some soil acceptable. Dolls in printed underwear are sometimes found dressed in old petticoats and frocks. Names such as: Art Fabric Mills, Dolly Dear, Merry Marie, Improved Foot Doll, Standish No Break Doll, and others:

7-9in (18-23cm)	$	75 - 95
16-18in (41-46cm)		135 - 160
22-24in (56-61cm)		150 - 195

Uncut sheet, bright colors,

13in (33cm) doll	125 - 150
20in (51cm) doll	175 - 200

Brownies: 1892. Designed by Palmer Cox; marked on foot.

8in (20cm)	75 - 85

Boys and Girls with printed outer clothes, Ca. 1903.

12-13in (31-33cm)	125 - 150
17in (43cm)	175 - 200

Darkey Doll, made up,		
16in (41cm)	$	225 - 250
Aunt Jemima Family,		
(four dolls)		65 - 75 each
Punch & Judy,		400 pair
Pitti Sing, uncut		65
Hen and Chicks, uncut sheet		65
Tabby Cat		80 - 90
Tabby's Kittens		55 - 65
Ball, uncut		250 - 275
Peck 1886 Santa		225
Topsy, uncut		
8-1/2 (22cm) Two dolls on sheet		195
E.T. Gibson, 1912.		
Red bathing suit		165 - 185
George & Martha Washington		400 pair
Pillow-type, printed and hand embroidered,		
1920s - 1930s, 16in (41cm)		65 - 85

BELOW: *Left:* 9in (23cm) printed cloth girl. *H & J Foulke, Inc. Right:* 14in (36cm) 1920-1930 embroidered pillow dolls. *H & J Foulke, Inc.*

CLOTH, RUSSIAN

Russian Cloth Doll: All-cloth with stockinette head and hands, molded face with hand-painted features; authentic regional clothes; all in very good condition.

6-1/2in (16cm) child	$	**45 - 50**
11in (28cm) child		**100 - 110**
15in (38cm)		**150 - 200**

Tea Cosy, 20in (51cm) **225 - 250**

FACTS
Unknown craftsmen. Ca. 1930.
Mark: "Made in Soviet Union" sometimes with identification of doll, such as "Ukrainian Woman," "Village Boy," "Smolensk District Woman."

15in (38cm) *Ukranian Woman. H & J Foulke, Inc.*

Dewees Cochran Doll: Latex with jointed neck, shoulders and hips; human hair wig, painted eyes, character face; dressed; all in good condition.

15-16in (38-41cm) Cindy, 1947-1948.
$ 800 - 900

Grow-up Dolls: Stormy, Angel, Bunnie, J.J. and Peter Ponsett each at ages 5, 7, 11, 16 and 20, 1952-1956.
$ 1800 - 2000

Look-Alike Dolls
(6 different faces) $ 1800 - 2000

Individual Portrait
Children $ 2000 - 2200
Composition American Children (see Effanbee, page 163).

FACTS
Dewees Cochran, Fenton, Calif., U.S.A. 1940-on.
Designer: Dewees Cochran.
Mark: Signed under arm or behind right ear.

14in (36cm) Frances Eason *Family Child Portrait Doll,* all original. *Ruth Covington West.*

COLUMBIAN DOLL

Columbian Doll: All-cloth with hair and features hand-painted on a flat face; treated limbs; appropriate clothes; all in very good condition, no repaint or touch up.

15in (38cm)	$	**5000**
20-22in (51-56cm)		**6000 - 7000**
Some wear,		
20-22in (51-56cm)		**4000 - 4200**
Worn,		
29in (74cm)		**2000**

```
━━━━━━━━━ FACTS ━━━━━━━━━
Emma and Marietta Adams. 1891-1910
or later. All-cloth. 15-29in (38-74cm).
Mark: Stamped on back of body.
Before 1900:
"COLUMBIAN DOLL
EMMA E. ADAMS
OSWEGO CENTRE
N.Y."
After 1906:
"THE COLUMBIAN DOLL
MANUFACTURED BY
MARIETTA ADAMS RUTTAN
OSWEGO, N.Y."
```

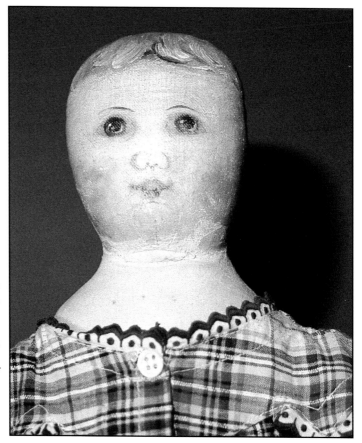

15in (38cm) unmarked *Columbian Doll.* *Doelman Collection. Courtesy of Richard W. Withington, Inc.*

COMPOSITION (AMERICAN)

All-Composition Child Doll: 1912-1920. Various firms, such as Bester Doll Co., New Era Novelty Co., New Toy Mfg. Co., Superior Doll Mfg. Co., Artcraft Toy Product Co., Colonial Toy Mfg. Co. Composition with mohair wig, sleep eyes, open mouth; ball-jointed composition body; appropriate clothes; all in good condition. These are patterned after German bisque head dolls. (For photograph see *10th Blue Book*, page 163.)

───────FACTS───────
Various United States firms, many unidentified. 1912-on.

   22-24in (56-61cm)   **$**   **300 - 350**
Character baby, all-composition
   19in (48cm)   **275 - 300**

16in (41cm) early composition character girl. *H & J Foulke, Inc.*

Early Composition Character Head: Ca. 1912. Composition head with molded hair and painted features; hard cloth body with composition hands; appropriate clothes; all in good condition.

12-15in (31-38cm)	$	**150 - 200**
18-20in (46-51cm)		**250 - 300**
24-26in (61-66cm)		**350 - 450**
Two-face toddler,		
14in (36cm)		**275 - 300**

Molded Loop Dolls: Ca. 1930s. All-composition with molded bobbed hair and loop for tying on a ribbon, painted eyes, closed mouth; composition or cloth torso, composition arms and legs; original or appropriate clothing; all in good condition. Quality is generally mediocre.

12-15in (31-38cm)	$	**135 - 165**

Patsy-type Girl: Ca. 1930s. All-composition with molded bobbed hair, sleep or painted eyes, closed mouth; jointed at neck, shoulders and hips; original clothes; all in very good condition, of good quality.

9-10in (23-25cm)	$	**150 - 175**
14-16in (36-41cm)		**225 - 250**
20in (51cm)		**300 - 325**

16in (41cm) Patsy-type composition girl. *H & J Foulke, Inc.*

18in (46cm) girl-type Mama doll, all original. *H & J Foulke, Inc.* (For further information see page 138.)

18in (46cm) composition, all original. *H & J Foulke, Inc.* (For further information see page 138.)

13in (33cm) Uneeda toddler twins, all original. *H & J Foulke, Inc.*

13in (33cm) **Ritzy Chubby Baby,** Natural Doll Co., all original. *H & J Foulke, Inc.*

Girl-type Mama Dolls: Ca. 1920-on. Made by various American companies. Composition head with hair wig, sleep eyes, open mouth with teeth; composition shoulder plate, arms and legs, cloth body; original clothes; all in good condition, of good quality. (See photograph on page 136.)

16-18in (41-46cm)	$	225 - 250
20-22in (51-56cm)		300 - 350
24-26in (61-66cm)		400 - 450
Acme,		
26in (66cm), excellent, at auction		850

Composition Baby: Ca. 1930. All-composition or composition head, arms and legs, cloth torso; with molded and painted hair, sleep eyes; appropriate or original clothes; all in very good condition, of good quality.

12-14in (31-36cm)	$	165 - 225
18-20in (46-51cm)		250 - 300
24in (61cm)		375 - 425
Acme twins,		
16in (44cm), all original in bunting		600

Dionne-type Doll: Ca. 1935. All-composition with molded hair or wig, sleep or painted eyes, closed or open mouth; jointed at neck, shoulders and hips; original clothes; all in very good condition, of good quality.

7-8in (18-20cm) baby	$	125 - 135
13in (33cm) toddler		225 - 250
18-20in (46-51cm) toddler		300 - 350

14in (36cm) Alexander-type girl, all original. *H & J Foulke, Inc.*

COMPOSITION (AMERICAN) *continued*

Alexander-type Girl: Ca. 1935. All-composition, jointed at neck, shoulders and hips; sleeping eyes, mohair wig, closed mouth, dimples. Original clothing. All in good condition, of good quality.

13in (33cm)	$	200 - 225
16-18in (41-46cm)		275 - 325
22in (56cm)		350 - 400

Shirley Temple-type Girl: Ca. 1935-on. All-composition, jointed at neck, shoulders and hips; blonde curly mohair wig, sleep eyes, open smiling mouth with teeth; original clothes; all in very good condition, of good quality.

16-18in (41-46cm)	$	350 - 400
19in (48cm) boxed		450

Costume Doll: Ca. 1940. All-composition, jointed at neck, shoulders and hips, sleep or painted eyes, mohair wig, closed mouth; original costume; all in good condition.

11in (28cm)

Excellent quality	$	150 - 175
Standard quality		65 - 75

Miscellaneous Specific Dolls: All original; very good condition:

Royal "Spirit of America"
15in (38cm) with original box and outfits	$	300 - 350

Jackie Robinson
13-1/2in (34cm)	700**

Trudy 3 faces, 1946.
14in (36cm)	250 - 295

Lone Ranger
16in (41cm)	500
20in (51cm) boxed, at auction	1400

Kewpie-type characters
12in (31cm)	80 - 90

Miss Curity
18in (46cm)	450 - 500

P.D. Smith
22in (56cm) at auction	2600

**Not enough price samples to compute a reliable average.

11in (28cm) *O-U-Kid*, Gem Toy Co. 1919. *H & J Foulke, Inc.*

11in (28cm) Paris Doll Co. bridesmaid, all original. *H & J Foulke, Inc.*

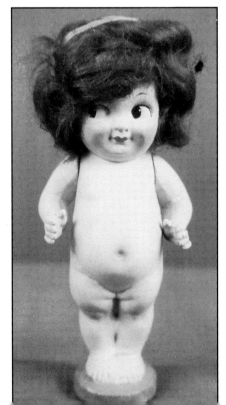

COMPOSITION (AMERICAN) *continued*

Buddy Lee
12in (31cm) all original
$ 255 - 275*
Uneeda Rita Hayworth,
red mohair wig
14in (36cm)   **400****
Hedwig/DiAngeli (See *6th Blue Book*, page 175.)
Elin, Hannah, Lydia, Suzanne
14in (36cm)   **450 - 500**
3 Pigs and Wolf boxed set, all original   **650**
Sterling Doll Co. Sports Dolls
29in (74cm) all original
250 - 300
Paris Doll Co. Peggy
28in (71cm) walker
350 - 400
Monica, 1941-1951.
18in (46cm)   **550**
Famlee, 1921. Boxed with 6 heads and 6 costumes **1000**
Cat or **Rabbit head doll**
10-11in (25-28cm)
150 - 175
Santa Claus
19in (48cm)   **400 - 500**
Pinocchio, Crown Toy, 1939.
12in (31cm)   **250 - 300**
Puzzy, 1948. H. of P.
15in (38cm)   **350 - 400**
Sizzy, 1948. H. of P.
14in (36cm)   **250 - 300**

*Depending upon costume.
** Not enough price samples to compute a reliable range.

10in (25cm) compositon cat head doll. *H & J Foulke, Inc.*

OPPOSITE PAGE: 14in (36cm) *Suzanne* by Hedwig/Di Angeli, all original. *H & J Foulke, Inc.*

COMPOSITION (German)

All-Composition Child Doll: Socket head with good wig, sleep (sometimes flirty) eyes, open mouth with teeth; jointed composition body; appropriate clothes; all in good condition, of excellent quality.

12-14in (31-36cm)	$ 225 - 275
18-20in (46-51cm)	375 - 425
22in (56cm)	450 - 500

Character face

18-20in (46-51cm)	$ 425 - 525

Character Baby: Composition head with good wig, sleep eyes, open mouth with teeth; bent-limb composition baby body or hard-stuffed cloth body; appropriate clothes; all in good condition, of excellent quality.

All-composition baby,

16-18in (41-46cm)	$ 375 - 425
Cloth body,	
18-20in (46-51cm)	300 - 350
All composition toddler,	
16-18in (41-46cm)	450 - 500

───── FACTS ─────

Various German firms such as König & Wernicke, Kämmer & Reinhardt and others. Ca. 1925.

20in (51cm) "O3V" German character baby, all original. *H & J Foulke, Inc.*

COMPOSITION SHOULDER HEAD

(Patent Washable Dolls)

Composition Shoulder Head: Composition shoulder head with mohair or skin wig, glass eyes, closed or open mouth; cloth body with composition arms and lower legs, sometimes with molded boots; appropriately dressed; all in good condition. (For additional photograph, see page 13.)

Superior Quality:

12-14in (31-36cm)	$ 425 - 475
16-18in (41-46cm)	525 - 575
22-24in (56-61cm)	750 - 825
30in (76cm)	1000 - 1200

Standard Quality:

11-12in (28-31cm)	150 - 175

14-16in (36-41cm)	200 - 225
22-24in (56-61cm)	300 - 350
30-33in (76-84cm)	400 - 500
38in (97cm)	600 - 700
Lady, 13-16in (33-41cm)	750 - 850
Oriental, 12in (31cm)	225 - 250

---FACTS---

Various German firms, such as Heinrich Stier, J.D. Kestner, F.M. Schilling and C. & O. Dressel. 1880-1915.
10-42in (25-107cm).
Mark: None.

24in (61cm) Patent Washable-type compositon shoulder head, standard quality.
H & J Foulke, Inc.

DANEL (LATER JUMEAU)

Marked Paris Bébé: 1889-1892. Perfect bisque socket head with Jumeau look, good wig, paperweight eyes, closed mouth, pierced ears; composition jointed body; appropriately dressed; all in good condition. This doll was a copy of a Jumeau.

Mark: On Head

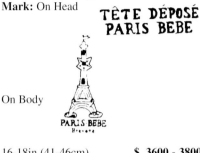

TÊTE DÉPOSÉ
PARIS BEBE

On Body

PARIS BEBE
Breveté

| 16-18in (41-46cm) | $ 3600 - 3800 |
| 22-24in (56-66cm) | 4200 - 4400 |

Marked Paris Bébé: 1892-on. Character face developed by Jumeau for use with this trademark after he won a lawsuit against Danel. (For photograph see *11th Blue Book*, page 144.)

18-19in (46-48cm)	$ 4800 - 5100
23-25in (58-64cm)	5500 - 6500
28in (71cm) with hairline, at auction	
	5500

Marked B.F.: Ca. 1891. Bébé Français was used by Jumeau after 1892. Perfect bisque head, appropriate wig, paperweight eyes, closed mouth, pierced ears; jointed composition body; appropriate clothes; all in good condition. (For photograph see *10th Blue Book*, page 173.)

Mark:

B 9 F

| 16-19in (41-48cm) | $ 4200 - 4500 |
| 23-25in (58-64cm) | 5200 - 5800 |

FACTS

Danel & Cie., Paris & Montreuil-sous-Bois, France. 1889-1895.
Trademarks: Paris Bébé, Bébé Français. Both used by Jumeau after winning an 1892 lawsuit.

16in (41cm) *Paris Bébé* with Jumeau-style face. *H & J Foulke, Inc.*

DEP

DEP Closed Mouth: Ca. 1890. Perfect bisque head, swivel neck, lovely wig, set paperweight eyes, upper and lower painted eyelashes, closed mouth, pierced ears; jointed French composition and wood body; pretty clothes; all in good condition.

Mark: **DEP**
         (size number)

15in (38cm)	$ **2600 - 2800**
18-20in (46-51cm)	**3500 - 3800**
25-27in (63-68cm)	**5000 - 5500**
Open mouth, 22in (56cm)	**1000 - 1200**

Jumeau DEP: Ca. 1899-on. Heads possibly by Simon & Halbig. Perfect bisque socket head (sometimes with Tête Jumeau stamp), human hair wig, deeply molded eye socket, sleeping eyes, painted lower eyelashes, upper hair eyelashes (sometimes gone), pierced ears; jointed French composition and wood body (sometimes with Jumeau label or stamp); lovely clothes; all in good condition.

Mark: **DEP**
         8

11-1/2in (29cm)	$ **750 - 850**
13-15in (33-38cm)	**800 - 900**
18-20in (46-51cm)	**1050 - 1200**
23-25in (58-64cm)	**1400 - 1700**
29-30in (74-76cm)	**2200 - 2500**
35in (89cm)	**3000 - 3200**
21in (53cm) with Parisian wardrobe and trunk, at auction	**5500**
16in (41cm) all original in elaborate French baby outfit	**1300**

23in (58cm) *DEP* Jumeau. *H & J Foulke, Inc.*

26-1/2in (67cm) *DEP*, closed mouth. *Kay & Wayne Jensen Collection.*

146

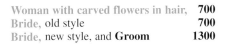
Door of Hope: Carved wooden head with painted and/or carved hair, carved features; cloth body, some with stubby arms, some with carved hands; original handmade clothes, exact costuming for different classes of Chinese people; all in excellent condition. 25 dolls in the series.

Adult,
11-13in (28-33cm)	$	**500 - 600**
Child,		
7-8in (18-20cm)		**550 - 650**
Amah and Baby,		**700 - 800**
Manchu Lady,		**1100 - 1200**
Kindergarten Girl,		
6in (15cm)		**600 - 675**

Woman with carved flowers in hair,	**700**
Bride, old style	**700**
Bride, new style, and **Groom**	**1300**

FACTS

Door of Hope Mission, China; heads by carvers from Ning-Po. 1901-on. Usually under 13in (33cm). **Mark:** Sometimes "Made in China" label.

Door of Hope woman, all original. *H & J Foulke, Inc.*

GRACE G. DRAYTON

Puppy Pippin: 1911. Horsman Co., New York, N.Y., U.S.A. Composition head with puppy dog face, plush body with jointed legs; all in good condition. Cloth label.

8in (20cm) sitting	**$ 400 - 450****
Pussy Pippin	**500 - 600****

Peek-a-Boo: 1913-1915. Horsman Co., New York, N.Y., U.S.A. Composition head, arms, legs and lower torso, cloth upper torso; character face with molded hair, painted eyes to the side, watermelon mouth; dressed in striped bathing suit, polka dot dress or ribbons only; cloth label on outfit; all in good condition. (For photograph see *7th Blue Book*, page 136.)

7-1/2in (19cm)	**$ 150 - 175**

Hug-Me-Tight: 1916. Colonial Toy Mfg. Co., New York, N.Y., U.S.A. Mother Goose characters and others in one piece, printed on cloth; all in good condition. (For photograph see *8th Blue Book*, page 149.)

11in (28cm)	**$ 225 - 250****

Captain Kiddo,

6-1/4in (16cm)	**$ 200 - 250****

Chocolate Drop: 1923. Averill Manufacturing Co., New York, N.Y., U.S.A. Brown cloth doll with movable arms and legs; painted features, three yarn pigtails; appropriate clothes; all in good condition. Stamped on front torso and paper label. (For photograph see page 148.)

11in (28cm)	**$ 450 - 500****
16in (41cm)	**650 - 750****

**Not enough price samples to compute a reliable range.

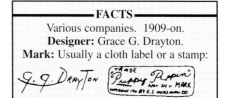

───── **FACTS** ─────
Various companies. 1909-on.
Designer: Grace G. Drayton.
Mark: Usually a cloth label or a stamp:

Puppy Pippin with label.
H & J Foulke, Inc.

GRACE G. DRAYTON *continued*

Dolly Dingle: 1923. Averill Manufacturing Co., New York, N.Y., U.S.A. Cloth doll with painted features and movable arms and legs; appropriate clothes; all in good condition. Stamped on front torso and paper label:

DOLLY DINGLE
COPYRIGHT BY
G.G. DRAYTON

11in (28cm)	$ 400 - 450**
16in (41cm)	600 - 650**
10in (25cm) double face	750**

Composition Child: Composition shoulder head, arms and legs, cloth torso; molded bobbed hair, watermelon mouth, painted eyes, round nose; original or appropriate clothes; in fair condition. (For photograph see *11th Blue Book*, page 147.)

Mark:

9 · 9 Drayton

14in (36cm)	$ 450 - 500**

Kitty-Puss: All-cloth with painted cat face, flexible arms and legs, tail; original clothing; all in good condition. (For photograph see *9th Blue Book*, page 145.)

Mark: Cardboard tag $ 500**

September Morn: All-bisque, molded hair, painted features; jointed shoulders and hips.

6in (15cm) at auction	$ 2250

**Not enough price samples to compute a reliable average.

11in (28cm) *Chocolate Drop.* H & J Foulke, Inc. (For further information see page 147.)

Crying side of double-face *Dolly Dingle. H & J Foulke, Inc.*

DRESSEL

Marked Holz-Masse Heads: 1875-on.
Composition shoulder head, molded hair or mohair wig, glass or painted eyes, sometimes pierced ears; cloth body with composition arms and legs with molded boots; old clothes; all in good condition, with some wear.

Mark:

Molded hair:
13-15in (33-38cm) $ **250 - 300**
23-25in (58-64cm)   **500 - 600**

Wigged with glass eyes:
(Patent Washable)
14-16in (36-41cm) $ **200 - 225**
22-24in (56-61cm)   **300 - 350**
19in (48cm) excellent condition with
   original shift and wig   **400**

FACTS

Cuno & Otto Dressel verlager & doll factory of Sonneberg, Thüringia, Germany. Bisque heads by Armand Marseille, Simon & Halbig, Ernst Heubach, Gebrüder Heubach. 1700-on.
Trademarks: Fifth Ave. Dolls (1903), Jutta (1907), Bambina (1909), Poppy Dolls (1912), Holz-Masse (1875).

21in (53cm) composition shoulder head of the type made by Dressel. *H & J Foulke, Inc.*

150

Child Doll: 1893-on. Perfect bisque head, original jointed kid or composition body; good wig, glass eyes, open mouth; suitable clothes; all in good condition.

Mark:

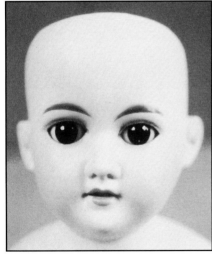

Composition body:

15-16in (38-41cm)	$	375 - 400
19-21in (48-53cm)		450 - 500
24in (61cm)		525 - 550
32in (81cm)		950
38in (96cm)		2000 - 2200

#93, 1896 Kid body,

19-22in (48-56cm)	$	500 - 550

Character-type face, similar to **K★R 117n**:

26in (66cm)	1000 - 1100

Portrait Series: 1896. Perfect bisque heads with portrait faces, glass eyes, some with molded mustaches and goatees; composition body; original clothes; all in good condition.

Some marked "S" or "D" with a number. (For photograph see *11th Blue Book*, page 149.)

13in (33cm) Uncle Sam	$	1200 - 1500
15in (38cm) Admiral Dewey and Officers		1200 - 1600
8in (20cm) Old Rip		600 - 700
10in (25cm) Farmer		700 - 800
10in (25cm) Buffalo Bill		750

Marked Jutta Child: Ca. 1906-1921. Perfect bisque socket head, good wig, sleep eyes, open mouth, pierced ears; ball-jointed composition body; dressed; all in good condition. Head made by Simon & Halbig. (For photograph see *10th Blue Book*, page 179.) Mold 1348 or 1349

Mark:

1349
Jutta
S & H
11

14-16in (36-41cm)	$	675*
19-21in (43-53cm)		700 - 800*
24-26in (61-66cm)		900 - 1000*
30-32in (76-81cm)		1600 - 1800
38-39in (96-99cm)		3000 - 3500

* Allow $150 extra for flapper body with high knee joint.

** Allow extra for flirty eyes.

5-1/2in (14cm) C.O.D. 93 A.M. shoulder head. *H & J Foulke, Inc.*

22in (56cm) 1912 child. *H & J Foulke, Inc.*

DRESSEL *continued*

Character Child: 1909-on. Perfect bisque socket head, ball-jointed composition body; mohair wig, painted eyes, closed mouth; suitable clothes; all in good condition. Glazed inside of head. (For photograph see *10th Blue Book*, page 179.)

Mark:

C.OD.
A/2

| 10-12in (25-31cm) | $ 1650 - 1850** |
| 16-18in (41-46cm) | 2600 - 2900** |

Composition head (For photogaph see *11th Blue Book*, page 150.)

| 19in (48cm) | 2600 - 3000** |

Marked C.O.D. Character Baby: Ca. 1910 -on. Perfect bisque character face with marked wig or molded hair, painted or glass eyes; jointed baby body; dressed; all in good condition. (For photogaph see *11th Blue Book*, page 149.)

12-13in (31-33cm)	$ 350 - 375
16-18in (41-46cm)	450 - 500
22-24in (56-61cm)	675 - 775

Marked Jutta Character Baby: Ca. 1910-1922. Perfect bisque socket head, good wig, sleep eyes, open mouth; bent-limb composition baby body; dressed; all in good condition. (For photograph see page 152.) Simon & Halbig:

| 16-18in (41-46cm) | $ 650 - 750 |
| 23-24in (58-61cm) | 1300 - 1500 |

Other Makers: (Armand Marseille, E. Heubach)

| 16-18in (41-46cm) | $ 450 - 500 |
| 23-24in (58-61cm) | 700 - 800 |

Mark:

Heubach 6½ Koppelsdorf
Jutta · Baby
Dressel
Germany
1922
10½

Jutta
1914
8

Toddler:

| 16-18in (41-46cm) | $ 1000 - 1100 |
| 22in (56cm) | 1600 - 1800 |

**Not enough price samples to compute a reliable range.

Lady Doll: Ca. 1920s. Bisque socket head with young lady face, good wig, sleep eyes, closed mouth; jointed composition body in adult form with molded bust, slim waist and long arms and legs, feet modeled to wear high-heeled shoes; all in good condition. (For photograph see page 152.)

Mark: 1469
C ⊙ Dressel
Germany
2

#1469:
14in (36cm)

| Naked | $ 2000 - 2300 |
| Original clothes | 3000 - 4200 |

Composition head (For photograph see *11th Blue Book*, page 152.)

| 14in (36cm) | 750 - 850 |

24in (61cm) C.O.D. girl with character face similar to K & R 117n. *H & J Foulke, Inc.*

23in (58cm) *Jutta* 1914
S & H character baby.
H & J Foulke, Inc.

14in (36cm) C.O.D. 1469 lady.
H & J Foulke, Inc.

E. D. BÉBÉ

Marked E. D. Bébé: Perfect bisque head, wood and composition jointed body; good wig, beautiful blown glass eyes, pierced ears; nicely dressed; good condition.

Closed mouth:

15-18in (38-46cm)	$ **2800 - 3200***
22-24in (56-61cm)	**3600 - 4000***
28in (71cm)	**4200 - 4400***

Open mouth:

18-20in (38-51cm)	**1800 - 2000***
25-27in (64-69cm)	**2500 - 2700***

*For a pretty face.

Note: Dolls with Jumeau look but signed E. D. are Jumeau factory dolls produced when Emile Douillet was director of the Jumeau firm, 1892-1899. They do not have the word "Déposé" under the E. D. They should be priced as Jumeau dolls. (For photograph see *10th Blue Book*, page 181.)

FACTS

Etienne Denamur of Paris, France. 1889-on.

Mark:　　E 8 D
　　　　　　DÉPOSÉ

17in (43cm) E.6.D. child.
Jensen's Antique Dolls.

EDEN BÉBÉ

Marked Eden Bébé: Ca. 1890. Perfect bisque head, fully-jointed or 5-piece composition jointed body; beautiful wig, large set paperweight eyes, closed or open/closed mouth, pierced ears; lovely clothes; all in nice condition.

Closed mouth,

14-16in (36-41cm)	$	**2200 - 2400**
21-23in (53-58cm)		**2800 - 3000**
5-piece body, 12in (31cm)		**1200 - 1500**

Open mouth,

19-20in (48-51cm)	**1900 - 2000**
6in (15cm) walker, all original boxed, at auction	**725**
DEP head, walking body, all original with Eden Bébé label.	
17in (43cm)	**1200 - 1500**

FACTS

Fleischmann & Bloedel, doll factory, of Fürth, Bavaria, and Paris, France. Founded in Bavaria in 1873. Also in Paris by 1890, then on into S.F.B.J. in 1899.
Trademark: Eden Bébé (1890), Bébé Triomphe (1898).
Mark: "EDEN BEBE, PARIS"

20in (51cm) *Eden Bébé. Jensen's Antique Dolls.*

EFFANBEE

Early Characters: Composition character face, molded painted hair, closed mouth, painted eyes; cloth stuffed body with metal disk joints at shoulders and hips, composition lower arms, sewn-on shoes; appropriate clothes; in good condition. Some marked "Deco." Sizes: 12-16in (30-41cm).

Baby Grumpy, 1912. Molds 172, 174 or
  176                                  $ **300 - 325****
Coquette, 1912.   **300 - 325****
Pouting Bess, 1915. Some mold 162 or
  166 (For photograph see *9th Blue Book*,
  page 152.)   **300 - 325****
Billy Boy, 1915. (For photograph see *11th
  Blue Book*, page 12.)   **300 - 325**
Whistling Jim, 1916.   **300 - 325**
Harmonica Joe, 1924. (For photograph see
  11th Blue Book, page 156.)   **300 - 325**
Katie Kroose, 1918. (For photograph see
  page 156.)   **300 - 325**
Buds, 1915-1918.   **175 - 195**
  Black   **200 - 225**

**Not enough price samples to compute a reliable average.

FACTS
EFFanBEE Doll Co., New York, N.Y., U.S.A. 1912-on.
Marks: Various, but nearly always marked "EFFanBEE" on torso or head, sometimes with doll's name. Wore a metal heart-shaped bracelet; later a gold paper heart label.

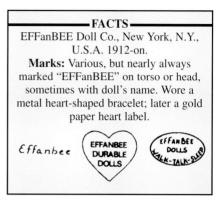

Metal Heart Bracelet and chain: $ **45 - 50**

16in (41cm) early **Baby Grumpy**. H & J Foulke, Inc.

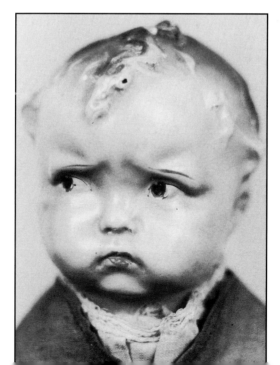

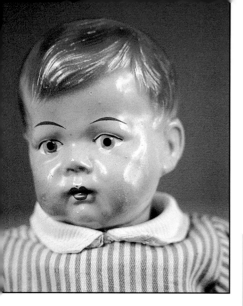

18in (46cm) *Katie Kroose*. *H & J Foulke, Inc.* (For further information see page 155.)

27in (69cm) early mama doll, all original. *H & J Foulke, Inc.* (For further information see page 158.)

12in (31cm) *Baby Grumpy,* all original. *H & J Foulke, Inc.* (For further information see page 158.)

19in (48cm) **Bubbles,** all original. *H & J Foulke, Inc.* (For further information see page 158.)

18in (46cm) **Sweetie Pie,** all original. *H & J Foulke, Inc.* (For further information see page 158.)

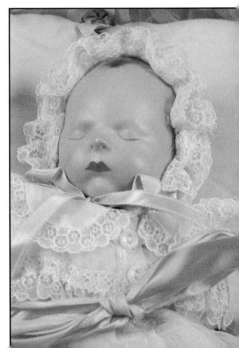

13in (33cm) **Babyette,** all original. *H & J Foulke, Inc.* (For further information see page 158.)

Shoulder Head Dolls: Composition shoulder head, painted molded hair or human hair wig, open or closed mouth, painted tin sleep eyes; cloth torso, composition arms and legs; original clothes; all in good condition. Came with metal heart bracelet.

Baby Grumpy, 1925-1939.
12in (31cm) white (For photograph see
    page 156.) $ **275 - 300***
Black   **325 - 350***

Pennsylvania Dutch Dolls: 1936-1940, all
    original and excellent. $ **225 - 275***
Baby Dainty, 1912-1922.
15in (38cm)   **225 - 250***
Rosemary, 1925. Marilee, 1924.
14in (36cm)   **275 - 300***
17in (43cm)   **325 - 375***
25in (64cm)   **450 - 550***
30in (76cm)   **600 - 625***
Mary Ann, 1928.
16in (41cm)   **325 - 375***
Mary Lee, 1928.
19in (48cm)   **375 - 425***
Early Mama Dolls, 1920s. (For photograph
    see page 156.)
20-22in (51-56cm)   **400 - 450***
26-28in (66-71cm)   **550 - 600***

*Deduct 30-35% if clothes are not original.

Mary Jane: 1917-1920. Composition "dolly face" head with metal sleeping eyes, painted eyebrows and eyelashes, open mouth with teeth, original human hair or mohair wig; jointed composition body with wood arms; dressed; all in very good condition. (For photograph see *7th Blue Book*, page 144.)
Mark:

Effanbee

back of head and torso in raised letters
20-24in (51-61cm) $ **300 - 350**

Babies: Composition head with painted hair or wigged, sleep eyes, open smiling mouth with teeth or closed mouth; cloth body,

curved composition arms and legs; original clothes; all in good condition. Came with metal heart bracelet, later with gold heart hang tag.
Bubbles, 1924. (For photograph see page 157.)
Mark:

19 © 24
EFFANBEE
DOLLS
WALK·TALK·SLEEP
MADE IN U S A

EFFANBEE
BUBBLES
COPYR 1924
MADE IN U.S.A.

16-18in (41-46cm) $ **350 - 400***
22-24in (56- 61cm)   **450 - 500***
26in (66cm) mint, all original with tag
    700 - 800*

Lovums, 1928. (For photograph see *11th Blue Book*, page 155.)
Mark:

EFFANBEE
LOVUMS
©
PAT No. 1,283,558

16-18in (41-46cm) $ **300 - 350***
22-24in (56-61cm)   **400 - 450***
Mickey, Baby Bright Eyes, Tommy Tucker, 1939-1949.
16-18in (41-46cm)   **300 - 350***
22-24in (56-61cm)   **400 - 450***
Sweetie Pie, 1942. (For photograph see page 157.)
16-18in (41-46cm)   **275 - 325***
22-24in (56-61cm)   **375 - 425***
Baby Effanbee, 1925.
12in (31cm)   **160 - 180***
Lambkin, 1930s.
16in (41cm)   **375 - 425***
Sugar Baby, 1936. Caracul wig,
16-18in (41-46cm)   **300 - 350***
Babyette, eyes closed, (For photograph see page 157.)
13in (33cm) boxed with pillow
    550 - 600

*Deduct 30-35% if clothes are not original.

Patsy Family: 1928-on. All-composition jointed at neck, shoulders and hips; molded hair (sometimes covered with wig), bent right arm on some members, painted or sleep eyes; original or appropriate old clothes; may have some crazing. Came with metal heart bracelet. (See previous *Blue Books* for **Patsy** dolls not pictured here.)

Mark:

EFFANBEE
PATSY JR.
DOLL

EFFANBEE
PATSY
DOLL

Bracelet

EFFANBEE
PATSY
BABY KIN

Wee Patsy, 6in (15cm)	$	325 - 375
boxed with extra outfits		525 - 625
Baby Tinyette, 7in (18cm) (For photograph see page 160.)		250 - 300
Patsy Babyette, 9in (23cm)		300 - 350
Patsyette, 9in (23cm)	.	350 - 400
Brown		450 - 500
Hawaiian		450 - 500
Patsy Baby, 11in (28cm) (For photograph see page 161.)		300 - 350
Brown		450 - 500
Patsy Jr., Patsy Kins, Patricia Kin, 11in (28cm)		350 - 400
Patsy, 14in (36cm) (For photograph see page 12.)		400 - 500
Patricia, 15in (38cm)		450 - 500
Patsy Joan, 16in (41cm)		450 - 500
Brown (For photograph see *11th Blue Book,* page 157.)		650 - 675
Patsy Ann, 19in (48cm) (For photograph see page 160.)		500 - 550
with large original wardrobe		950
Patsy Lou, 22in (56cm)		525 - 575
Patsy Ruth, 26in (66cm)		800 - 900
Patsy Mae, 30in (76cm)		800 - 900

Skippy: 1929. All-composition, jointed at neck, hips and shoulders, (later a cloth torso, still later a cloth torso and upper legs with composition molded boots for lower legs); molded hair, painted eyes to the side; original clothes; all in good condition. Came with metal heart bracelet. (For photograph see *11th Blue Book,* page 159.)

Mark:

EFFANBEE
SKIPPY
©
P.L. Crosby

14in (36cm)	$	500 - 600
Redressed		350 - 400
Brown		800 - 900**

**Not enough price samples to compute a reliable average.

W. C. Fields: 1930. Composition head, hands and feet, cloth body, painted hair and eyes; original clothes; all in very good condition.

Mark: W.C. FIELDS
AN EFFANBEE PRODUCT

19in (48cm)	$	850 - 950

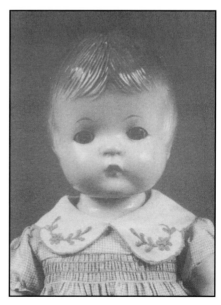

16in (41cm) *Patsy Joan,* all original. *H & J Foulke, Inc.*

8in (20cm) *Tinyette* Dutch Twins **Kit** and **Kat**, all original. *H & J Foulke, Inc.* (For further information see page 159.)

19in (48cm) *Patsy Ann,* all original. *H & J Foulke, Inc.* (For further information see page 159.)

11in (28cm) *Patsy Baby* twins, all original. *H & J Foulke, Inc.* (For further information see page 159.)

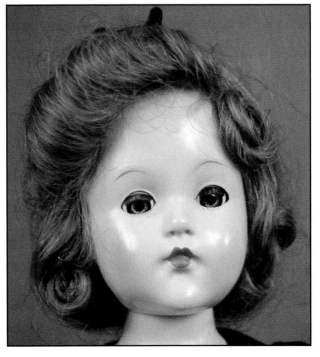

21in (53cm) *Anne Shirley*, all original. *H & J Foulke, Inc.* (For further information see page 162.)

162

Dy-Dee Baby: 1933-on. First dolls had hard rubber head with soft rubber body, caracul wig or molded hair, open mouth for drinking, soft ears (after 1940). Later dolls had hard plastic heads with rubber bodies. Still later dolls had hard plastic heads with vinyl bodies. Came with paper heart label. Various sizes from 9-20in (23-51cm). Very good condition.

Mark:

> *"EFF-AN-BEE*
> *DY-DEE BABY*
> *US PAT.-1-857-485*
> *ENGLAND-880-060*
> *FRANCE-723-980*
> *GERMANY-585-647*
> *OTHER PAT PENDING"*

Rubber body:

14-16in (36-41cm)	$	225 - 275
24in (61cm)		400 - 450
14in (36cm) boxed with layette and accessories		450 - 475
Carded 5-piece nursey set with **Dy-Dee** booklet		100
Dy-Dee pajamas		16

All-Composition Children: 1933-on. All-composition jointed at neck, shoulders and hips; human hair or mohair wigs, sleep eyes, closed mouths; original clothes; all in very good condition. Came with metal heart bracelet or cardboard gold heart tag.

Anne Shirley, 1935-1940. (For photograph see page 161.) Marked on back.

14-15in (36-38cm)	$	275 - 300*
17-18in (43-46cm)		300 - 325*
21in (53cm)		400 - 450*
with 5 extra outfits		850
27in (69cm)		450 - 500*

*Deduct 30-35% if clothes are not original.

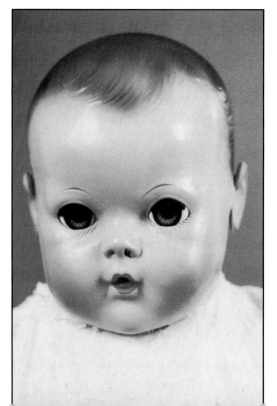

20in (51cm) *Dy-Dee Baby. H & J Foulke, Inc.*

American Children, 1936-1939.
Open mouth, unmarked.
Barbara Joan, 15in (38cm) **$ 550 - 650***
Barbara Ann, 17in (43cm) (For photograph
see page 164.)   **650 - 750***
Barbara Lou, 21in (53cm)   **750 - 850***

Closed mouth. (For photograph see *9th Blue
Book*, page 157.)
19-21in (48-53cm) marked head on
Anne Shirley body, sleep or
painted eyes   **$ 1300 - 1500**

17in (43cm) boy, unmarked, painted eyes.
(For photograph see page 165.)
$ 1500 - 1600

Suzette, 1939. Painted eyes. (For photograph
see *9th Blue Book*, page 159.)
11-1/2in (29cm)   **$ 250 - 300***
Suzanne, 1940. (For photograph see *8th
Blue Book*, page 165.)
14in (36cm)   **$ 300 - 350***
Little Lady, 1940-1949. Same prices
as **Anne Shirley**

Portrait Dolls, 1940. Ballerina, **Bo-Peep**,
Gibson Girl, bride, groom, dancing couple,
colonial. (For photograph see page 164.)
11in (28cm)   **$ 275 - 325**

Candy Kid, 1946. Toddler, molded hair. (For
photograph see *10th Blue Book*, page 190.)
12in (31cm)   **$ 300 - 350***
Betty Brite, 1933. Caracul wig. (For photograph see *6th Blue Book*, page 130.)
16-1/2in (42cm)   **325 - 375***
Button Nose, 1939. (For photograph see
11th Blue Book, page 163.)
9in (23cm)   **250 - 275***

*Deduct 30-35% if clothes are not original

Charlie McCarthy: 1937. Composition
head, hands and feet, cloth body; painted hair
and eyes; strings at back of head to operate
mouth; original clothes; all in very good condition. (For photograph see *11th Blue Book*,
page 164.)

Mark:
"EDGAR BERGEN'S CHARLIE
McCARTHY,
AN EFFanBEE PRODUCT"

17-20in (43-51cm)   **$ 650 - 750**
Mint-in-box with button   **850 - 950**

Historical Dolls: 1939. All-composition,
jointed at neck, shoulders and hips. Three
each of 30 dolls portraying the history of
American fashion, 1492-1939. "American
Children" heads used with elaborate human
hair wigs and painted eyes; elaborate original
costumes using velvets, satins, silks, bro-
cades, and so forth; all in excellent condition.
Came with metal heart bracelet. (For photograph see *11th Blue Book*, page 165.)

Marks: On head:
"EFFanBEE AMERICAN
CHILDREN"

On body:
"EFFanBEE ANNE SHIRLEY"

21in (53cm)   **$1300 - 1500**

17in (43cm) **Barbara Ann,** all original. *H & J Foulke, Inc.* (For further information see page 163.)

11in (28cm) Portrait, all original. *H & J Foulke, Inc.* (For further information see page 163.)

17in (43cm) *American Child* boy, all original. *H & J Foulke, Inc.*
(For further information see page 163.)

Historical Doll Replicas: 1939. All-composition, jointed at neck, shoulders and hips. Series of 30 dolls, popular copies of the original historical models (see above). Human hair wigs, painted eyes; original costumes all in cotton, copies of those on the original models. Came with metal heart bracelet. All in excellent condition. (For photograph see *11th Blue Book*, page 165.)
Mark: On torso:

"EFFanBEE
ANNE SHIRLEY"

14in (36cm) $ **500 - 600**

Howdy Doody: 1949-1950. Hard plastic head and hands, molded hair, sleep eyes; cloth body; original clothes; all in excellent condition.

19-23in (48-58cm)	$	**300 - 400**
Mint-in-Box		**525 - 575**

Honey: 1949-1955. All-hard plastic, jointed at neck, shoulders and hips; synthetic, mohair or human hair, sleep eyes; original clothes; all in excellent condition.
Mark: EFFANBEE

14in (36cm)	$	**275 - 300**
18in (46cm)		**325 - 375**
24in (61cm)		**450 - 500**
Prince Charming		**375 - 400**
Cinderella		**375 - 400**
Alice		**350 - 375**

16in (41cm) ***Honey***.
H & J Foulke, Inc.

EFFanBEE *continued*

Vinyl Dolls: All original and excellent condition.
Mickey, 1956.
   10-11in (25-28cm)   **$**   **125 - 135**
Champagne Lady, 1959.
   19in (48cm)   **250 - 300****
Fluffy Girl Scout, 1957 on.
   11in (28cm)   **60 - 70**
Patsy Ann Girl Scout, 1960-1961. (For photograph see *7th Blue Book*, page 154.)   **165 - 185**
Mary Jane Nurse, 1959.
   32in (81cm)   **275 - 325**

Effanbee Club Limited Edition Dolls: 1975-on. All-vinyl jointed dolls; original clothes; excellent condition.

1975 **Precious Baby**	**$**	**200 - 300**
1976 **Patsy**		**200 - 225**
1977 **Dewees Cochran**		**75 - 100**
1978 **Crowning Glory**		**50 - 60**
1979 **Skippy**		**200 - 225**
1980 **Susan B. Anthony**		**50 - 60**
1981 **Girl with Watering Can**		**65 - 75**
1982 **Princess Diana**		**50 - 60**
1983 **Sherlock Holmes**		**50 - 60**
1984 **Bubbles**		**65 - 75**
1985 **Red Boy**		**50 - 60**
1986 **China Head**		**35**

**Not enough price samples to compute a reliable average.

19in (48cm) vinyl head lady, all original. *H & J Foulke, Inc.*

FRENCH FASHION-TYPE (POUPÉE)

French Fashion Lady (Poupée): Perfect unmarked bisque shoulder head, swivel or stationary neck, kid body or cloth body with kid arms — some with wired fingers; original or old wig, lovely blown glass eyes, closed mouth, earrings; appropriate old clothes; all in good condition. Fine quality bisque.

12-13in (31-33cm)	$	**2200 up***
15-16in (38-41cm)		**2500 up***
18-19in (46-48cm)		**3200 up***
21in (53cm)		**3500 up***
33in (84cm)		**6750**

Fully-jointed wood body, naked,
15-17in (38-43cm)	**5000 - 5500+**

19in (48cm) with fabulous original trousseau, trunk and accessories, at auction, **17,820**

Dainty oval face,
12-14in (31-36cm)	**2300 - 2500**

Round face, cobalt eyes (shoulder head),
13-15in (33-38cm)	**2300 - 2500**

Portrait face, wood body,
18in (46cm)	**30,000 up**

Twill-over-wood body (Simon & Halbig-type),
9-10in (23-25cm)	**4000 - 4500**
15-17in (38-43cm)	**5000 - 6000**

Swivel head on shoulderplate, full face, original wig
5-1/2 (13cm)	**$ 1400**
Kubelka Lady, 26in (66cm)	no prices available

Period Clothes, Fashion Lady clothing:
Dress	**$ 500 - 1000 up**
Boots	**300**
Elaborate wig	**300 - 400**
Nice wig	**150 - 250**

* Allow extra for original clothing. Value of doll varies greatly depending upon the appeal of the face. Also, allow additional for kid-over-wood upper and bisque lower arms.
+ Allow extra for joints at ankle and waist.

FACTS

Various French firms. Ca. 1860-1930. Bisque shoulder head, gusseted kid body (*poupée peau*), some with bisque lower limbs or wood arms; or fully-jointed wood body (*poupée bois*) sometimes covered with kid; or cloth body with kid arms.
(See also ***Bru, Jumeau, Gaultier, Gesland, Huret, Rohmer*** and ***Barrois***.)

14in (36cm) *poupée peau.*
H & J Foulke, Inc.

12in (31cm) *poupée peau. H & J Foulke, Inc.*

21in (53cm) B6S *poupée peau.*
Private Collection.

26in (66cm) Kubelka Lady, human hair inset in wax pate, 1884. *Private Collection.*

FREUNDLICH

General Douglas MacArthur: Ca. 1942. All-composition portrait doll, molded hat, painted features, one arm to salute if desired; jointed shoulders and hips; original khaki uniform; all in good condition. (For photograph see *11th Blue Book*, page 171.)
Mark: Cardboard tag: "General MacArthur"
18in (46cm) $ **300 - 350**

─────**FACTS**─────
Freundlich Novelty Corp., New York, N.Y., U.S.A. 1923-on.

Military Dolls: Ca. 1942. All-composition with molded hats, jointed shoulders and hips, character face, painted features; original clothes. Soldier, Sailor, WAAC, and WAVE, all in good condition.
Mark: Cardboard tag.
15in (38cm) $ **200 - 250**

15in (38cm) sailor, all original.
H & J Foulke, Inc.

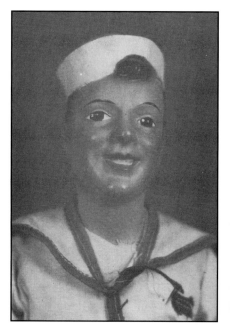

15in (38cm) WAAC, all original.
H & J Foulke, Inc.

Baby Sandy: 1939-1942. All-composition with swivel head, jointed shoulders and hips, chubby toddler body; molded hair, smiling face, larger sizes have sleep eyes, smaller ones painted eyes; appropriate clothes; all in good condition. (For photograph see *11th Blue Book*, page 172.)
Mark: On head; "Baby Sandy"

8in (20cm)$	**165 - 185**
12in (31cm)	**275 - 300**
14-15in (36-38cm)	**350 - 400**
15in (38cm) all original, boxed	**500 - 600**

Other Composition Dolls:
Orphan Annie & Sandy,
12in (30cm)$ **275 - 325**
Red Ridinghood, Wolf & Grandmother Set, all original
9in (23cm) **400 - 500****
Dionne Quints and Nurse Set **400 - 500**
Dummy Dan,
15in (38cm)$ **100 - 125**

Goo Goo Eva,
20in (51cm) **90 - 110**
Goo Goo Topsy (black),
20in (51cm) **110 - 135**
Wolf, naked **150**

**Not enough price samples to compute a reliable average.

9in (23cm) wolf.
H & J Foulke, Inc.

FROZEN CHARLOTTE

(Bathing Doll)

Frozen Charlotte: All-china doll, black or blonde molded hair parted down the middle, painted features; hands extended, legs separated but not jointed; no clothes; perfect condition. Good quality.

2-3in (5 - 8cm)	$	**50 - 65***
4-5in (10-13cm)		**110 - 135***
6-7in (15-18cm)		**165 - 185***
9-10in (23-25cm)		**275 - 325***
14-15in (36-38cm)		**500 - 550***
Pink tint, early hairdo,		
2-1/2–3-1/2in (6-9cm)		**200 - 225**
5in (13cm)		**300 - 350**
Pink tint with bonnet,		
3-1/2 (9cm)		**350 - 375**
5in (13cm)		**425 - 475**
Black china, 5in (13cm)		**165 - 195**
Black boy, molded turban and pants,		
3in (8cm)		**275 - 300**

Black boy, molded shift,		
5in (13cm)		**300 - 350**
Blonde hair, molded bow,		
5-1/2in (14cm)		**175 - 200**
Wig, lovely boots, 5in (13cm)		**175 - 195**
All-Bisque:		
5in (13cm)	$	**135 - 160**
Parian-type (1860s style),		
5in (13cm)		**175 - 195**
Alice style with pink boots,		
5in (13cm)		**325 - 350**
Fancy hairdo and boots,		
4-1/2in (11cm)		**275 - 300**
Molded clothes,		
3-1/4in (9cm)		**225**

*Allow extra for pink tint, fine decoration and modeling, unusual hairdo.

FACTS
Various German firms.
Ca. 1850s-early 1900s.
1-18in (3-46cm).
Mark: None, except for "Germany," or numbers or both.

3-1/4in (9cm) bisque girl with molded clothes. *H & J Foulke, Inc.*

Early pink tint girl with café-au-lait hair. *H & J Foulke, Inc.*

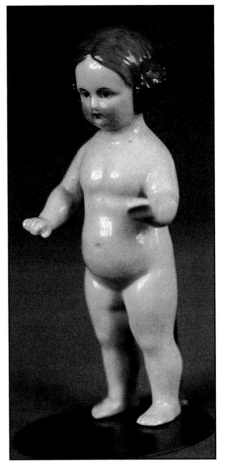

Early black girl, all original. *H & J Foulke, Inc.*

FULPER

Fulper Child Doll: Perfect bisque head, good wig; kid jointed or composition ball-jointed body; set or sleep eyes, open mouth; suitably dressed; all in good condition. Good quality bisque.

Kid body,
18-21in (46-53cm)   **$**   **375 - 425***
Composition body,
16-18in (41-46cm)   **450 - 500***
22-24in (56-61cm)   **550 - 600***

Fulper Baby:
16-18in (41-46cm)   **550 - 650***
22-24in (56-61cm)   **750 - 850***
Toddler:
15-17in (38-43cm) very cute   **800 - 900**

* Allow more for an especially pretty or cute doll.

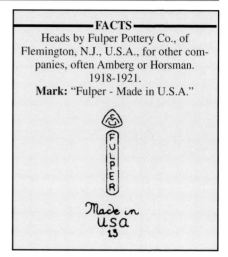

FACTS
Heads by Fulper Pottery Co., of Flemington, N.J., U.S.A., for other companies, often Amberg or Horsman. 1918-1921.
Mark: "Fulper - Made in U.S.A."

18in (46cm) Fulper character baby. *H & J Foulke, Inc.*

G. I. JOE®

Marked G.I. Joe: Molded and painted hair and features, scar* on right cheek; fully-jointed body; complete original outfit; all in perfect condition. Dolls less than perfect sell for considerably less. (See following page for photographs.)

* All G.I. Joe dolls have a scar on the right cheek except Foreign dolls and the Nurse

Action Soldier, all original, boxed	
$	285 - 300
Action Sailor (painted hair), boxed	450
Action Marine, boxed	350
Action Pilot, boxed	600
Action Soldier Black	
(painted hair), boxed	1300
Naked Dolls:	
Action Soldier (painted hair)	75
Adventure Team (flocked hair*)	50 - 60
Adventure Team (flocked hair and	
beard*)	45 - 50
Black Action Soldier (painted hair) (For	
photograph see page 176.)	300 - 350

*Hair must be in excellent condition.

Action Soldiers of the World (painted hair, no scars):

German Soldier,	
boxed, large box	1200
boxed, small box	600
dressed doll only, no accessories	
	200 - 225
Russian Infantry Man, (For photograph see page 176.)	
boxed, large box	1200
boxed, small box	600
dressed doll only, no accessories	
	200 - 225
British Commando,	
boxed, large box $	1250
boxed, small box	225
dressed doll only, no accessories	
	200 - 225
French Resistance Fighter,	
boxed, large box	900
boxed, small box	500
dressed doll only, no accessories	
	200 - 225
Australian Jungle Fighter,	
boxed, large box	700

boxed, small box	400
dressed doll only, no accessories	
	150 - 175
Japanese Imperial Soldier (unique model used only for this type) (For photograph see page 176.)	
boxed, large box	1300
boxed, small box	800
dressed doll only, no accessories	
	275 - 300
Talking Action Soldier, boxed	400
Talking Action Sailor, boxed	575
Talking Action Marine, boxed	475
Talking Action Pilot, boxed	800
Nurse Action Girl, boxed	1800
dressed doll only	800
naked doll	150
Adventurer (lifelike hair) Black,	
boxed	300
Man of Action (lifelike hair),	
boxed	200 - 225
Man of Action with Kung-Fu Grip (lifelike hair), boxed	200 - 225
Talking Man of Action (lifelike hair)	
boxed	225 - 250
Land Adventurer (lifelike hair and beard),	
boxed	185 - 200
Talking Astronaut (lifelike hair),	
boxed	400 - 425
dressed doll	275 - 300

Accessories:		
Footlocker, green	$	40
Space Capsule, boxed		325
Five Star Jeep, boxed		350
Desert Patrol Jeep, boxed		1500

FACTS

Hasbro (Hassenfeld Brothers, Inc.)
Pawtucket, RI, U.S.A. 1964 - 1979.
Hard plastic and vinyl. 12in (31cm)
fully-jointed.
Mark: G.I. Joe   After 1967 added:
Copyright 1964   Pat. No. 3,277,602
By Hasbro
Patent Pending
Made in U.S.A.

Outfits in unopened packages:

#7532 Green Beret Special Forces $	500
#7521 Military Police (brown)	400
#7521 Military Police (aqua)	1250
#7531 Ski Patrol	250
#7620 Deep Sea Diver	300
#7710 Dress Parade Set	225
#7824 Astronaut Suit	250
#7537 West Point Cadet	1200
#7624 Annapolis Cadet	1200
#7822 Air Cadet	1200
#7612 Shore Patrol	300
#7807 Scramble Set	275

(See preceding page for information about dolls pictured here.)

Right: #7900 Action Soldier (Black). 1965. Loose with heavy weapons, flak vest. $350. *Matthew McKeeby Collection.* **BOTTOM:** *Left: #8101 Japanese Imperial Soldier.* 1966. Missing medal, loose. NM. $425. *Matthew McKeeby Collection.* *Right: #8102 Russian Infantry Man.* 1966. Complete, loose. NM. $350. *Matthew McKeeby Collection.*

GAULTIER

Marked F.G. Fashion Lady (Poupée Peau): 1860 to 1930. Bisque swivel head on bisque shoulder plate, original kid body, kid arms with wired fingers or bisque lower arms and hands; original or good French wig, lovely glass stationary eyes, closed mouth, ears pierced; appropriately dressed; all in good condition.
Mark: "F.G." on side of shoulder.

12-13in (30-33cm)	$	1800 - 2100*
16-17in (41-43cm)		2500 - 2600*
20in (51cm)		2800 - 2900*
23in (58cm)		3200 -3400*
35in (89cm)		6750**

14in (36cm) all original provincial
    costume   **2800**
16in (41cm) all original Nun   **3000**
17in (43cm) all original communion
    outfit, boxed   **3800**
15in (38cm) wood arms, naked   **3000**
Wood body, *(Poupée Bois):*
  16-18in (41-46cm) $ **4000 - 4300**
Late doll in ethnic costume:
  8-9in (20-23cm)   **700 - 800**

Painted eyes:
  16-17in (41-43cm)   **1600 - 1800**
Approximate size chart:
Size 3/0 = 10-1/2in (27cm)
   2/0 = 11-1/2in (29cm)
     1 = 13-1/2in (34cm)
     2 = 15in (38cm)
     3 = 17in (43cm)
     5 = 20in (51cm)
     6 = 22in (56cm)

*Allow extra for original clothes.

**Not enough price samples to compute a
  reliable average.

FACTS

Francois Gauthier (name changed to
Gaultier in 1875); St. Maurice,
Charenton, Seine, Paris, France. (This
company made only porcelain parts, not
bodies.) 1860 to 1899
(then joined S.F.B.J.)

15in (38cm) *poupée peau* young lady, all original. *H & J Foulke, Inc.*

14in (36cm) *poupée peau. H & J Foulke, Inc.*

178

Marked F.G. Bébé: Ca. 1879-1887. Bisque swivel head on shoulder plate and gusseted kid body with bisque lower arms or chunky jointed composition body; good wig, large bulgy paperweight eyes, closed mouth, pierced ears; dressed; all in good condition. So-called "Block letters" mark.
Mark:

$$F . 7.G$$

Composition body:	
10in (25cm)	$ 2600 - 2800
13-15in (33-38cm)	4000 - 4400
18-20in (46-51cm)	4800 - 5000
22-23in (56-58cm)	5200 - 5500
27-28in (69-71cm)	6300 - 7000
33-35in (84-89cm)	7500 - 8000
Kid body:	
13in (33cm)	$ 4000 - 5000
16in (41cm)	5500
20-22in (51-56cm)	6500 - 7000

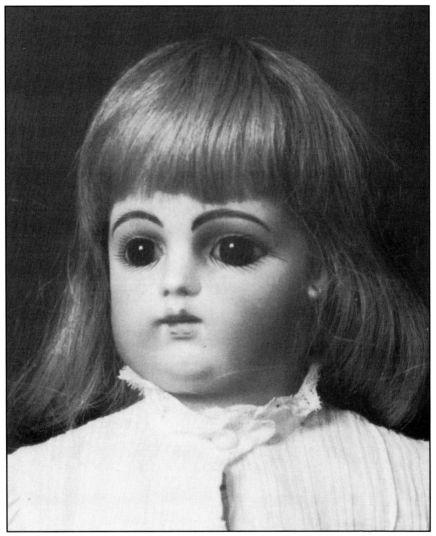

18in (46cm) F.7.G block letters. *Joanna Ott Collection.*

GAULTIER *continued*

Marked F.G. Bébé: Ca. 1887-1900 and probably later. Bisque head, composition jointed body; good French wig, beautiful large set eyes, closed mouth, pierced ears; well dressed; all in good condition. So-called "Scroll" mark.
Mark:

5-6in (13-15cm)	$ **725 - 775**
15-17in (38-43cm)	**2600 - 2900**
22-24in (56-61cm)	**3400 - 3700***
27-28in (69-71cm)	**4100 - 4400***
Open mouth:	
15-17in (38-43cm)	**1750 - 1950**
20-22in (51-56cm)	**2100 - 2400**

*Allow more for an especially pretty doll.

21in (53cm) "Scroll" mark Bébé. *Private Collection.*

GESLAND

Fashion Lady (Poupée): Perfect bisque swivel head, good wig, paperweight eyes, closed mouth, pierced ears; stockinette body on metal frame with bisque hands and legs; dressed; all in good condition.
Early face:

16-20in (41-51cm)	$ 5500 - 6200*

F.G. face:

14in (36cm)	3600 - 3800*
16-20in (41-51cm)	4000 - 4500*
28in (71cm)	5500 - 6000*

*Allow extra for original clothes.

Bébé: Perfect bisque swivel head; composition shoulder plate, good wig, paperweight eyes, closed mouth, pierced ears; stockinette body on metal frame with composition lower arms and legs; dressed; all in good condition.

(For photograph see *8th Blue Book*, page 183.)
Beautiful early face:

14-16in (36-41cm)	$ 4800 - 5000
22-24in (56-61cm)	5700 - 6200

"Scroll" mark face:

14-16in (36-41cm)	2500 - 2800
22-24in (56-61cm)	4000 - 4500

———— FACTS ————

Heads: Francois Gaultier, Paris, France.
Bodies: E. Gesland, Paris, France.
1860-1928.
Mark: Head: *F. G.*

Body: Sometimes stamped E. Gesland

19-1/2in (50cm) *poupée* incised "E 5 B" on Gesland-type body. *Private Collection.*

GODEY'S LITTLE LADY DOLLS

Ruth Gibbs Doll: Pink or white china head with painted black, brown, blonde or auburn hair and features; pink or white cloth body with china limbs and painted slippers which often matched the hair color; original clothes, usually in an old-fashioned style.

7in (18cm)	$	85 - 95
7in (18cm) boxed		95 - 110
10in (25cm) skin wig		295
12in (31cm) original underclothes		
		185 - 210
12in (31cm) boxed		215 - 235
Little Women, set of 5		750 - 850
Trousseau, boxed set		575
Fairy Tale, boxed		575

```
FACTS
Ruth Gibbs, Flemington, N.J., U.S.A.
1946.
Designer: Herbert Johnson.
Mark: Paper label inside skirt "Godey's
Little Lady Dolls;" "R.G." incised on
back plate.
```

7in (18cm) Ruth Gibbs doll, all original.
H & J Foulke, Inc.

10in (25cm) *Godey's Little Lady* with skin wig, all original. *H & J Foulke, Inc.*

GOOGLY-EYED DOLLS

All-Bisque Googly: Jointed at shoulders and hips, molded shoes and socks; mohair wig, glass eyes, impish mouth; undressed; in perfect condition.

#217, 501, 330 and others:

4-1/2–5in (11-13cm)	$	**500 - 550**
5-1/2–6in (14-15cm)		**625 - 675**

#189, 192 swivel necks:

4-1/2–5in (11-13cm)	$	**650 - 750**
5-1/2–6in (14-15cm)		**800 - 900**
7in (18cm)		**1000 - 1200**

#405:

6-1/2in (17cm)	$	**950**

Jointed elbows and knees (Kestner), swivel neck,

6-7in (15-18cm)	$	**2500 - 3000**
Stiff neck, 5in (13cm)		**1500 - 1650**

Baby, 4-1/2in (12cm)   **400 - 450**
Painted eyes, molded hair:

4-1/2 (12cm)	**375 - 400**
6in (15cm)	**525 - 550**

K & R 131, 7in (18cm)   **$2600 - 3000****

**Not enough price samples to compute a reliable average.

FACTS

J.D. Kestner, Armand Marseille, Hertel, Schwab & Co., Heubach, H. Steiner, Goebel and other German and French firms. Ca. 1911-on.

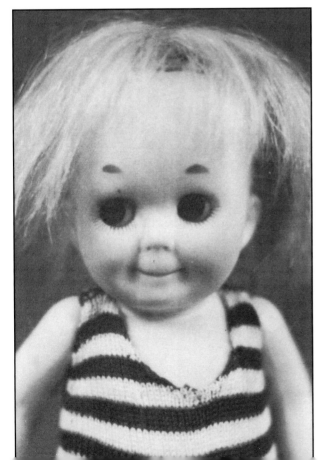

6-1/2in (17cm) S.W. 405 all-bisque googly. *H & J Foulke, Inc.*

GOOGLY-EYED DOLLS *continued*

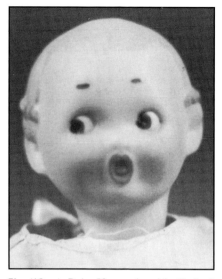

7in (18cm) R.A. 50 googly girl. *H & J Foulke, Inc.*

Painted eyes, composition body: Perfect bisque swivel head with molded hair, painted eyes to the side, impish mouth; 5-piece composition toddler or baby body jointed at shoulders and hips, some with molded and painted shoes and socks; cute clothes; all in good condition.

A.M., E. Heubach, Goebel, R.A.:
6-7in (15-18cm)	$	450 - 500*
9-10in (23-25cm)		850 - 900*
#252 A.M. Kewpie-type baby,		
9in (23cm)	$	1200

Gebrüder Heubach:
6-7in (15-18cm)	$	525 - 600*
7in (18cm) Winker		850
9in (23cm) with top knot		1350
9in (23cm) #8995		2650 - 3000

*Allow extra for unusual models.

Glass eyes, composition body: Perfect bisque head, mohair wig or molded hair, sleep or set large googly eyes, impish mouth closed; original composition body jointed at neck, shoulders and hips, sometimes with molded and painted shoes and socks; cute clothes; all in nice condition.

JDK 221:
12-15in (30-38cm) toddler	**$4500 -5500**

A.M. #323 and other similar models by H. Steiner, E. Heubach, Goebel and Recknagel:
6-7in (15-18cm)	$	800 - 900
9-10in (23-25cm)		1300 - 1400
Baby body,		
10-11in (25-28cm)		1100 - 1200

A.M. #253 (watermelon mouth):
6-7in (15-18cm)	$	900 - 1000
9in (23cm)		1400 - 1600

A.M. #200, 241:
8in (20cm)	$	1200 - 1500
11-12in (28-31cm)		2000 - 2200

A.M. #240:
10in (25cm) toddler	$	3000**

B.P. 686: 12in (31cm), at auction   **$ 3600**

Demalcol (Dennis, Malley, & Co. London, England):
9-10in (23-25cm)	**$ 700 - 800**

E. Heubach:
#419, 7in (18cm), at auction	$	2750
#322, 8-1/2in (21cm)		1100

**Not enough price samples to compute a reliable average.

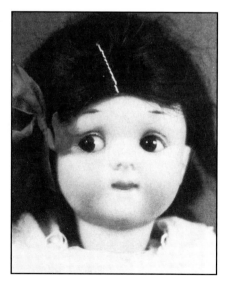

10in (25cm) A.M. 200 googly. *H & J Foulke, Inc.*

12in (31cm) H.S. & Co. 165 googly. *Jensen's Antique Dolls.*

For further information about dolls pictured on this page, see pages 183 & 186.

6-1/2in (17cm) E.H. 264 googly boy. *H & J Foulke, Inc.*

7in (18cm) A.M. 323 googly. *H & J Foulke, Inc.*

See page 186 for further information about
these dolls.

Right & Below: 9-1/2in (24cm) double-faced
googly with molded hat. *H & J Foulke, Inc.*

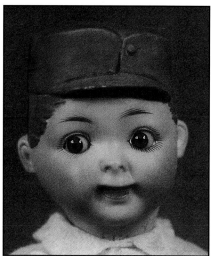

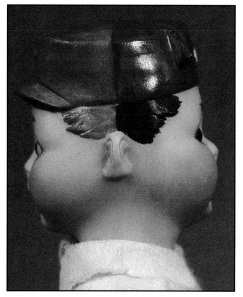

10in (25cm) ***Hug Me Kid,***
all original. *H & J Foulke,
Inc.*

GOOGLY-EYED DOLLS *continued*

Hertel, Schwab & Co.:
#163, toddler, 15-16in (38- 41cm)
$ 5000 - 5600

#165, baby:
12-13in (31-33cm)	$ 3300 - 3800
16in (41cm)	4800 - 5000
19in (48cm)	5500
Toddler 15in (38cm)	3800 - 4200

#172, 173:
Baby, 16in (41cm)	5000**
Toddler,	
10-12in (25-31cm)	4000 - 5000**
16in (41cm)	6000 - 7000**

#222, Our Fairy:
5in (13cm)	600 - 700
10in (25cm)	1200 - 1500
11in (28cm)	1700

G. Heubach:
Einco,
11in (28cm) 5-piece body	$ 3200
14-15in (36-38cm)	4000 - 5000
Elizabeth, 7-9in (18-23cm)	1650 - 1850

#8678, 9573:
6-7in (15-18cm)	$ 850 - 950
9in (23cm)	1250 - 1500

K ★ R 131:
8in (20cm), 5-piece body	$2400 - 2500**
15-16in (38-41cm)	7500

Kley & Hahn 180:
16-1/2in (43cm)	$ 3500**

P.M. 950:
11in (28cm)	$ 1600**

SFBJ #245:
8in (20cm), 5-piece body	$ 1500 - 1700**
11in (28cm) jointed body, with wardrobe	
at auction	3750
15in (38cm)	4200 - 4600**

SFBJ Black #52: 13in (33cm) $ 1350

Schieler: 12in (31cm) $ 3200**

Disc Eyes:
DRGM 954642 black or white
11-12in (28-31cm)	$ 1250 - 1500**

Composition face: 1911-1914. Made by various companies in 9-1/2–14in (24-36cm) sizes; marked with paper label on clothing. Called Hug Me Kids, Little Bright Eyes, as well as other trade names. Round all-composition or composition mask face, wig, round glass eyes looking to the side, watermelon mouth; felt body; original clothes; all in very good condition. (For photograph see page 185.)
10in (25cm)	$ 650 - 700
14in (36cm)	850 - 950

Googly with molded hat: 1915. Perfect bisque head with glass side-glancing eyes, watermelon mouth, molded hat; jointed composition body. Made for Max Handwerck, possibly by Hertel, Schwab & Co. All were soldiers: "U.S." (Uncle Sam hat); "E," (English Bellhop-type hat); "D," (German); "T," (Austrian/Turk-two faces) and Japanese.
Mark: "Dep
Elite"

10-13in (25-33cm)	$ 2000 - 2200
Double-Faced (See photograph on page 185.)	2200 - 2500

**Not enough price samples to compute a reliable average.

GREINER

―――― FACTS ――――

Ludwig Greiner of Philadelphia, Pa.,
U.S.A. 1858-1883, but probably as early
as 1840s. Heads of papier-mâché, cloth
bodies, homemade in most cases, but
later some Lacmann bodies were used.
Various sizes, 13-38in (33-97cm) and
perhaps larger, sizes "0" to "13."
Mark: Paper label on back shoulder:

GREINER'S
IMPROVED
PATENTHEADS
Pat.March 30th'58
or
GREINER'S
PATENT DOLL HEADS
No7
Pat. Mar.30'58.Ext.'72

Greiner: Blonde or black molded hair, painted features; homemade cloth body, leather arms; nice old clothes; entire doll in good condition.

'58 label:

15-17in (38-43cm)	$ 800 - 950
20-23in (51-58cm)	1150 - 1350
28-30in (71-76cm)	1500 - 1800
38in (97cm)	2500
Much worn:	
20-23in (51-58cm)	650 - 750
28-30in (71-76cm)	850 - 950
Glass eyes,	
20-23in (51-58cm)	2200 - 2500

'72 label:

19-22in (48-56cm)	$ 500 - 550
29-31in (71-79cm)	800 - 900
35in (89cm)	1100 - 1200

Two views of a 24in (61cm) 1858 Greiner with label, all original. *Carol Corson Collection.*

HEINRICH HANDWERCK

Marked Handwerck Child Doll: Ca. 1885 -on. Perfect bisque socket head, original or good wig, sleep or set eyes, open mouth, pierced ears; composition ball-jointed body with Handwerck stamp; dressed; entire doll in good condition.

#69, 89, 99 or no mold #*:

10-12in (25-31cm)	$	500 - 600
14-16in (36-41cm)		650 - 700
19-21in (43-53cm)		700 - 800
23-25in (58-64cm)		800 - 900
28-30in (71-76cm)		1200 - 1400
32-33in (79-84cm)		1700 - 1800
36in (91cm)		2200 - 2500
42in (107cm)		3800 - 4200

#79, 109, 119:

14-16in (36-41cm)	$	700 - 750
22-24in (56-61cm)		900 - 1000
41in (104cm)		4300

*Must have pretty face.

#139 and other shoulder heads, kid body :

16-18in (41-46cm)	$	350 - 400
22-24in (56-61cm)		450 - 500

#79, 89 closed mouth:

18-20in (46-51cm)	$	2300 - 2500
24in (61cm)		2800 - 3200

#189, open mouth,

18-20in (46-51cm)	900 - 950

———— FACTS ————

Heinrich Handwerck, doll factory, Waltershausen, Thüringia, Germany. Heads by Simon & Halbig. 1855-on.
Trademarks: Bébé Cosmopolite, Bébé de Réclame, Bébé Superior.
Mark:

Germany   HANDWERCK

HEINRICH HANDWERCK   109-11
SIMON B HALBIG

Germany

15in (38cm) Handwerck/S & H (no mold number). *H & J Foulke, Inc.*

MAX HANDWERCK

FACTS

Max Handwerck, doll factory, Waltershausen, Thüringia, Germany. Some heads by Goebel. 1900-on. **Trademarks:** Bébé Elite, Triumph-Bébé.

Mark:

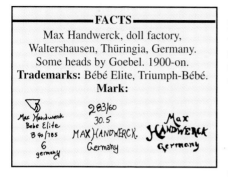

Marked Max Handwerck Child Doll: Perfect bisque socket head, original or good wig, set or sleep eyes, open mouth, pierced ears; original ball-jointed body; well dressed; all in good condition. Some mold **#283, 297** or **421.**

16-18in (41-46cm)	**$ 375 - 400**
22-24in (56-61cm)	**525 - 575**
31-32in (79-81cm)	**1000 - 1100**
38-39in (97-99cm)	**2000 - 2200**

Marked Bébé Elite Character: Perfect socket head with sleep eyes, open mouth with upper teeth, smiling character face; bent-limb composition baby body; appropriate clothes; all in good condition. (For photograph see *6th Blue Book*, page 171.)

14-16in (36-41cm)	**$ 425 - 475**
19-21in (48-53cm)	**550 - 650**
25in (64cm)	**800 - 900**

25in (64cm) Max Handwerck girl. *H & J Foulke, Inc.*

HARD PLASTIC, AMERICAN

Unmarked Hard Plastic Doll: All hard plastic, jointed at neck, shoulders and hips; sleeping eyes with real eyelashes, synthetic wig in original set, open or closed mouth; original clothes; all in excellent condition.

14in (36cm)	**$ 225 - 250**
18in (46cm)	**275 - 300**
24in (61cm)	**300 - 325**

Buddy Lee, 12in (31cm)	**$250 - 500***
Mary Jane, 16in (41cm)	**$ 275 - 300**

*Depending upon outfit.

FACTS
Various United States companies.
1948 into 1950s.
Mark: None, or various letters and numbers, or "Made in U.S.A."

16in (41cm) *Mary Jane.*
H & J Foulke, Inc.

12in (31cm) *Buddy Lee. H & J Foulke, Inc.*

OPPOSITE PAGE: 15in (38cm) *Paradise Dolls* bride, all original. *H & J Foulke, Inc.*

HARD PLASTIC (ITALIAN)

Italian Hard Plastic: Heavy, fine quality hard plastic, sometimes painted, or plastic coated papier-mâché, jointed at shoulders and hips; human hair wig, sleep eyes, sometimes flirty, often a character face; original clothes; all in excellent condition.

12in (31cm)	$	**125**
15-17in (38-43cm)		**150 - 200**
19-21in (48-53cm)		**255 - 250**

FACTS

Bonomi, Ottolini, Ratti, Furga and other Italian firms. Later 1940s and 1950s.
Mark: Usually a wrist tag; company name on head;
Ottolini-Lion head trademark.

16in (41cm) Bonomi girl, all original.
H & J Foulke, Inc.

HARMUS | KARL HARTMANN

Marked Harmus Child: Ca. 1920s. Perfect bisque socket head, sleeping eyes, real upper eyelashes, painted lower lashes, open mouth with teeth, original or appropriate wig; ball-jointed composition body; dressed; all in good condition.

20in (51cm)   **$ 775 - 825****

**Not enough price samples to compute a reliable average.

FACTS

Carl Harmus, Jr., Sonneberg, Thüringia, Germany. 1873 on. Doll factory, produced and exported dolls; bisque heads by various porcelain factories.
Trademark: Our Bobby, 1926.
Mark: HARMUS
800.0

Marked Karl Hartmann Doll: Perfect bisque head, good wig, glass eyes, open mouth; jointed composition body; suitable clothing; all in good condition.

18-20in (46-51cm)	**$ 400 - 450***
22-24in (56-61cm)	**525 - 575***
28-30in (71-76cm)	**800 - 900***

*Allow more for an especially pretty doll.

FACTS

Karl Hartmann, doll factory, Stockheim/Upper Franconia, Germany. 1911-1926. Bisque head, jointed composition body.
Mark:

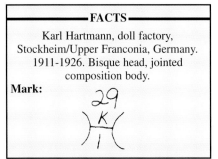

20in (51cm) Harmus girl. *H & J Foulke, Inc.*

22in (56cm) Karl Hartmann girl. *H & J Foulke, Inc.*

CARL HARTMANN

HELLER

Marked Globe Baby: Perfect bisque head, mohair or human hair wig, sleep eyes, multi-stroked eyebrows, open mouth with upper teeth; good quality 5-piece composition body with molded shoes and socks; dressed; all in very good condition.

   8in (20cm)   **$ 325 - 350**

   8in (20cm), all original clothes
      and wig   **375 - 425**

Marked Adolf Heller Child: Perfect bisque socket head, sleeping eyes, open mouth, original or appropriate wig; jointed composition body; appropriate clothes; all in good condition.

   20-22in (51-56cm)   **$ 775 - 825****

**Not enough price samples to compute a
   reliable average.

————— FACTS —————

Carl Hartmann, Neustadt, Thüringia;
Stockheim, Bavaria, Germany. 1889-on.
Trademark: Globe Baby 1898.
Mark:
          Globe Baby
            DEP
          Germany
           C : H

————— FACTS —————

Adolf Heller, Waltershausen, Thüringia,
Germany. 1909-1930. Doll factory.
Trademarks: My Good Child,
           My Gold Pearl
Mark:

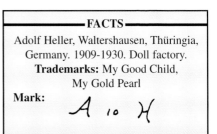

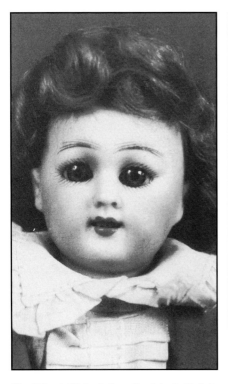

8in (20cm) *Globe baby,* all original. *H & J Foulke, Inc.*

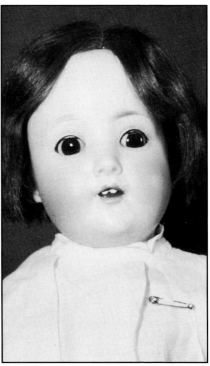

21in (53cm) A.H. flapper girl. *H & J Foulke, Inc.*

HERTEL, SCHWAB & Co.

Marked Character Baby: Perfect bisque head, molded and painted hair or good wig, sleep or painted eyes, open or open/closed mouth with molded tongue; bent limb baby body; dressed; all in good condition.

#130, 142, 150, 151, 152:
10-12in (25-31cm)	$	425 - 475
15-17in (38-43cm)		550 - 650
19-21in (48-53cm)		700 - 750
24-25in (61-64cm)		900 - 1000

#125 (so-called "Patsy Baby"):
11-12in (28-31cm)	$	800 - 900**

#126 (so called "Skippy"):
10-12in (25-31cm)	$	900 - 1100**
19in (48cm) mulatto toddler		1650**

#142 All-bisque, painted eyes,
11in (28cm)	$	800 - 900

#169 (open mouth):
18-20in (46-51cm)	**$1000 - 1200****

**Not enough price samples to compute a reliable range.

FACTS
Stutzhauser Porzellanfabrik, Hertel Schwab & Co., Stutzhaus, near Ohrdruf, Thüringia, Germany. 1910-on.
Bisque heads to be used on composition, cloth or leather bodies, all-bisque dolls, pincushion dolls.
Mark:

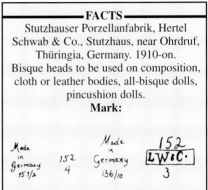

12in (31cm) 151 baby. *H & J Foulke, Inc.*

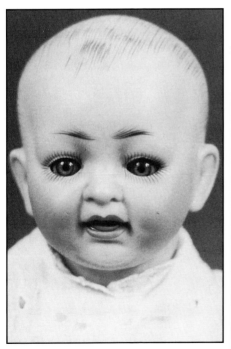

19in (48cm) 126 mulatto toddler. *H & J Foulke, Inc.*

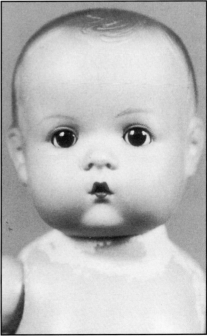

Child Doll: Ca. 1910. Perfect bisque head, mohair or human hair wig, sleep eyes, open mouth with upper teeth; good quality jointed composition body (some marked K & W); dressed; all in good condition. Mold **#136**. (For photograph see *11th Blue Book*, page 197.)

14-17in (36-43cm)	**$ 475 - 525**
20-22in (51-56cm)	**575- 625**
24-25in (61-64cm)	**700 - 750**

Marked Character Child: Perfect bisque head, painted or sleeping eyes, closed mouth; jointed composition body; dressed; all in good condition. (For photograph see page 13.)

#134, 149, 141:

11in (28cm)	**$ 3500**
16-18in (41-46cm)	**6500 - 8500****

#154 (closed mouth):

14-16in (36-41cm)	**$ 2300 - 2500**
19in (48cm)	**3100**

#154 (open mouth):

16-18in (41-46cm)	**$ 1200 - 1400**

#169 (closed mouth):

19-21in (48-53cm) toddler	**$ 3500 - 4000**

#127 (so-called "Patsy"):

16in (41cm)	**$1100 - 1250****

**Not enough price samples to compute a reliable range.

All-Bisque Doll: Jointed shoulders and hips; good wig, glass eyes, closed or open mouth; molded and painted shoes and stockings; undressed; all in good condition. Mold **#208** often with **Prize Baby** label.

4-5in (10-13cm)	**$ 225 - 275***
6in (15cm)	**350 - 375**
8in (20cm)	**500 - 550**
Swivel neck,	
7in (18cm)	**550 - 600**

#150 character baby

7-1/2in (19cm)	**$ 550**

*Do not pay as much for poor quality bisque.

7-1/2in (19cm) 150 all-bisque baby. *H & J Foulke, Inc.*

ERNST HEUBACH

FACTS

Ernst Heubach, porcelain factory,
Köppelsdorf, Thüringia, Germany.
1887 - on. Bisque heads for use on kid,
cloth or composition bodies.
Mark:

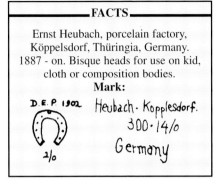

D.E.P. 1902   Heubach · Kopplesdorf.
300·14/0
2/0   Germany

Heubach Child Doll: Ca. 1888-on. Perfect bisque head, good wig, sleep eyes, open mouth; kid, cloth or jointed composition body; dressed; all in good condition.

#275 or horseshoe, kid or cloth body:

13-15in (33-38cm)	$	**175 - 225**
19-21in (48-53cm)		**275 - 325**
24in (61cm)		**425 - 450**

#250, 251. composition body:

8-9in (20-23cm)	**210 - 235**
16-18in (41-46cm)	**350 - 400**
23-24in (58-61cm)	**500 - 550**
29-30in (74-76cm)	**750 - 850**

Painted bisque, **#250, 407,**

7-8in (18-20cm)	**100 - 125**

#312 SUR (for Seyfarth & Reinhard):

14in (36cm)	**375 - 400**
28in (71cm)	**850 - 900**
45-46in (113-115cm)	**3500**

7in (18cm) painted bisque 250 flapper, all original. *H & J Foulke, Inc.*

24in (61cm) SUR 312 flapper. *H & J Foulke, Inc.*

Character Children: 1910-on. Perfect bisque shoulder head with molded hair in various styles, some with hair bows, painted eyes, open/closed mouth; cloth body with composition lower arms.
#261, 262, 271 and others,
  12in (31cm)   **$ 400 - 450****

** Not enough price samples to compute a
  reliable range.

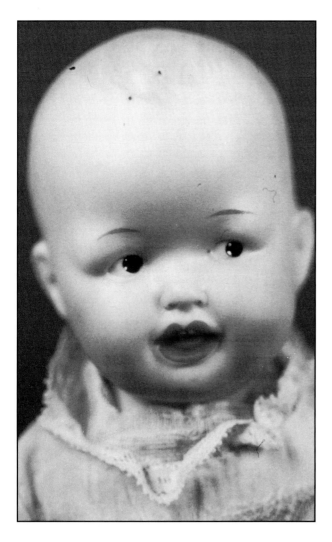

10in (25cm) 261 character. *H & J Foulke, Inc.*

Character Baby: 1910-on. Perfect bisque head, good wig, sleep eyes, open mouth (sometimes also wobbly tongue and pierced nostrils); composition bent-limb baby or toddler body; dressed; all in good condition.

#300, 320, 342 and others:

5-1/2–6in (14-15cm)	$	250 - 275
8-10in (20-25cm)		250 - 275
14-17in (36-43cm)		425 - 475
19-21in (48-53cm)		550 - 600
24-25in (61-64cm)		850 - 900

#300, 320, jointed composition body:

17in (43cm)	450
24in (61cm)	650

Toddler:

9in (23cm) 5-piece body	350 - 400
15-17in (38-43cm)	525 - 600
23-25in (58-64cm)	950 - 1100

Infant: Ca. 1925. Perfect bisque head, molded and painted hair, sleep eyes, closed mouth; cloth body, composition or celluloid hands, appropriate clothes; all in good condition. (For photograph see *11th Blue Book,* page 200.)

#349, 339, 350:

13-16in (33-41cm)	$	575 - 675**

#338, 340:

14-16in (36-41cm)	725 - 825**

**Not enough price samples to compute a reliable range.

Black Dolls #399, 414, 452, 444, 463:
See pages 95 and 96.

5-1/4in (13cm) 300 character baby.
H & J Foulke, Inc.

20in (51cm) 342 toddler, flirty eyes.
H & J Foulke, Inc.

GEBRÜDER HEUBACH

Heubach Character Child: Ca. 1910. Perfect bisque head, molded hair, glass or intaglio eyes, closed or open/closed mouth, character face; jointed composition or kid body; dressed; all in good condition. (For photographs of Heubach dolls see *Focusing On Dolls*, pages 30-68 and previous *Blue Books*.)

#5636, 7663, laughing child, glass eyes:

12in (31cm)	$	**1500 - 1700**
15-18in (38-46cm)		**2500 - 2800**

#5689 smiling child. (For photograph see *6th Blue Book*, page 197.)

27in (69cm)	$	**4000**

#5730 Santa. (For photograph see *11th Blue Book*, page 201.)

19-21in (48-53cm)	$	**1800 - 2200**

#5777 Dolly Dimple:

19-22in (48-56cm)	$	**3500 - 4000**
Shoulder head, 15in (38cm)		**1000**

#6969, 6970, 7246, 7347, 7407, 8017, 8420 pouty child (must have glass eyes):

12-13in (31-33cm)		**1800 - 2200**
16-19in (41-48cm)		**3500 - 4000**
24in (61cm)		**5500 - 6000**

#6692 and other shoulder head pouties:

14-16in (36-41cm)	$	**750 - 950**

FACTS

Gebrüder Heubach, porcelain factory, Licht and Sonneberg, Thüringia, Germany. 1820-on; doll heads, 1910-on. Bisque heads, all-bisque.

Mark:

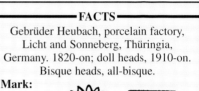

15in (38cm) 7663 laughing child. *H & J Foulke, Inc.*

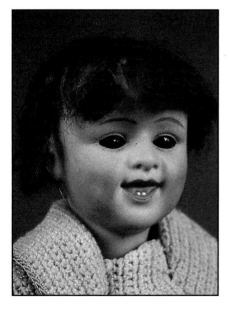

12in (31cm) 7246 pouty. *H & J Foulke, Inc.*

13-1/2in (35cm) 7603 pouty boy. *H & J Foulke, Inc.*

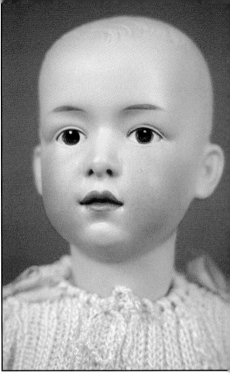

13-1/2in (35cm) 8191 laughing boy. *H & J Foulke, Inc.*

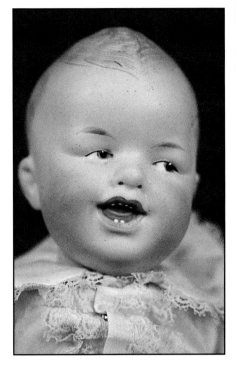

11-1/2in (30cm) girl with blue hair band, no mold number. *H & J Foulke, Inc.*

#7604, 7623 and other smiling socket heads,
14-16in (36-41cm) **$ 800 - 1000**
#7602, 6894 and other socket head pouties,
14-16in (36-41cm) **750 - 950**
#7622 and other socket head pouties (wide
lips), 14-17in (36-43cm) **1000 - 1250**
#7661 squinting eyes, crooked mouth,
19in (48cm) **6750**
#7665 Smiling, 16in (41cm) **1800**
#7679 Whistler socket head:
10in (25cm) **800 - 900**
14in (36cm) **1100 - 1300**
#7684 Screamer. (For photograph see *11th
Blue Book*, page 201.)
16-19in (41-48cm) **2500 - 3000**
#7743 big ears, 17in (43cm) **5500 - 6000**
#7764 singing girl, 16in (41cm) **10,000**
#7788 Coquette:
14in (36cm) **1150**
Shoulder head, 12in (31cm) **700 - 775**
#7865, 14in (36cm) **3000**
#7852 shoulder head, molded coiled
braids, 16in (41cm) **2200**
#7853 shoulder head, downcast eyes,
14in (36cm) **1650 - 1850**
#7911, 8191 grinning:
11in (28cm) **900 - 1000**
15in (38cm) **1300 - 1400**
#7925, 7926 lady. (For photograph see *9th
Blue Book*, page 167.)
16in (41cm) **2500**
21-22in (53-56cm) **3700**
#8050 smiling girl with hairbow. (For photo-
graph see *10th Blue Book*, page 157.)
18in (46cm) **10,000**
#8192:
9-11in (23-28cm) **450 - 550**
14-16in (36-41cm) **750 - 800**
18-22in (46-56cm) **1000 - 1200**
#8381 Princess Juliana,
16in (41cm) **10,000 - 12,000**
#8550 molded tongue sticking out:
13in (33cm) intaglio eyes **950 - 1050**
13in (33cm) glass eyes **1300 - 1400**
#8556 (For photograph see *10th Blue Book*,
page 157.) **11,500**
#9102 Cat, 6in (15cm) **1150**
#9141 Winker:
9in (23cm) glass eye **1500**
7in (18cm) painted eye **850 - 950**
#9467 Indian, 14in (36cm) **2500 - 3000**
#10532, 20-22in (51-53cm) **1200 - 1300**

#10586, 10633,
18-20in (46-51cm) **750 - 850**

#11173 Tiss Me. (For photograph see *8th
Blue Book*, page 224.)
8in (20cm) **$ 1850 - 2000**
Baby Bokaye, Bonnie Babe,
7-8in (18-20cm) **900 - 950**
#1907 Jumeau. (For photograph see *10th
Blue Book*, page 156.)
20-22in (51-56cm) **$ 2400 - 2500**

All-Bisque. (For photographs see *Focusing
on Dolls*, pages 71-77.):
Position Babies and Action Figures:
5in (13cm) **$ 350 - 500**
Girl with bobbed hair:
7in (18cm) **800 - 900**
9in (23cm) **1200 - 1300**
Girl with head band:
7in (18cm) **950 - 1050**
9in (23cm) **1500 - 1600**
Girl with three bows:
7in (18cm) **1100 - 1300**
9in (23cm) **1800 - 2000**
Boy, 8in (20cm) **1200 - 1300**
Boy or girl, 4-1/2in (11cm) **300 - 400**
Chin Chin, 4in (10cm) **275 - 325**
Bunny Boy or Girl:
5-1/2in (14cm) **350 - 400**
9in (23cm) **700 - 800**
Piano Babies, various positions,
9in (23cm) **550 up**

Heubach Babies: Ca. 1910. Perfect bisque head, molded hair, intaglio eyes, open or closed mouth, character face; composition bent-limb body; dressed; all in nice condition.

#6894, 7602, 6898, 7759 and other pouty babies:

4-1/2in(12cm)	$	225 - 275
6in (15cm)		275 - 300
10in (25cm)		450 - 500
12in (31cm)		650 - 700
14in (36cm)		750 - 800

#7604 laughing,

13-14in (33-36cm)		700 - 800

#7877, 7977 Baby Stuart:

10in (25cm)	$	1100 - 1200
16in (41cm)		1800
12in (31cm) glass eyes		2100

#8228 shoulder head **Baby Stuart,**

10-1/2in (26cm)	$	750

#7959 molded pink cap,

10in (25cm)	$	2000

9in (23cm) all-bisque *Coquette*. *H & J Foulke, Inc.*

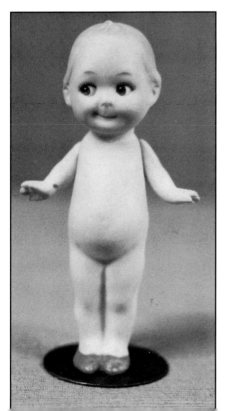

9-1/2in (24cm) *Baby Stuart*. *H & J Foulke, Inc.*

4-1/2in (12cm) all-bisque child. *H & J Foulke, Inc.*

HIMSTEDT

Marked Himstedt Doll: Hard vinyl head swivels on long shoulder plate, cloth lower torso, vinyl arms and curved legs; inset eyes with real eyelashes, painted feathered eyebrows, molded upper eyelids, open nose, human hair wig; original cotton clothing, bare feet. All in excellent condition, with original box.

Barefoot Children, 1986, 26in (66cm):

Ellen	$	700 - 800
Kathe		700 - 800
Paula		650 - 700
Fatou		900 - 1100
Bastian		600 - 650
Lisa		700 - 800

American Heartland Dolls, 1987, 19-20in (48-51cm):

Timi	$	400 - 450
Toni		400 - 450

The World Child Collection, 1988, 31in (79cm):

Kasimir	$	1300 - 1500
Malin		1100 - 1300
Michiko		900 - 1000
Frederike		1000 - 1100
Makimura		750 - 850

Reflections of Youth, 1989, 26in (66cm):

Adrienne	$	650 - 750
Janka		550 - 650
Ayoka		900 - 1000
Kai		750 - 850

1990:

Fiene	$	600 - 650
Taki (Baby)		650 - 750
Annchen (Baby)		550 - 650

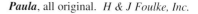

FACTS

1986-on. Hard vinyl and cloth.
Designer: Annette Himstedt
Distributor: Mattel, Inc., Hawthorne, CA., U.S.A. Dolls made in Spain.
Mark: Wrist tag with doll's name; cloth signature label on clothes; signature on lower back plate and on back of doll's head under wig.

Paula, all original. *H & J Foulke, Inc.*

HORSMAN

Billiken: 1909. Composition head with peak of hair at top of head, slanted slits for eyes, watermelon mouth; velvet or plush body; in very good condition.
Mark: Cloth label on body; "Billiken" on right foot.
12in (31cm) $ **350 - 400**

Can't Break 'Em Characters: Ca. 1911. Heads and hands of "Can't Break 'Em" composition, hard stuffed cloth bodies with swivel joints at shoulders and hips; molded hair, painted eyes, character faces; appropriate clothes; all in good condition.
Mark: "E.I.H.1911"
11-13in (28-33cm) $ **200 up**

Polly Pru, 13in (33cm)   **325****
Cotton Joe, black, 13in (33cm)**400 - 475****
Baby Bumps   **200 - 250**
  black   **250 - 300**

**Not enough price samples to compute a reliable range.

FACTS

E.I. Horsman Co., New York, N.Y., U.S.A. Also distributed dolls as a *verlager* for other manufacturers and imported French and German dolls. 1878-on.

12in (31cm) *Billiken*. *Private Collection.*

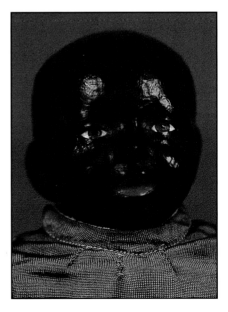

12in (31cm) black ***Baby Bumps***. *H & J Foulke, Inc.*

Campbell Kid: 1910-1914. Designed by Grace Drayton. Marked composition head with flange neck, molded and painted bobbed hair, painted round eyes to the side, watermelon mouth; original cloth body, composition arms, cloth legs and feet; all in fair condition. (For photograph see page 208.)
Mark: On head:

E.I.H. © 1910

Cloth label on sleeve:

> The Campbell Kids
> Trademark by
> Joseph Campbell
> Mfg. by E. I. HORSMAN Co.

10-13in (25-33cm)	$	250 - 300
16in (41cm)		350 - 400

Peterkin: 1914-1930. All-composition with character face, molded hair, painted eyes to side, watermelon mouth; various boy and girl clothing or simply a large bow; all in good condition. (For photograph see *9th Blue Book*, page 234.)

11in (28cm)	$	300 - 350

Gene Carr Character: 1916. Composition head with molded and painted hair, eyes painted open or closed, wide smiling mouth with teeth; cloth body with composition hand; original or appropriate clothes; all in good condition. Names such as: Snowball (black boy); Mike and Jane (eyes open); Blink and Skinney (eyes closed). Designed by Bernard Lipfert from Gene Carr's cartoon characters. (For photograph see page 208.)
Mark: None.

8in (20cm)	$	200 - 225
13-14in (33-36cm)		300 - 350
Black Snowball		450 - 550

Mama Dolls: Ca. 1920-on. Composition head, cloth body, composition arms and lower legs; mohair wig or molded hair, sleep eyes; original clothes; all in very good condition. (For photograph see page 208.)
Mark: "E. I. H. Co." or "HORSMAN"
Babies:

12-14in (31-36cm)	$	150 - 185
18-20in (46-51cm)		250 - 275

Girls, including Rosebud and Peggy Ann:

14-16in (36-41cm)		**250 - 275**
22-24in (56-61cm)		**325 - 375**

Jackie Coogan: 1921. Composition head with molded hair, painted eyes, closed mouth; cloth torso with composition hands; appropriate clothes; all in good condition. (For photograph see *8th Blue Book*, page 228.)
Mark: "E.I.H. Co. 19©21"

14in (36cm)	$	500 - 550

HEbee-SHEbee: 1925. All-composition, jointed at shoulders and hips, painted eyes, molded white chemise and real ribbon or wool ties in molded shoes; all in good condition. Blue shoes indicate a **HEbee**, pink ones a **SHEbee**. (For photograph see *11th Blue Book*, page 208.)

11in (28cm)	$	550 - 600
Fair condition (some peeling)		325 - 375
Mint, all original		750 - 800

Ella Cinders: 1925. Composition head with molded hair, painted eyes; cloth body with composition arms and lower legs; original clothes; all in fair condition. From the comic strip by Bill Conselman and Charlie Plumb for the Metropolitan Newspaper Service. (For photograph see *8th Blue Book*, page 229.)
Mark: "1925 © MNS"

18in (46cm)	$	550 - 650

Baby Dimples: 1928. Composition head with molded and painted hair, tin sleep eyes, open mouth, smiling face; soft cloth body with composition arms and legs; original or appropriate old clothes; all in good condition. (For photograph see page 209.)
Mark: "©
E. I. H. CO. INC."

16-18in (41-46cm)	$	250 - 300
22-24in (56-61cm)		350 - 400

HORSMAN *continued*

Child Dolls: Ca. 1930s and 1940s. All-composition with swivel neck, shoulders and hips; mohair wig, sleep eyes; original clothes; all in excellent condition. (For photograph see page 209.)

Mark: "HORSMAN"

13-14in (33-36cm)	$	**225 - 250**
16-18in (41-46cm)		**275 - 325**
Chubby toddler,		
16-18in (41-46cm)		**300 - 350**
Jo-Jo, 1937. 12in (31cm) toddler		**225 - 250**
Jeanie, 1937. 14in (36cm)		**300**
Naughty Sue, 1937. 16in (41cm)		**400 - 450**
Roberta, 1937. 16in (41cm)		**400 - 450**
Bright Star, 1940.		
17-20in (43-51cm)		**400 - 500**

Cindy: Ca. 1950. All-hard plastic, sleep eyes, open mouth with upper teeth and tongue, synthetic wig with braids.

Mark: "170 made in USA."

Walker, 16in (41cm)	$	**225 - 275**

Campbell Kid: 1948. Unmarked all-composition, molded painted hair, painted eyes to the side, watermelon mouth; painted white socks and black slippers; original clothes; all in good condition. (For photograph see page 209.)

12in (31cm)	$	**350 - 425**
With Campbell Soup outfit and label,		
at auction		**600**

Marked Tynie Baby: 1924. Bisque solid dome infant head with sleep eyes, closed mouth, slightly frowning face; cloth body with composition arms; appropriate clothes; all in good condition. Designed by Bernard Lipfert. (For photograph see *11th Blue Book*, page 210.)

Mark:

© 1924
E.I. Horsman Inc.
Made in
Germany

Bisque head,

8-1/2–9-1/2in (21-23cm) h.c.	$	**550 - 600**
11-12in (28-31cm) h.c.		**750 - 800**
Composition head,		
15in (38cm) long		**275 - 300**

All-bisque with swivel neck, glass eyes, wigged or solid dome head. (For photograph see page 209.)

8-10in (20-25cm)	**1800 - 2200**

Vinyl, Ca. 1950 crying face. (For photograph see *11th Blue Book*, page 210.)

15in (38cm) boxed	**90 - 110**

See photographs on following pages.

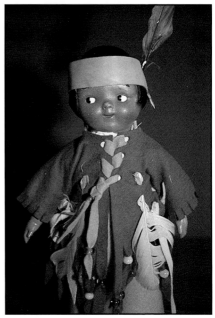

TOP: *Left:* 8in (20cm) Gene Carr *Blink*, all original. *H & J Foulke, Inc.* (For further information see page 206.) *Right:* 13in (33cm) *Campbell Kid* Indian, all original. *H & J Foulke, Inc.* (For further information see page 206.) **BOTTOM:** *Left:* 24in (61cm) mama doll, all original. *H & J Foulke, Inc.* (For further information see page 206.) *Right:* 24in (61cm) Horsman-type unmarked baby, all original. *H & J Foulke, Inc.*

TOP: *Left:* 19in (48cm) *Dimples*. H & J *Foulke, Inc.* (For further information see page 206.) *Right:* 15in (38cm) child doll, all original. *H & J Foulke, Inc.* (For further information see page 207.) **BOTTOM:** *Left:* 12in (31cm) *Campbell Kid* 1948, all original. *H & J Foulke, Inc.* (For further information, see page 207.) *Right:* 8-1/2in (22cm) all-bisque *Tynie Baby*. *H & J Foulke, Inc.* (For further information see page 207.)

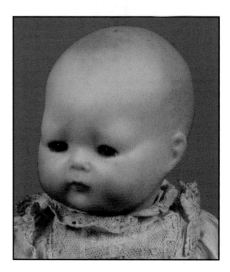

MARY HOYER

Marked Mary Hoyer: Material as above; swivel neck; jointed shoulders and hips, original wig, sleep eyes with eyelashes, closed mouth; all in excellent condition. Original tagged factory clothes or garments made at home from Mary Hoyer patterns.

Composition, 14in (36cm) $ 350 - 450
Boxed and all original with 2 extra outfits, pajamas and shoes, at auction **600**
Hard plastic:
14in (36cm) **425 - 500**
14in (36cm) boy with
caracul wig **500 - 550**
18in (46cm), **Gigi** **550 - 700**

FACTS

The Mary Hoyer Doll Mfg. Co., Reading Pa., U.S.A. Ca. 1925-on.
Mark: Embossed on torso:
"The
Mary Hoyer
Doll"
or in a circle:
"ORIGINAL
Mary Hoyer
Doll"

14in (36cm) hard plastic Mary Hoyer, all original. *H & J Foulke, Inc.*

HÜLSS

━━━━━━ FACTS ━━━━━━
Adolf Hülss, doll factory, Waltershausen, Thüringia, Germany; heads by Simon & Halbig. 1913-on.

Mark:

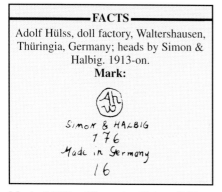

Simon & Halbig
7 7 6
Made in Germany
1 6

Marked Hülss Character Baby: 1925-on. Mold number **156**. Perfect bisque head with good wig, sleep eyes, open mouth with teeth and tongue, smiling face; composition bent-limb body; nicely dressed; all in good condition. (For photograph see *11th Blue Book*, page 212.)

15-17in (38-43cm)	$ 600 - 700*
23in (58cm)	1250 - 1350*
Toddler:	
10-11in (25-28cm)	750 - 850*
15-16in (38-41cm)	850 - 950*
22-24in (56-61cm)	1350 - 1650*

Marked Hülss Child: 1920s. Mold number **176**. Perfect bisque head with good wig, flirty sleep eyes, open mouth with teeth and tongue. Jointed composition body with high knee joint; dressed; all in good condition.

18in (46cm)	$ 750 - 850**
30in (76cm)	1500 - 1650**

* Allow $50-100 extra for flirty eyes.
**Not enough price samples to compute a reliable range.

30in (76cm) 176 flapper with flirty eyes.
H & J Foulke, Inc.

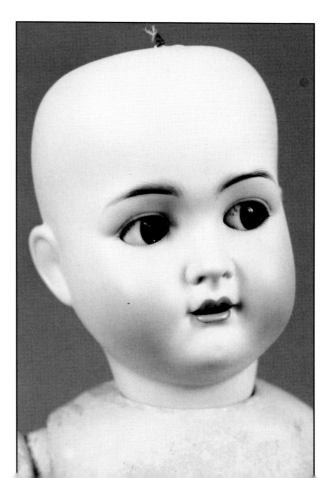

HURET

Marked Huret Poupée: China or bisque shoulder head, good wig, painted eyes, closed mouth; kid body; beautifully dressed; all in good condition.

17in (43cm)	**$ 15,000 - 20,000**
Swivel neck	**32,000**
Gutta-percha body	**20,000****
Child, wood body,	
18in (46cm)	**25,000 - 30,000****

**Not enough price samples to compute a reliable range.

FACTS

Maison Huret, Paris, France. 1850-on.
Mark: "Huret" or "Maison Huret" stamped on body.

17-1/2in (44cm) Huret *poupée* with swivel neck and jointed wood body. *Private Collection.*

IDEAL

Uneeda Kid: 1914-1919. Composition head with molded brown hair, blue painted eyes, closed mouth; cloth body with composition arms and legs with molded black boots; original bloomer suit, yellow slicker and rain hat; carrying a box of Uneeda Biscuits; all in good condition, showing some wear. (For photograph see *11th Blue Book*, page 216.)

16in (41cm)	$	450 - 475
24in (61cm)		650 - 700**

Snoozie: 1933. Composition head, character expression with yawning mouth, sleeping eyes, molded hair, composition arms and legs or rubber arms, cloth body; baby clothes; all in good condition. 13, 16 and 20 in (33, 41 and 51cm). (For photograph see *7th Blue Book*, page 216.)

Mark: ©

By B. LIPFERT

16-20in (41-51cm) $ **275 - 350**

**Not enough price samples to compute a reliable range.

Shirley Temple: 1935. For detailed information see pages 328-329.

Mama Doll: Ca. 1920-on. Composition head, cloth body, composition arms and lower legs; mohair wig or molded hair, sleep eyes; appropriate old clothes; all in very good condition.

Mark:

14-16in (36-41cm)	$	225 - 250
Characters,		
14-16in (36-41cm)		225 - 250

Flossie Flirt: (For photograph see *11th Blue Book*, page 216.)

20in (51cm)	$	275 - 325
Flirty-eyed baby, 1938.		
16-18in (41-46cm)		225 - 275

Betsy Wetsy: 1937-on. Composition head with molded hair, sleep eyes; soft rubber body jointed at neck, shoulders and hips; drinks, wets; appropriate clothes; all in good condition. This doll went through many changes including hard plastic head on rubber body, later vinyl body, later completely vinyl. Various sizes.

Mark: "IDEAL"

Rubber body,

14-16in (36-41cm) $ **125 - 165**

════════ FACTS ════════

Ideal Novelty and Toy Co., Brooklyn, N.Y., U.S.A. 1907-on.

15-1/2in (40cm) character doll, all original. *H & J Foulke, Inc.*

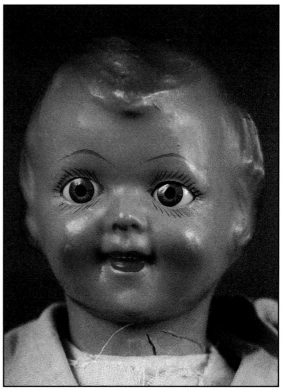

IDEAL *continued*

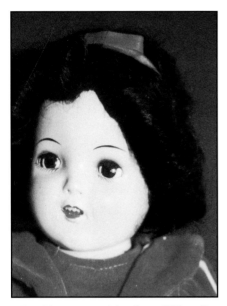

18in (46cm) composition *Snow White*, all original. *H & J Foulke, Inc.*

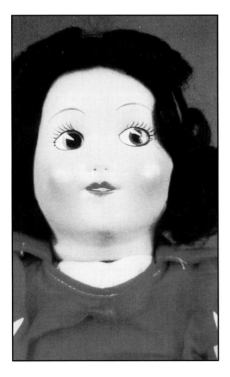

Snow White: 1937. All-composition, jointed at neck, shoulders and hips; black mohair wig, lashed sleep eyes, open mouth; original dress with velvet bodice and cape, and rayon skirt, with figures of seven dwarfs; in excellent condition. 11in (28 cm), 13in (33cm) and 18in (46cm) sizes.

Mark: On body:
"SHIRLEY TEMPLE/18"
On dress: "An Ideal Doll"

11-13in (28-33cm)	$	500 - 525
18in (46cm)		600 - 700

Molded black hair, painted blue bow, painted eyes,

13-14in (33-36cm)		190 - 225
All cloth, 16in (41cm)		500 - 550

Shirley Temple-Type Girl: 1930s-1940s. All-composition with jointed neck, shoulders and hips; lashed sleeping eyes (sometimes flirty), open mouth with teeth; all original; excellent condition. Some have marked **Shirley Temple** bodies.

Mark: IDEAL
18

Betty Jane, Little Princess or **Cinderella:**

14in (36cm)	$	275 - 300
18in (46cm)		375 - 425

Deanna Durbin: 1938. All-composition, jointed at neck, shoulders and hips; original human hair or mohair wig, sleep eyes, smiling mouth with teeth; original clothing; all in good condition. Various sizes.

Mark: Metal button with picture:
"DEANNA DURBIN,
IDEAL DOLL, U.S.A."

14in (36cm)	$	550 - 600
20-21in (51-53cm)		750 - 850
24in (61cm)		1000

16in (41cm) cloth *Snow White*, all original. *H & J Foulke, Inc.*

IDEAL *continued*

Judy Garland as Dorothy of the Wizard of Oz: 1939. All-composition, jointed at neck, shoulders and hips; dark human hair wig, dark sleep eyes, open mouth with teeth; original dress; all in good condition. (For photograph see *10th Blue Book*, page 159.)
Mark: On head:
"IDEAL DOLL"
MADE IN U.S.A.
Body: U.S.A.
16
16in (41cm)   **$ 1200 - 1400**
Soldier: Ca. 1942. All-composition, character face. All original and excellent. (For photograph see page 216.)
13in (33cm)   **400 - 425**

Flexy Dolls: 1938-on. Head, hands and feet of composition; arms and legs of flexible metal cable, torso of wire mesh; in original clothes; all in good condition. 12in (31cm).
Mark: On head: "Ideal Doll".
Baby Snooks (Fanny Brice) (For photograph see *11th Blue Book*,
page 216.)   **$ 250 - 275**
Mortimer Snerd   **$ 250 - 275**
Soldier   **200 - 225**
Children   **200 - 225**

Composition and wood segmented characters: 1940. Molded composition heads with painted features, wood segmented bodies. Label on front torso gives name of character. (For photograph see *10th Blue Book*, page 160.)
Pinocchio, 10-1/2in (27cm) **$ 350 - 450**
King-Little, 14in (36cm)   **275 - 325**
Jiminy Cricket, 9in (23cm) **400 - 450**
Gabby, 11in (28cm)   **375 - 425**

Magic Skin Baby and Plassie: 1940-on. Composition or hard plastic head with molded hair, sleep eyes, closed or open mouth; stuffed latex rubber body; appropriate clothes; all in good condition. (For photograph see page 217.)
Mark: On head: "IDEAL".
14-15in (36-38cm)   **$ 125 - 150**
22in (56cm)   **200 - 225**
Sparkle Plenty, 1947.
15in (38cm) Baby   **100 - 135**
Toddler   **125 - 175**

16in (41cm) *Deanna Durbin*, original dress. *H & J Foulke, Inc.*

18in (46cm) "Magic Eyes" *Cinderella*. *H & J Foulke, Inc.*

13in (33cm) all-composition *Soldier*, all original (missing jacket). *H & J Foulke, Inc.* (For further information see page 215.)

14in (36cm) *Harriet Hubbard Ayer*, mint-in-box. *June & Norman Verro.* (For further information see page 218.)

14in (36cm) *Magic Skin Baby*, all original. *H & J Foulke, Inc.* (For further information see page 215.)

22in (56cm) *Saucy Walker*, mint-in-box. *June & Norman Verro.* (For further information see page 218.)

218

Toni and P-90 and P-91 Family: 1948 - on. Series of girl dolls. Most were completely of hard plastic with jointed neck, shoulders and hips, nylon wig, sleep eyes, closed mouth; original clothes; all in excellent condition. (For photograph see *11th Blue Book,* page 218.)

Mark: On head: "IDEAL DOLL"
On body: "IDEAL DOLL
       P-90
       Made in USA"

Toni:

14-15in (36-38cm) P-90	$	325 - 375
Naked, untidy hair		70 - 80
Mint-in-box		550 - 650
21in (53cm) P-93		500 - 600
22-1/2in (57cm) P-94		750**

Mary Hartline:

14in (36cm) P-90	350 - 400
22in (56cm) P-94	750**

Betsy McCall, vinyl head,

14in (36cm)	250 - 300
Mint-in-box	450 - 500

Harriet Hubbard Ayer, vinyl head. (For photograph see page 216.)

14in (36cm)	200 - 225
Mint-in-box	400
Miss Curity, 14in (36cm)	300 - 350
Sara Ann, 14in (36cm)	275 - 325

**Not enough price samples to compute a reliable range.

Saralee: 1950. Black vinyl head, painted hair, sleep eyes, open/closed mouth; cloth body, vinyl limbs; original clothes; all in excellent condition. Designed by Sarah Lee Creech; modeled by Sheila Burlingame. (For photograph see *11th Blue Book,* page 216.)

17-18in (43-46cm)	$	300 - 350
Undressed		125

Bonny Braids: 1951. Vinyl character head, molded hair, sleeping eyes; hard plastic body; original clothes; all in excellent condition. (For photograph see *11th Blue Book,* page 219.)

13in (33cm)	$	150 - 200
Mint in comic strip box		325 - 350

Saucy Walker: 1951. All-hard plastic, jointed at neck, shoulders and hips with walking mechanism; synthetic wig, flirty eyes, open mouth with tongue and teeth; original clothes; all in excellent condition. (For photograph see page 217.)

Mark: "IDEAL DOLL"

16-17in (41-43cm)	$	125 - 150
20-22in (51-56cm)		175 - 200
22in (56cm) mint-in-box		400

Miss Revlon: 1955. Vinyl head with rooted hair, sleep eyes, closed mouth, earrings; hard plastic body with jointed waist and knees, high-heeled feet, vinyl arms with polished nails; original clothes; all in excellent condition. (For photograph see *6th Blue Book,* page 213.)

Mark: On head and body:
    "IDEAL DOLL"

18in (46cm)	$	165 - 200
20in (51cm)		225 - 250
Little Miss Revlon,		
10-1/2in (27cm)		100 - 135

Peter and Patti Playpal: 1960. Vinyl heads with rooted hair, sleep eyes; hard vinyl body, jointed at shoulders and hips; appropriate clothes; all in excellent condition. (For photograph see *7th Blue Book,* page 221.)

Mark: Peter: "IDEAL TOY CORP.
       BE-35-38"
    Patty: "IDEAL DOLL
       G-35"

Peter, 35in (89cm)	$	400 - 450
Patti, 35in (89cm)		300 - 325
Platinum hair, at auction		1300
Red hair, at auction		950
Patti, 18in (46cm)		175 - 200
Daddy's Girl, 42in (107cm)		850 - 950
Miss Ideal, 29in (74 cm)		400 - 450
25in (63 cm)		375 - 400
Patti, Ca. 1980. Mint-in-box	$	100 - 110

JULLIEN

FACTS

Jullien, Jeune of Paris, France. 1875-1904 when joined with S.F.B.J.
Mark: "JULLIEN" with size number

JuLLiEN
1

Marked Jullien Bébé:
Bisque head, lovely wig, paperweight eyes, closed mouth, pierced ears; jointed wood and composition body; pretty old clothes; all in good condition.

17-19in (43-48cm)	$ 3500 - 3700
24-26in (61-66cm)	4200 - 4500
Open mouth,	
19-21in (48-53cm)	1600 - 1800
29-30in (74-76cm)	2600 - 2900

25in (63cm) Jullien. *Jensen's Antique Dolls.*

JUMEAU

Poupée Peau Fashion Lady: Late 1860s-on. Usually marked with number only on head, blue stamp on body. Perfect bisque swivel head on shoulder plate, old wig, paperweight eyes, closed mouth, pierced ears; all-kid body or kid with bisque lower arms and legs; appropriate old clothes; all in good condition.

Mark:

> JUMEAU
> MEDAILLE D'OR
> PARIS

Standard face:
11-1/2–13in (29-33cm)	$	2600 - 3000*
17-18in (43-46cm)		3200 - 3800*
20in (51cm)		3800 - 4000*

Very pretty face:
15-17in (38-43cm)	$	3500 - 4000*

Poupée Bois, wood body with bisque limbs,
18in (46cm)	5000*

Later face with large eyes:
10-12in (25-31cm)	1800 - 2000*
14-15in (36-38cm)	2400 - 2500*

So-called "Portrait Face": (See *11th Blue Book*, page 221.)
19-21in (48-53cm)	6000 - 7000*
27in (68cm) all original, at auction	11,000

Poupée Bois, wood body
20in (51cm)	12,000
Very rare lady face, 22in (56cm)	30,000 up
Creole Lady, at auction	231,000

Period Clothes for Bébés:
Jumeau shift	$	300 - 350
Jumeau shoes		400 - 500
Jumeau dress		650 up

*Allow extra for original clothes.

```
┌─────────── FACTS ───────────┐
│ Maison Jumeau, Paris, France. 1842- on. │
│ Trademark:  Bébé Jumeau (1886)  │
│             Bébé Prodige (1886)  │
│             Bébé Francais (1896) │
└─────────────────────────────┘
```

22in (56cm) very rare lady face. *Richard Wright Antiques.*

18in (46cm) *Poupée peau* standard face. *Private Collection.*

32in (81cm) Jumeau *Triste*. *Private Collection*. (For further information see page 222.)

Long-Face Triste Bébé: 1879-1886. Designed by Carrier-Belleuse. Marked with size (9-16) number only on head, blue stamp on body. Perfect bisque socket head with beautiful wig, paperweight eyes, closed mouth, applied pierced ears; jointed composition body with straight wrists (separate ball joints on early models); lovely clothes; all in good condition. (For photograph see page 221.)

20-21in (51-53cm)	**$ 16,000 - 20,000**
28-30in (71-76cm)	**25,000**
Size 9 = 21in (53cm)	
11 = 24in (61cm)	
13, 14 = 29-30in (74-76cm)	

Portrait Jumeau: 1877-1883. Usually marked with size number only on head, blue stamp on body; skin or other good wig; spiral threaded enamel paperweight eyes, closed mouth, pierced ears; jointed composition body with straight wrists and separate ball joints; nicely dressed; all in good condition.

Premiere Jumeau Portrait: (For photograph see page 224.)

10-12in (25-30cm)	**$ 5000 - 5500***
14-15in (36-38cm)	**6000 - 7000***
18-19in (46-48cm)	**7000 - 8000***

*Expect dust specks and uneven eye cuts and uneven eyebrows.

Almond-Eyed: (For photograph see page 224.)

Sizes: 4/0 = 12in (30cm)
      3/0 = 13-1/2in (34cm)
      2/0 = 14-1/2in (37cm)
      0 = 16in (41cm)
      1 = 17in (43cm)
      2 = 18-1/2in (47cm)
      3 = 20in (51cm)
      4 = 23in (58cm)
      5 = 25in (64cm)

12-14-1/2in (30-37cm)	**$ 7500 - 8500***
16-18-1/2in (41-47cm)	**13,000 - 15,000***
20in (51cm)	**20,000***
23in (58cm)	**28,000***
25in (64cm)	**35,000 up***

*Allow extra for unusually large eyes.

E.J.Bébé: 1881-1886. Head incised as below, blue stamp on body. Perfect bisque socket head with good wig, paperweight eyes, closed mouth, pierced ears; jointed composition body with straight wrists, early models with separate ball joints; lovely clothes; all in good condition. (See photographs on pages 4 and 224.)

Early Mark:

$$\frac{8}{E.J.}$$

17-18in (43-46cm) size 6	**$**	**10,500**
19-21in (48-53cm) size 8		**12,500**
23in (58cm) size 9		**22,000**
EJA, 25in (64cm)		**30,000**

Mid-Period Mark:

E. 8 J.

10in (25cm)	**$**	**5000 - 5500**
14-16in (36-41cm)		**5800 - 6300**
19-21in (48-53cm)		**6700 - 7300**
25-26in (64-66cm)		**8500 - 9500**
30in (76cm)		**10,000 - 11,000**

Later Tête-style face ("DEPOSÉ" above "E.J."):

18-19in (46-48cm)	**5000 - 5500**
25-26in (64-66cm)	**6800 - 7500**
30in (76cm)	**8800**

Incised "Jumeau Déposé" Bébé: 1886-1889. Head incised as below, blue stamp on body. Perfect bisque socket head with good wig, paperweight eyes, closed mouth, pierced ears; jointed composition body with straight wrists; lovely clothes; all in good condition. (For photograph see page 225.)
Mark: Incised on head:

DÉPOSÉ
JUMEAU
8

14-15in (36-38cm)	$	4500 - 5000
18-20in (46-51cm)		5500 - 6000
24-25in (61-64cm)		6800 - 7200

Tête Jumeau Bébé: 1885-on, then through S.F.B.J. Red stamp on head as indicated below, blue stamp or "Bebe Jumeau" oval sticker on body. Perfect bisque head, original or good French wig, beautiful stationary eyes, closed mouth, pierced ears; jointed composition body with jointed or straight wrists; original or lovely clothes; all in good condition. (See photographs on page 225.)
Mark:

DÉPOSÉ
TETE JUMEAU
B^{TE} SGDG
6

10in (25cm) #1	$	4200 - 4800*
12-13in (31-33cm)		3100 - 3400*
15-16in (38-41cm)		3700 - 4100*
18-20in (46-51cm)		4200 - 4500*
21-23in (53-58cm)		4500 - 4700*
25-27in (64-69cm)		4700 - 5300*
30in (76cm)		6000*
34-36in (86-91cm)		7000 - 7500
Lady body, 20in (51cm)		5000 - 5500
Open mouth:		
14-16in (36-41cm)		2200 - 2500
20-22in (51-56cm)		2800 - 3000
24-25in (61-64cm)		3200 - 3300
27-29in (69-74cm)		3500 - 3600
32-34in (81-86cm)		3800 - 4000

*Allow extra for original clothes.

Marked B.L. Bébé: Ca. 1880. For the Louvre department store. Perfect bisque socket head, closed mouth, paperweight eyes, pierced ears, good wig; French-style jointed composition body; appropriate clothes; all in good condition. (See photograph see *Doll Classics*, page 41 or *5th Blue Book*, page 54.)
Mark:

B.9 L.

18-21in (46-53cm)	$	4200 - 4700

Marked R.R. Bébé: Ca. 1880s. Perfect bisque head, closed mouth, paperweight eyes, pierced ears, good wig; French-style jointed composition body; appropriate clothes; all in good condition. (For photograph see *9th Blue Book*, page 180.)
Mark:

R 10 R

21-23in (53-58cm)	$	4900 - 5300

Approximate sizes of E.J.s and Têtes:
1	=	10in (25cm)
2	=	11in (28cm)
3	=	12in (31cm)
4	=	13in (33cm)
5	=	14-15in (36-38cm)
6	=	16in (41cm)
7	=	17in (43cm)
8	=	19in (48cm)
9	=	20in (51cm)
10	=	21-22in (53-56cm)
11	=	24-25in (61-64cm)
12	=	26-27in (66-69cm)
13	=	29-30in (74-76cm)

#230 Character Child: Ca. 1910. Perfect bisque socket head, open mouth, set or sleep eyes, good wig; jointed composition body; dressed; all in good condition. (For face, see *10th Blue Book* page 369. Same mold as S.F.B.J. **230**.)

16in (41cm)	$	1600
21-23in (53-58cm)		2000

14in (36cm) Premiere Jumeau Portrait. *H & J Foulke, Inc.* (For further information see page 222.)

25in (64cm) Almond-eyed Portrait Jumeau, with unusually large eyes. *Richard Wright Antiques.* (For further information see page 222.)

26in (66cm) E 12 J standard face. *H & J Foulke, Inc.* (For further information see page 222.)

TOP: *Right:* 17in (43cm) incised "*Jumeau Déposé*." *H & J Foulke, Inc.* (For further information see page 223.) *Left:* 17in (43cm) *Tête Jumeau*, size 7, all original. *Private Collection.* (For further information see page 223.)
BOTTOM: *Right:* 23in (58cm) *Tête Jumeau*, size 11. *Kay & Wayne Jensen Collection.* (For further information see page 223.) *Left:* 24in (61cm) *Tête Jumeau*, size 10 with rare smiling face. *Private Collection.* (For further information see page 223.)

21in (53cm) 1907 Jumeau.
H & J Foulke, Inc.

#1907 Jumeau Child: Ca. 1907-on. Sometimes red-stamped "Tête Jumeau." Perfect bisque head, good quality wig, set or sleep eyes, open mouth, pierced ears; jointed composition body; nicely dressed; all in good condition.

14in (36cm)	$	2000 - 2200
16-18in (41-46cm)		2300 - 2500
24-25in (61-64cm)		3000 - 3200
33-34in (84-87cm)		3800 - 4000

Papier-mâché face:

22-24in (56-61cm)	$	800 - 1000**

Jumeau Characters: Ca. 1900. Tête Jumeau mark. Perfect bisque head with glass eyes, character expression; jointed composition body; appropriately dressed; all in good condition.

#203, 208 and others:	$	50,000 up
#221 Great Ladies,		
10-11in (25-28cm) all original		550 - 650

Princess Elizabeth Jumeau: 1938 through S.F.B.J. Perfect bisque socket head highly colored, good wig, glass flirty eyes, closed mouth; jointed composition body; dressed; all in good condition. (For photograph see *9th Blue Book*, page 254.)

Mark: **Body Incised:**

JUMEAU
1938
PARIS

JUMEAU
PARIS
Princess

18-19in (46-48cm)	$	1600 - 1800
32-33in (81-84cm)		2700 - 3200**

**Not enough price samples to compute a reliable range.

Papier-mâché face Jumeau. *Betty Harms Collection.*

KAMKINS

FACTS

Louise R. Kampes Studios, Atlantic City,
N.J. U.S.A. 1919-1928 and
perhaps longer.
Mark: Red paper heart on left side
of chest:

Also sometimes stamped with black on
foot or back of head:

KAMKINS
A DOLLY MADE TO LOVE
PATENTED BY L.R. KAMPES
ATLANTIC CITY,   N.J.

Marked Kamkins: Molded mask face with painted features, wig; cloth body and limbs; original clothing; all in excellent condition.

18-20in (46-51cm)	$	**1200***
Fair to good condition		**750 - 850**

*Allow more for an especially nice example.

18in (46cm) *Kamkins*. *Kay & Wayne Jensen Collection.*

KÄMMER & REINHARDT

Child Doll: 1886-1895. Perfect bisque head, original or good wig, sleep or set eyes, open or closed mouth, pierced ears; ball-jointed composition body; dressed; all in good condition.

#192:

Closed mouth:

6-7in (15-18cm)	$ 600 - 700*
10in (25cm)	900 - 1000
16-18in (41-46cm)	2800 - 3200
22-24in (56-61cm)	3400 - 3800

Open mouth:

7-8in (18-20cm)	550 - 600*
12in (31cm)	700 - 800
14-16in (36-41cm)	900 - 1000
20-22in (51-56cm)	1300 - 1500
26-28in (66-71cm)	1900 - 2100

*Allow extra for a fully-jointed body.

18-1/2in (47cm) 192 child with closed mouth. *H & J Foulke, Inc.*

FACTS

Kämmer & Reinhardt of Waltershausen, Thüringia, Germany. Bisque heads often by Simon & Halbig. 1886-on. Later papier-mâché, rubber or celluloid heads. Size: 4-1/2–45in (11-112cm).
Trademarks: Majestic Doll, Mein Liebling (My Darling), Der Schelm (The Flirt), Die Kokette (The Coquette), My Playmate.
Mark: In 1895 began using K(star)R, sometimes with "S & H." Mold number for bisque socket head begins with a 1; for papier-mâché, 9; for celluloid, 7. Size number is height in centimeters.

K ☆ R

SIMON & HALBIG
116/A
50

KÄMMER & REINHARDT *continued*

Child Doll: 1895-1930s. Perfect bisque head, original or good wig, sleep eyes, open mouth, pierced ears; dressed; K & R ball-jointed composition body; all in good condition. Numbers 15-100 low on neck are centimeter sizes, not mold numbers.

#191, 290, 403 or size number only:

12-14in (31-36cm)	$	600 - 700*+
16-17in (41-43cm)		750 - 800*+
19-21in (48-53cm)		850 - 950*+
23-25in (58-64cm)		1050 - 1150*
29-31in (74-79cm)		1400 - 1600*
35-36in (89-91cm)		2200 - 2500*
39-42in (99-107cm)		3600 - 4200*

* Allow $50-100 additional for flirty eyes; allow $200 extra for flapper body; allow $100 for walking body.

+ Allow 50% additional for fantastic totally original clothes, wig and shoes in pristine condition.

Child Doll: Shoulder head, kid body; all in good condition.

17-18in (41-46cm)	$	450 - 500
22in (56cm)		550 - 650

Tiny Child Doll: Perfect bisque head, mohair wig, sleep eyes, open mouth; K & R 5-piece composition body with molded and painted shoes and socks.

4-1/2–5in (11-13cm)	$	400 - 425
6-7in (15-18cm)		425 - 475
8-9in (20-23cm)		500 - 550
Walker, 6-7in (15-18cm)		500 - 550
Closed mouth, 6in (15cm)		600
Jointed body,		
8-10in (20-25cm)		700 - 800

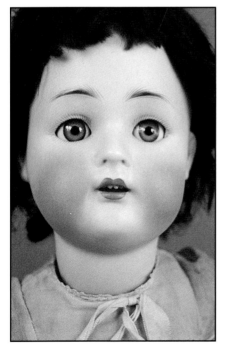

6in (15cm) tiny child, closed mouth, all original. *H & J Foulke, Inc.*

22in (56cm) flapper. *H & J Foulke, Inc.*

Character Babies or Toddlers: 1909-on. Perfect bisque head, original or good wig, sleep eyes, open mouth; K & R composition bent-limb or jointed toddler body; nicely dressed; may have voice box or spring tongue; all in good condition. (See *Simon & Halbig Dolls, The Artful Aspect* for photographs of mold numbers not pictured here.)

#100 Baby, painted eyes:

12in (31cm)	$	575 - 625
14-15in (36-38cm)		725 - 800
18-20in (46-51cm)		1000 - 1200
Glass eyes, 16in (41cm)		2000

#126, 22 baby body:

10-12in (25-31cm)	$	525 - 550*
14-16in (36-41cm)		600 - 650*
18-20in (46-51cm)		750 - 850*
22-24in (56-61cm)		950 - 1100*
30-33in (76-84cm)		1800 - 2200*

#126 all-bisque baby:

6in (15cm)	$	750 - 800
8-1/2in (21cm)		1000 - 1100**

#126, 22 5-piece toddler body:

6-7in (15-18cm)	$	750 - 800+
9-10in (23-25cm)		850 - 900+
15-17in (38-43cm)		900 -950
23in (58cm)		1250

#126 all-bisque toddler,

7in (18cm)	$	1400 - 1500**

#126 toddler fully-jointed:

12in (31cm)	$	700 - 750
15-17in (38-41cm)		900 - 1100*
23-25in (58-64cm)		1600 - 1700*
28-30in (71-76cm)		2200 - 2300*
32in (81cm)		2500 - 2800*

*Allow $50-75 extra for flirty eyes.

#128 baby body:

20in (51cm)	$	1600

#121, 122 baby body:

10-11in (25-28cm)	$	700 - 750
15-16in (38-41cm)		900 - 1100
23-24in (58-61cm)		1400 - 1600

#121, 122, 128 toddler body:

13-14in (33-36cm)	$	1150 - 1300
20-23in (51-58cm)		1600 - 1800
27-28in (69-71cm)		2300 - 2500

#118A baby body:

18in (46cm)		2500 - 2600**

#119 baby body:

24in (61cm), at auction		16,000

Composition Head **#926**, 5-piece toddler body: (For photograph see *11th Blue Book*, page 234.)

17in (43cm)	$	500 - 600*
23in (58cm)		750 - 850
Baby, 18in (46cm)		550*

"Puz": (For photograph see *11th Blue Book*, page 234.)

8-1/2in (21cm)		225 - 250*
17-19in (43-48cm)		400 - 450
25in (64cm)		650 - 750*

*Allow $50 additional for flirty eyes.
+With "Star fish" hands.
**Not enough price samples to compute a reliable range.

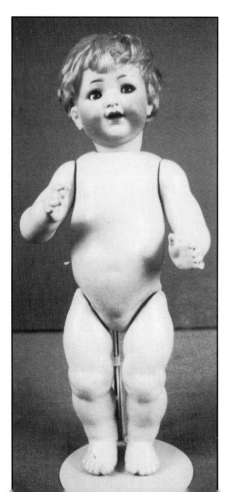

18in (46cm) 22 toddler. *H & J Foulke, Inc.*

Character Children: 1909-on. Perfect bisque-socket head, good wig, painted or glass eyes, closed mouth; K & R composition ball-jointed body; nicely dressed; all in good condition. (See *Simon & Halbig, The Artful Aspect* for photographs of mold numbers not pictured here.)

#101 (Peter or Marie):
8-9in (20-23cm)		
5-piece body	$	**1500**
8-9in (20-23cm)		
jointed body		**1800 - 2000**
12in (31cm)		**2500 - 2800**
15-16in (38-41cm)		**3800 - 4200**
19-20in (48-51cm)		**5000 - 5500**
Glass eyes:		
15in (38cm)		**11,500**
20in (51cm)		**14,000 - 15,000**

#102: (See photograph on page 233.)
12in (31cm)	$	**30,000 - 35,000****
22in (55cm)		**50,000 - 60,000****

#103, 104, 105, 106: (seldom available)
22in (56cm)	$	**75,000 up**

#107 (Carl):
12in (30cm)	$	**13,000 - 15,000**
22in (55cm)		**50,000 - 55,000**

#108: at auction $ **277,095**

#109 (Elise):
9-10in (23-25cm)	$	**3000 - 3500**
14in (36cm)		**7500 - 8500**
19-21in (48-53cm)		**13,000 - 15,000**
Glass eyes:		
20in (51cm)	$	**18,000 - 20,000**

#112, 112x:
16-18in (41-46cm)	$	**16,000**

#114 (Hans or Gretchen): (For photograph see page 232.)
8-9in (20-23cm) jointed body	**1800 - 2200**
12in (31cm)	**3200**
15-16in (38-41cm)	**4200 - 4500**
19-20in (48-51cm)	**5500 - 6000**
Glass eyes:	
15in (38cm)	**8000 - 9000**
20in (51cm)	**12,000 - 14,000**

#115:
15-16in (38-41cm)		
toddler	$	**5500 - 6000****

**Not enough price samples to compute a reliable range

#115A: (For photograph see page 232.)
Baby, 14-16in (36-41cm)	$	**3500 - 3850**
Toddler, 15-16in (38-41cm)		**4200 - 4500**
19-20cm (48-51cm)		**5500 - 6000**

#116: (For photograph see page 5.)
16in (41cm) toddler	**4500 - 5000****

#116A, open/closed mouth:
Baby 14-16in (36-41cm)	**2300 - 2600**
Toddler,	
16in (41cm)	**3000**
22in (56cm)	**4000 - 4500**

#116A, open mouth: (For photograph see page 232.)
Baby, 14-16in (36-41cm)	**2000 - 2200**
Toddler, 16-18in (41-46cm)	**2200 - 2500**

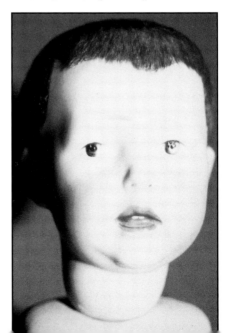

17in (43cm) 112x, flocked hair. *Doelman Collection. Courtesy of Richard W. Withington, Inc.*

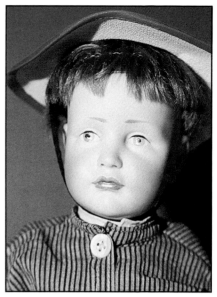

116A, open mouth. *Mary Barnes Kelley Collection.* (For further information see page 231.)

15in (38cm) 114. *Doelman Collection. Courtesy of Richard W. Withington, Inc.* (For further information see page 231.)

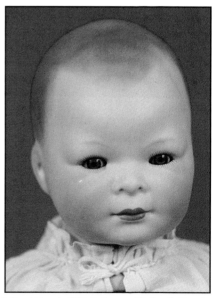

19in (48cm) 115A toddler. *H & J Foulke, Inc.* (For further information see page 231.)

16in (41cm) 172 infant. *Richard Wright Antiques.* (For further information see page 234.)

12-1/2in (32 cm) 102. *Private Collection.* (For further information see page 231.)

#117, 117A, closed mouth (may have an H. Handwerck body):

12in (30cm)	$ **3200 - 3500**
14-16in (36-41cm)	**3800 - 4300**
18in (46cm)	**4800 - 5200**
22-23in (56-58cm)	**6300 - 6800**
30-32in (76-81cm)	**7500 - 8500**

#117n, flirty eyes:

14-16in (36-41cm)	**1300 - 1400***
20-22in (51-56cm)	**1800 - 2000***
28-30in (71-76cm)	**2400 - 2500***

#117n, sleep eyes:

14-16in (36-41cm)	**1000 - 1100**
22-24in (56-61cm)	**1500 - 1600**
30-32in (76-81cm)	**1900 - 2100**

#117, open mouth:

27in (69cm)	**4700 - 5000***

#123, 124 (Max & Moritz): (For photograph see *11th Blue Book*, page 232.)

17in (43cm)	**15,000 - 20,000***

#127:

Baby, 10in (25cm)	**800 - 850**
14-15in (36-38cm)	**1300 - 1400**
20-22in (51-56cm)	**1800 - 2000**

Toddler or child,

15-16in (38-41cm)	**1250 - 1500**
Toddler, 25-27in (64-69cm)	**2200 - 2500**

#135 Child, 14-16in (36-41cm) **1900 - 2200**

#201, 13in (33cm)	**1500***
#214, 15in (38cm)	**2100***

Infant: 1924-on. Perfect bisque head, molded and painted hair, glass eyes; cloth body, composition hands; nicely dressed; all in good condition. (For photograph see page 232.)

#171, 172:

14-15in (36-38cm)	$ **3500***

#175:

11in (28cm) h.c.	**1100 - 1200***

*Allow extra for flapper body.
**Not enough price samples to compute a reliable range.

14-1/2in (37cm) 127 toddler. *H & J Foulke, Inc.*

KESTNER

Child doll, early socket head: Ca. 1880. Perfect bisque head, plaster dome, good wig, paperweight or sleep eyes; Kestner composition ball-jointed body, some with straight wrists and elbows; well dressed; all in good condition. Many marked with size numbers only.

#169, 128, long-face and round face with no mold number, closed mouth:

12in (31cm)	$	**2000***
14-16in (36-41cm)		**2200 - 2400***
19-21in (48-53cm)		**2600 - 2800***
24-25in (61-64 cm)		**2900 - 3200***
29in (74cm)		**3500***

Face with square cheeks, face with white space between lips, no mold number, closed mouth:

11-12in (28-30cm)	**$ 2200 - 2500***
14-16in (36-41cm)	**2600 - 2800***
19-21in (48-53cm)	**3000 - 3300***
24-25in (61-64cm)	**3500 - 3600***

#XI, 103 and very pouty face, closed mouth:

10-12in (25-31cm)	**$ 2600 - 2800***
14-16in (36-41cm)	**3000 - 3300***
19-21in (48-53cm)	**3600 - 3800***
24-25in (61-64cm)	**4000 - 4100***

27in (69cm)	**4300 - 4500***
32in (81cm)	**4800 - 5000***

*Allow 20% more for original clothes, wig and shoes. Allow more for an especially beautiful face.

A.T.-type: (For photograph see *11th Blue Book*, page 237.)

Closed mouth, any size	$	**15,000 up**
Open mouth, 19in (48cm)		**2500**

Bru-type, molded teeth, jointed ankles (For photograph see *11th Blue Book*, page 236.):

20in (51cm)	$	**5000**
Kid body, 24in (61cm)		**3200**

Open mouth, square cut teeth:

12-14in (31-36cm)	$	**1000 - 1200**
16-18in (41-46cm)		**1400 - 1600**
24-25in (61-64cm)		**1900 - 2000**

FACTS
J.D. Kestner, Jr., doll factory, Waltershausen, Thüringia, Germany. Kestner & Co., porcelain factory, Ohrdruf. 1816-on. Up to 42in (107cm), size Q 20.

13in (33cm) 128 pouty.
H & J Foulke, Inc.

15in (38cm) "10" pouty, white space between lips. *H & J Foulke, Inc.*

25in (64cm) unmarked pouty face with square cheeks. *H & J Foulke, Inc.*

18-1/2in (49cm) 148 shoulder head. *H & J Foulke, Inc.*

20in (51cm) "H," fashion body. *H & J Foulke, Inc.*

16in (41cm) "E" shoulder head with closed mouth. *H & J Foulke, Inc.*

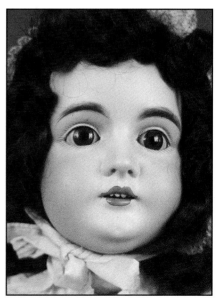

30in (76cm) 164. *H & J Foulke, Inc.*

Child doll, early shoulder head: Ca. 1880s. Perfect bisque head, plaster dome, good wig, set or sleep eyes; sometimes head is slightly turned; kid body with bisque lower arms; marked with size letters or numbers. (No mold numbers.)

Closed mouth:

12in (31cm)	$	850*
14-16in (36-41cm)		900 - 950*
20-22in (51-56cm)		1100 - 1250*
26in (66cm)		1500 - 1650*

A.T.-type, closed mouth any size:

        10,000 up

Open/closed mouth:

16-18in (41-46 cm)	750 - 850

Open mouth:

16-18in (41-46cm)	500 - 600
22-24in (56-61cm)	700 - 750

Open mouth, square cut teeth:

14-16in (36-41cm)	1200

* Allow $100-200 extra for a very pouty face or swivel neck.

Child doll, bisque shoulder head, open mouth: Ca. 1892. Kid body, some with rivet joints. Plaster dome, good wig, sleep eyes, open mouth; dressed, all in good condition. (See *Kestner, King of Dollmakers* for photographs of mold numbers not pictured here.)

HEAD MARK: *154 8 dep*
D made in Germany

BODY MARK:

#145, 154, 147, 148, 166, 195:

8in (20cm)	$	275 - 300
12-13in (31-33cm)		350 - 400*
16-18in (41-46cm)		500 - 550*
20-22in (51-56cm)		600 - 650*
22in (56cm) all original, at auction		950
26-28in (66-71cm)		900 - 1000*

*Allow additional for a rivet jointed body.

Child doll, open mouth: Bisque socket head on Kestner ball-jointed body; plaster dome, good wig, sleep eyes, open mouth; dressed; all in good condition. (See *Kestner, King of Dollmakers* for photographs of mold numbers not pictured here.)

HEAD MARK: *made in Germany. 8.*
162.

BODY MARK:

Germany 5-1/2   or   *Excelsior DRP N. 70686 Germany*

Mold numbers 142, 144, 146, 164, 167, 171:

10-21in (25-31cm)	$	550 - 600*
14-16in (36-41cm)		700 - 800*
18-21in (46-53cm)		850 - 950*
24-26in (61-66cm)		1000 - 1100*
30-32in (76-81cm)		1200 - 1500
36in (91cm)		2000 - 2500
42in (107cm)		3750 - 4250

#129, 149, 152, 160, 161, 173, 174:

10-12in (25-31cm)	$	700 - 800*
14-16in (36-41cm)		900 - 1000*
18-21in (46-53cm)		1100 - 1250*
24-26in (61-66cm)		1300 - 1400*

*Allow 30% additional for all original clothes, wig and shoes.

#155: fully-jointed body,

7-8in (18-20cm)	$	800 - 850
10in (25cm) 5-piece body		700

#171: Daisy, blonde mohair wig,

18in (46cm) only	1000

#168, 196, 214:

18-21in (46-53cm)	700 - 750
26-28in (66-71cm)	800 - 900
32in (81cm)	1000 - 1100

KESTNER *continued*

Character Child: 1909-on. Perfect bisque head character face, plaster pate, wig, painted or glass eyes, closed, open or open/closed mouth; Kestner jointed composition body; dressed; all in good condition. (See *Kestner, King of Dollmakers* for photographs of mold numbers not pictured here.)

#143 (Pre 1897): (For photograph see page 5.)

7in (18cm)	$	725 - 750
9-10in (23-25cm)		800 - 850
12-14in (31-36cm)		900 - 1000
18-20in (46-51cm)		1300 - 1400
27in (69cm)		1800

#178-190:

Painted eyes:

12in (31cm)	$	1800 - 2200
15in (38cm)		3000 - 3400
18in (46cm)		4000 - 4500

Glass eyes:

12in (31cm)		2800 - 3200
15in (38cm)		4000 - 4500
18in (46cm)		5000 - 5500
Boxed set, 15in (38cm) painted eyes		9500
Boxed set, 15in (38cm) glass eyes		15,000

#191, glass eyes, 19in (48cm)

at auction	6200

#206:

12in (31cm)	$	4000 - 5000**
19in (48cm)		12,000 - 15,000**

#208:

Painted eyes:

12in (31cm)	4000 - 5000**
23-24in (58-61cm)	12,000 - 15,000**

#220 toddler:

16in (41cm)	5000 - 6000**
24in (61cm)	7500 - 8000**

#239 toddler:

15-17in (38-43cm)	4000**

#241:

21-22in (53-56cm)	7000 - 7500**

#249:

13-14in (33-36cm)	1100 - 1200
20-22in (51-56cm)	1800

**Not enough price samples to compute a reliable range.

TOP: 19in (48cm) 129. *H & J Foulke, Inc.*
BOTTOM: 10in (25cm) 155. 5-piece body. *H & J Foulke, Inc.*

9in (23cm) 260 toddler, all original. *H & J Foulke, Inc.* (For further information see page 242.)

15in (38cm) 182, painted eyes. *Doelman Collection. Courtesy of Richard W. Withington, Inc.* (For further information see page 239.)

16in (41cm) JDK 12 solid dome baby. *H & J Foulke, Inc.* (For further information see page 242.)

15in (38cm) JDK 257 toddler. *H & J Foulke, Inc.* (For further information see page 242.)

15in (38cm) JDK fat-cheeked baby. *H & J Foulke, Inc.* (For further information see page 242.)

19in (48cm) **Gibson Girl** 172, all original. *H & J Foulke, Inc.* (For further information see page 242.)

#260: (For photograph see page 240.)
Toddler,

8-10in (20-25cm)	$	**850 - 950**
19in (48cm) jointed body		**1100**
12-14in (31-36cm)		**800 - 850**
18-20in (46-51cm)		**900 - 1100**
29in (75cm)		**1400 - 1500**
35in (88cm)		**1800 - 2000**

Character Baby: 1910-on. Perfect bisque head, molded and/or painted hair or good wig, sleep or set eyes, open or open/closed mouth; Kestner bent-limb body; well dressed; nice condition. (See *Kestner, King of Dollmakers* for photographs of mold numbers not pictured here.)

Mark:

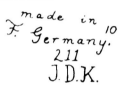

#211, 226:

11-13in (28-33cm)	$	**625 - 725***
16-18in (41-46cm)		**800 - 900***
20-22in (51-56cm)		**1050 - 1200***
25in (64cm)		**1500 - 1750***

* Allow $50-100 extra for an original skin wig.

JDK solid dome: (For photograph see page 240.)

12-14in (31-36cm)	$	**600 - 700**
18in (46cm)		**800**
23-25in (58-64cm)		**1200 - 1500**

#262, 263:

16-18in (41-46cm)	**700 - 800**
21-23in (53-58cm)	**950 - 1050**
16in (41cm) 5-piece toddler body	**950**

#210, 234, 235, 238 shoulder heads:

14-16in (36-41cm)	$	**1000**

Hilda, **#237, 245,** solid dome baby:

11-13in (28-33cm)	**2800 - 3200**
16-17in (41-43cm)	**3800 - 4200**
20-22in (51-56cm)	**4800 - 5300**
24in (61cm)	**6000 - 6500**

Toddler:

14in (36cm)	**4500 - 5000**
17-19in (43-48cm)	**5500 - 6000**

27in (69cm)	**7500 - 8500**

#247: (For photograph see *11th Blue Book*, page 241.)

11in (28cm)	**1100**
14-16in (36-41cm)	**1800 - 2100**
13in (33cm) toddler	**2200 - 2300**

#257: (For photograph see page 240.)

9-10in (23-25cm)	**600 - 700**
14-16in (36-41cm)	**750 - 850**
18-21in (46-53cm)	**1000 - 1150**
16in (41cm) toddler	**1100 - 1200**

JDK solid dome, fat-cheeked (so-called Baby Jean): (For photograph see page 241.)

12-13in (31-33cm)	$	**1100 - 1250**
17-18in (43-46cm)		**1500 - 1650**
23-24in (58-61cm)		**2000 - 2100**
15in (38cm) toddler		**1300 - 1500**

All-bisque:

Painted eyes, stiff neck,

5-6in (13-15cm)	**225 - 275**

Swivel neck, painted eyes

7-1/2in (19cm)	**425 - 450**
9in (23cm)	**600 - 650**
12in (31cm)	**850**

Glass eyes, swivel neck,

9-10in (23-25cm)	**900 - 1000**

#177: Toddler, 8in (16cm) | **800 - 850**

All-Bisque Child: Perfect all-bisque child jointed at shoulders and hips; mohair wig, sleeping eyes, open mouth with upper teeth; blue or pink painted stockings, black strap shoes. Naked or with appropriate clothes. Very good quality.

#130, 150, 160, 184 and 208:

4-5in (10-13cm)	$	**225 - 325***
6in (15cm)		**350 - 375***
7in (18cm)		**400 - 450***
8in (20cm)		**500 - 550***
9in (23cm)		**700 - 800**
11in (28cm)		**1100 - 1200**
12in (31cm)		**1300 - 1400**

* Allow 30-40% extra for swivel neck; allow $25-50 extra for yellow boots.

Early All-Bisque Dolls: see page 42.

Gibson Girl: Ca. 1910. Perfect bisque shoulder head with good wig, glass eyes, closed mouth, up-lifted chin; kid body with bisque lower arms (cloth body with bisque lower limbs on small dolls); beautifully dressed; all in good condition; sometimes marked "Gibson Girl" on body. (For photograph see page 241.)

#172:

10in (25cm)	**$ 1100 - 1300**
15in (38cm)	**2000 - 2400**
20-21in (51-53cm)	**3600**

Lady Doll: Perfect bisque socket head, plaster dome, wig with lady hairdo, sleep eyes, open mouth with upper teeth; jointed composition body with molded breasts, nipped-in waist, slender arms and legs; appropriate lady clothes; all in good condition.

Mark:

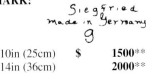

#162:

16-18in (41-46cm)
	$ 1600 - 1800
Naked, 16-18in (41-46cm)	**1200**
All original clothes,	
16-18in (41-46cm)	**2300**

O.I.C. Baby: Perfect bisque solid dome head with glass eyes, open mouth with molded tongue; cloth body, dressed; all in good condition.

MARK: "255
            3
            O.I.C."

10in (25cm) h.c.	**$ 1500 - 1800**

Siegfried: Perfect bisque solid dome head with molded hair and flange neck, sleep eyes, closed mouth, side nose, pronounced philtrum; cloth body with composition hands; dressed; all in good condition. Mold #272.

MARK:

10in (25cm)	**$**	**1500****
14in (36cm)		**2000****

**Not enough price samples to compute a reliable average.

5in (13cm) 208/184 boy with swivel neck. *H & J Foulke, Inc.*

KEWPIE

All-Bisque: Made by J. D. Kestner and other German firms. Often have imperfections in making. Sometimes signed on foot "O'Nei ⅄". Standing, legs together, arms jointed, blue wings, painted features, eyes to side.

2-1/2in (5-6cm)	$ **100 - 110**
4in (10cm)	**125 - 135***
5in (13cm)	**150 - 165***
6in (15cm)	**200 -225***

7in (18cm)	**250 - 300***
8in (20cm)	**400 - 450***
9in (23cm)	**550 - 600***
10in (25cm)	**750 - 800***
12in (31cm)	**1300 - 1500**
Jointed hips:	
4in (10cm)	**500 - 550**
6in (15cm)	**750**
8in (20cm)	**950**
Shoulder head, 3in (8cm)	**425**
Perfume bottle,	
4-1/2in (11cm)	**550 - 600**
Black Hottentot,	
5in (13cm)	**550 - 600**
Button hole,	
2in (5cm)	**165 - 175**
Pincushion,	
2-3in (5-8cm)	**250 - 300**
Painted shoes and socks:	
5in (13cm)	**550 - 600**
11in (28cm)	**1500 - 1800**
With glass eyes and wig,	
6in (15cm) at auction	**2400**

* Allow extra for original clothes.

FACTS

Various makers. 1913-on. 2in (5cm) up.
Designer: Rose O'Neill, U.S.A. U.S. Agent: George Borgfeldt & Co., New York, N.Y., U.S.A.
Mark: Red and gold paper heart or shield on chest and round label on back.

5-1/2in (14cm) all-bisque **Kewpie** with label. *H & J Foulke, Inc.*

Action Kewpies (sometimes stamped: ©):

Thinker:

4in (10cm)	$ 275 - 325
7in (18cm)	500 - 550

Kewpie with cat,
3-1/2in (9cm)	450 - 500

Kewpie holding pen,
3in (8cm)	425 - 475
Kneeling, 4in (10cm)	700 - 775

Reclining or sitting,
3-4in (8-10cm)	425 - 475

Gardener, Sweeper, Farmer,
4in (10cm)	475 - 525

Kewpie 2in (5cm) with rabbit,
rose, turkey, pumpkin,
shamrock, etc.	325 - 375

Doodledog:
3in (9cm)	1500 - 1800
1-1/2in (4cm)	750 - 800
Huggers, 3-1/2in (9cm)	200 - 225
Guitar player, 3-1/2in (9cm)	350 - 400
Traveler, 3-1/2in (9cm)	325 - 350

Governor or Mayor,
4in (10cm)	450 - 500

Kewpie and Doodledog on bench,
3-1/2in (9cm)	3000 up

Kewpie sitting on inkwell,
3-1/2in (9cm)	650 - 750

Kewpie Traveler with Doodledog,
3-1/2in (9cm)	1250 - 1350

Kewpie Soldiers,
5-6in (13-15cm)	750 - 850

Kewpie reading book,
3in (8cm) sitting	850

Two Kewpies reading book,
3-1/2in (9cm), standing	850
Kewpie at tea table	1800 up
Kewpie with basket, 4in (10cm)	1000

Kewpie Mountain with
17 figures	17,000 up

Kewpie holding teddy bear,
4in (10cm)	750

Kewpie in bisque swing,
2-1/2in (6cm)	4000

Glazed Kewpie shaker with animal,
2in (5cm)	275 - 300

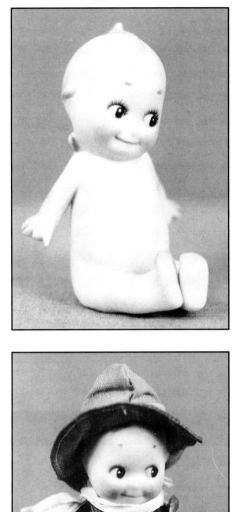

TOP: 3-1/4in (8cm) sitting *Kewpie*. *H & J Foulke, Inc.* **Right:** 4-1/2in (11cm) standing *Kewpie* with painted shoes and original cowboy outfit. *H & J Foulke, Inc.*

Bisque head on chubby jointed composition toddler body, glass eyes: Made by J.D. Kestner. (For photograph see *9th Blue Book*, page 276.)

Mark: "Ges.gesch.
                O'Neill J.D.K."

10in (25cm) 5-piece body $ **4000**
12-14in (31-36cm)   **5000 - 6000**

Bisque head on cloth body: Mold **#1377** made by Alt, Beck & Gottschalck. (For photograph see *10th Blue Book*, page 282.)
12in (31cm) glass eyes $ **2600 - 2800****
Painted eyes   **1600 - 2000****

Celluloid: Made by Karl Standfuss, Deuben near Dresden, Saxony, Germany. Straight standing, arms jointed, blue wings; very good condition.

2-1/2in (6cm)	$	**35 - 40**
5in (13cm)		**75 - 85**
8in (20cm)		**160 - 185**
12in (31cm)		**300 - 350**
22in (56cm)		**500 - 550**
Black, 2-1/2in (6cm)		**85 - 90**
5in (13cm)		**150 - 165**
Kewpie/Billiken double face,		
2-1/2 (6cm)		**75 - 85**

**Not enough price samples to compute a reliable range.

11in (28cm) *Kewpie* with bisque head. *Richard Wright Antiques.*

All-Composition: Made by Cameo Doll Co., Rex Doll Co., and Mutual Doll Co., all of New York, N.Y., U.S.A. All-composition, jointed at shoulders, some at hips; good condition.

8in (20cm)	$	**150 - 175**
11-12in (28-31cm)		**225 - 275**
13in (33cm) mint-in-box, at auction		**700**
Black, 12-13in (31-33cm)		**350 - 400**
Talcum container, 7in (18cm)		**175 - 225**

Composition head, cloth body,

12in (31cm)	**250 - 275**

All-Cloth: Made by Richard G. Krueger, Inc. or King Innovations, Inc., New York, N.Y., U.S.A. Patent number 1785800. Mask face with fat-shaped cloth body, including tiny wings and peak on head. Cloth label sewn in side seam. Good condition.

10-12in (25-31cm)	$	**200 - 225**
18-22in (46-56cm)		**375 - 425**

10in (25cm) cloth
Cuddle Kewpie.
H & J Foulke, Inc.

8in (20cm) hard plastic
Kewpie. H & J Foulke, Inc.

Hard Plastic: Ca. 1950s.
Standing Kewpie, 1-piece with jointed arms
   8in (20cm)   **$ 125 - 135**
Boxed   **200 - 250**
Fully-jointed with sleep eyes; all original
clothes, 13in (33cm)   **450 - 500**

Vinyl: Ca. 1960s.
  Kewpie Baby with hinged body,
    16in (41cm)   **$ 200 - 225**
    16in (41cm) standing, white   **95**
    16in (41cm) standing, black   **135 - 150**

11in (28cm) black vinyl *Kewpie* all original
with tag. *H & J Foulke, Inc.*

KLEY & HAHN

Character Baby: Perfect bisque head with molded hair or good wig, sleep or painted eyes, open or closed mouth; bent-limb baby body; nicely dressed; all in good condition.

#138, 158, 160, 167, 176, 458, 525, 531, 680 and others:

11-13in (28-33cm)	$	500- 525
18-20in (46-51cm)		750 - 850
24in (61cm)		1000 - 1100
28in (71cm)		1500 - 1600

Toddler, glass eyes:

15-16in (38-41cm)	1200 - 1500
22-23in (56-58cm)	1800 - 2000

Two-face baby,

13in (33cm)	2000 - 2200

Character Child: Perfect bisque head, wig, glass or painted eyes, closed mouth; jointed composition child or toddler body; fully dressed; all in good condition.
#520, 526:

15-16in (38-41cm)	$	3100 - 3500
19-21in (48-53cm)		4000 - 4500

#536, 546, 549:

15-16in (38-41cm)	$	3800 - 4200
19-21in (48-53cm)		4800 - 5300

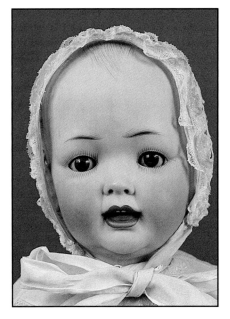

24in (61cm) 158 character baby. *H & J Foulke, Inc.*

FACTS

Kley & Hahn, doll factory, Ohrdruf, Thüringia, Germany. Heads by Hertel, Schwab & Co. (100 series), Bähr & Pröschild (500 series) and J.D. Kestner (200 Series, 680 and Walküre). 1902-on. Bisque head, composition body.
Trademarks: Walküre, Meine Einzige, Special, Dollar Princess.
Mark:

```
∑K&H∑      K H
Germany    Walküre
```

22in (56cm) 520 character boy. *Joanna Ott Collection.*

KLEY & HAHN *continued*

#547, 18-1/2in (47cm)
at auction $ 6825
#154, 166, closed mouth, toddler or jointed body,
16-17in (41-43cm) 2500 - 2650
19-20in (48-51cm) 3200
#154, 166, open mouth:
17-18in (43-46cm) jointed body 1400
25in (64cm) 1850 - 1950
20in (51cm) baby 1300 - 1400
#169, closed mouth:
13-14in (33-36cm) toddler 2200 - 2400
17-19in (43-48cm) toddler 3400 - 3500
#169, open mouth,
23in (58cm) baby $1500 - 1650**

Child Doll: Perfect bisque head, wig, glass eyes, open mouth; jointed composition child body; fully dressed; all in good condition.
#250, 282 or Walküre:
7-1/2in (19cm) $ 325 - 375
12-13in (31-33cm) 425 - 450
16-18in (41-46cm) 500 - 550
22-24in (56-61cm) 600 - 700
28-30in (71-76cm) 900 - 1000
35-36in (89-91cm) 1500 - 1600
Special, Dollar Princess,
23-25in (58-64cm) $ 525 - 575

**Not enough price samples to compute a reliable range.

32in (81cm) Walküre 282 child. *H & J Foulke, Inc.*

KLING

Bisque shoulder head: Ca. 1880. Molded hair or mohair wig, painted eyes, closed mouth; cloth body with bisque lower limbs; dressed; in all good condition. Mold numbers in **100** Series.

12-14in (31-36cm)	$	**300 - 375***
18-20in (46-51cm)		**500 - 550***
23-25in (58-64cm)		**600 - 700***

Glass eyes and molded hair,

15-16in (38-41cm)	**600 - 700***

Boy styles, such as **131**:

11in (28cm)	**600 - 650**
16-18in (41-46cm)	**900 - 1000**

Girl styles, such as **#186, 176**,

15-17in (38-43cm)	**900 - 1000**

Lady styles with decorated bodice, such as **#135, 170**, 21-23in (53-58cm) **1500 up**

*Allow extra for unusual or elaborate hairdo.

All-Bisque Child: Jointed shoulders and hips; wig, glass eyes, closed mouth; molded footwear, usually two-strap boots with heels, blue shirred hose with brown strap shoes or black hose with green shoes. (For photograph see *11th Blue Book*, page 251.)

Mark: on back or in leg joint

#36 or 69:

4in (10cm)	$ 200 - 225
5-1/2in (14cm)	**300**

#99 baby with bare feet,

4in (10cm)	$	**225****

**Not enough price samples to compute a reliable average.

── FACTS ──
Kling & Co., porcelain factory, Ohrdruf, Thüringia, Germany. 1836-on (1870-on for dolls). Bisque or china shoulder head, bisque socket head, all-bisque.
Mark:

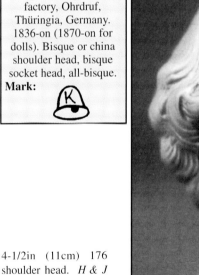

4-1/2in (11cm) 176 shoulder head. *H & J Foulke, Inc.*

China shoulder head: Ca. 1880. Black- or blonde-haired china head with bangs, sometimes with a pink tint; cloth body with china limbs or kid body; dressed; all in good condition.

#188, 189, 200 and others:

13-15in (33-38cm)	$	275 - 325
18-20in (46-51cm)		400 - 450
24-25in (61- 64cm)		525 - 575

Bisque head: Ca. 1890. Perfect bisque head, mohair or human hair wig, glass sleep eyes, open or closed mouth; kid or cloth body with bisque lower arms or jointed composition body; dressed; all in good condition.

#123, closed mouth shoulder head:

10-12in (25-31cm)		
Original costume	$	500 - 700
Redressed		250 - 300

#166 or 167, closed mouth shoulder head,

16-18in (41-46cm)	$	1000 - 1100

#373 or 377 shoulder head, open mouth:

13-15in (33-38cm)	$	375 - 425**
19-22in (48-56cm)		475 - 525**

#370, 372, 182 socket head, open mouth:

14-16in (36-41cm)	$	450 - 500
22-24in (56-61cm)		600 - 700
27in (69cm)		900 - 1000

**Not enough price samples to compute a reliable range.

18in (46cm) 189 china head. *H & J Foulke, Inc.*

19in (48cm) 167 bisque shoulder head. *H & J Foulke, Inc.*

KNICKERBOCKER

FACTS

Knickerbocker Doll & Toy Co., New York, N.Y., U.S.A. 1937.
Mark:
"WALT DISNEY
KNICKERBOCKER TOY CO."

Composition Snow White: All-composition jointed at neck, shoulders and hips; black mohair wig with hair ribbon, brown lashed sleep eyes, open mouth; original clothing; all in very good condition.

  20in (51cm)   **$ 500 - 600**
With molded black hair and blue ribbon,
  13-15in (33-38cm)   **300 - 400**

Composition Seven Dwarfs: All-composition jointed at shoulders, stiff hips, molded shoes, individual character faces, painted features; mohair wigs or beards; jointed shoulders, molded and painted shoes; original velvet costumes and caps with identifying names: Sneezy, Dopey, Grumpy, Doc, Happy, Sleepy and Bashful. Very good condition.

  9in (23cm)   **$ 225 - 275 each**
Additional composition dolls:
  Jiminy Cricket, 10in (25cm) **$450 - 550**
  Pinocchio, 13in (33cm)   **250 - 275**
Additional cloth dolls:
  Seven Dwarfs,
    14in (36cm)   **$ 250 - 275 each**
  Snow White, 16in (41cm)   **350 - 400**
  Donald Duck   **500 up**
  Mickey Mouse   **500 up**
  Minnie Mouse   **500 up**
  Two-Gun Mickey, 12in (31cm)   **1300**

9in (23cm) composition
Grumpy, all original.
*Rhoda Shomaker
Collection.*

KÖNIG & WERNICKE

K & W Character: Bisque head with good wig, sleep eyes, open mouth; composition baby or toddler body; appropriate clothes; all in good condition.

#98, 99, 100, 1070:

8-1/2in (21cm)	$	350 - 375
10-11in (25-28cm)		450 - 475
14-16in (36- 41cm)		600 - 650
19-21in (48-53cm)		750 - 850
24-25in (61-64cm)		1100
Toddler:		
15in (38cm)		1200 - 1300
20in (51cm)		1600 - 1700

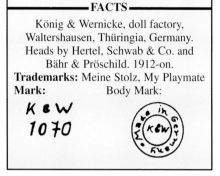

─── **FACTS** ───

König & Wernicke, doll factory, Waltershausen, Thüringia, Germany. Heads by Hertel, Schwab & Co. and Bähr & Pröschild. 1912-on.

Trademarks: Meine Stolz, My Playmate

Mark: Body Mark:

K & W
1070

16in (41cm) 99 character baby. *Ruth Covington West.*

RICHARD G. KRUEGER, INC.

FACTS

Richard G. Krueger, Inc., New York, N.Y., U.S.A. 1917-on.
Mark: Cloth tag or label.

All-Cloth Doll: Ca. 1930. Mask face with painted features, rosy cheeks, yarn hair or curly mohair wig on cloth cap; oil cloth body with hinged shoulders and hips; original clothes; in excellent condition.

Label: Krueger, N.Y.
              Reg, U.S. Pat Off.
              Made in U.S.A.

16in (41cm)	$	125 - 140
20in (51cm)		175 - 195

Pinocchio: Ca. 1940. Mask character face with black yarn hair, attached ears, round nose, large oval eyes, curved mouth; cloth torso, wood jointed arms and legs; original clothes, all in good condition. (For photograph see *10th Blue Book*, page 230.)

15in (38cm)	$	400 - 450**

Kewpie: See page 247.

Dwarfs: Ca. 1937. All cloth, mask face.

12in (30cm)	$	175 - 200

**Not enough price samples to compute a reliable average.

One of the Seven Dwarfs from *Snow White*.
H & J Foulke, Inc.

KÄTHE KRUSE

Cloth Käthe Kruse: Molded muslin head, hand-painted; jointed at shoulders and hips:

Doll I (1910-1929), 16in (41cm),
Early model, wide hips:
  Mint, all original   **$ 4000 - 5000**
  Very good   **2700 - 3500**
  Fair   **1500 - 2000**
  Jointed knees (For photograph see *11th Blue Book*, page 258.)   **5500 up****
Doll I (1929-on), 17in (43cm),
Later model, slim hips:
  Molded hair, mint   **$ 3000 - 3500**
  Very good   **2000 - 2500**
Doll 1H (wigged):
  Mint, all original   **$ 2800 - 3200**
  Very good   **1700 - 2200**

** Not enough price samples to compute a reliable average.

FACTS

Käthe Kruse, Bad Kösen, Germany; after World War II, Donauworth. 1910-on.
Mark: On cloth: "Käthe Kruse" on sole of foot, sometimes also "Germany" and a number.

Hard plastic on back: Turtle mark and "Käthe Kruse."

16in (41cm) *Doll IH*, all original. *Rosemary Dent Collection.*

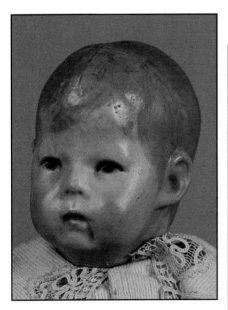

16in (41cm) *Doll I*. *H & J Foulke, Inc.*

Doll II "Schlenkerchen" Smiling Baby (1922-1936). (For photograph see *10th Blue Book*, page 292.)

13in (33cm) at auction   **$ 7600 - 9400***

Very worn   **2300**

Doll V & VI Babies "Traumerchen" (five-pound weighted Sand Baby) and Du Mein (unweighted). (For photograph see *9th Blue Book*, page 287.)

Cloth head,
19-1/2–23-1/2in (50-60cm)**$ 3500 - 4000**

Magnesit head, 21in (53cm)   **1500**

Doll VII (1927-1952) and Doll X (1935-1952), 14in (35cm):

Redressed   **$ 1300**

All original   **1800 - 2000**

Mint-in-box, at auction   **4000**

With Du Mein head (1928-1930), (For photograph see *11th Blue Book*, page 257.)

14in (36cm):

Showing wear   **1600 - 1800**

Mint   **2900**

*Due to demand in Germany.

Doll VIII "German Child" (1929-on), 20-1/2in (52cm) wigged, turning head:

Mint, all original   **$ 2500 - 3000**

Good condition, suitably dressed
   1500 - 1800

Doll IX "Little German Child" (1929-on), wigged, turning head, 14in (36cm):

Redressed   **$ 1300**

All original, mint   **1800 - 2200**

U.S. Zone Germany: Dolls IX or X with cloth or Magnesit heads, very thick paint finish; all original, very good condition (1945 - 1951):

14in (35cm)

Cloth head, mint   **$ 1200 - 1500**

Magnesit, mint   **750 - 850**

Hard plastic, mint   **600 - 700**

17-18in (43-46cm)

Doll I, mint   **$ 2500 - 3000**

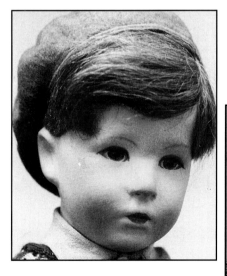

14in (35cm) **Doll IX** (boy) and **Doll X** (girl), all original. *H & J Foulke, Inc.*

20-1/2in (52cm) **Doll VIII**, all original. *H & J Foulke, Inc.*

Hard Plastic Head: Ca. 1952-on. Hard plastic head with human hair wig, painted eyes; pink muslin body; original clothes; all in excellent condition.

Ca. 1952-1975:

14in (35cm)	$	375 - 425
19-21in (48-53cm)		500 - 575

1975-on:

14in (35cm)	300 - 350*
19-21in (48-53cm)	400 - 450*
20in (51cm) **Du Mein**	550 - 650*

Hanna Kruse Dolls:

10in (25cm) **Däumlinchen** with foam rubber stuffing (1957-on) $ 200 - 225*
13in (33cm) **Rumpumpel Baby** or **Toddler,** 1959-on. 350 - 400
10in (25cm) **Doggi,** 1964-1967. (For photograph see *10th Blue Book,* page 293.) 200 - 225**

*Retail store prices may be higher.

14in (35cm) **Doll XI**, hard plastic head, U.S. Zone Germany, **Friedebald**, all original. *H & J Foulke, Inc.*

All-Hard Plastic (Celluloid) Käthe Kruse: Wig or molded hair and sleep or painted eyes; jointed neck, shoulders and hips; original clothes; all in excellent condition. Turtle mark. 1955-1951.

16in (41cm)	$	450 - 500

** Not enough price samples to compute a reliable range.

16in (41cm) all-hard plastic boy, all original. *H & J Foulke, Inc.*

KRUSE-TYPE

Bing Art Dolls: Nurnberg, Germany. 1921-1932. Cloth or composition head, molded face, hand-painted features, painted hair or curly wig; cloth body with jointed shoulders and hips (some with pinned joints), mitten hands; all original clothing; very good condition. "Bing" stamped or impressed on sole of shoe.

Cloth head, painted hair
10-12in (25-30cm)	$	**500 - 600**
14in (35cm)		**850 - 950**
Cloth head, wigged 10in (25cm)		**250 - 300**
Composition head, wigged		
7in (18cm)		**100 - 120**

Heine & Schneider Art Doll: Bad-Kösen, Germany. 1920-1922. All cloth or head of pressed cardboard covered with cloth, molded hair, painted eyes, closed mouth, oil-painted features; cloth body with jointed shoulders and hips (some with cloth covered composition arms and hands.) Appropriate or original clothes; all in good condition. Mark stamped on foot.

17-19in (43-48cm)   **$1300 - 1500****

Unmarked Child Dolls: Ca. 1920s. Depending upon quality $ **300 up**.

**Not enough price samples to compute a reliable average.

FACTS

Various German firms in imitation of the Käthe Krüse children

14in (35cm) Bing Boy, all original, signed on shoe. *H & J Foulke, Inc.*

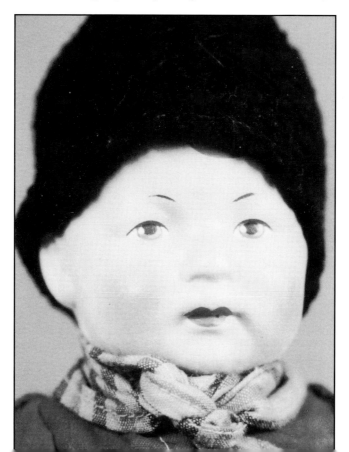

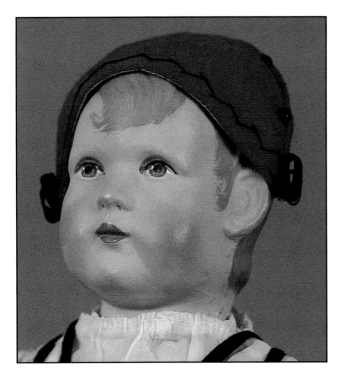

Heine & Schneider child, all original. *Nancy A. Smith Collection.*

See page 259 for further information about the dolls shown on this page.

15in (38cm) unmarked Kruse-type girl, all original, mediocre quality. *H & J Foulke, Inc.*

GEBRÜDER KUHNLENZ

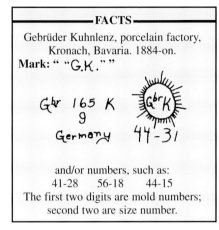

and/or numbers, such as:

41-28   56-18   44-15

The first two digits are mold numbers;
second two are size number.

21in (53cm) 32 child. *H & J Foulke, Inc.*

G. K. doll with closed mouth: Ca. 1885-on.
Perfect bisque socket head (some with closed
Belton-type crown), inset glass eyes, closed
mouth, round cheeks; jointed composition
body; dressed; all in good condition.

#32, 31:

8-10in (20-25cm)	$ 850 - 1100*
15-16in (38-41cm)	1600 - 1900*
21-23in (53-58cm)	2400 - 2900*

#34, Bru-type, French body:

18in (46cm)	$3000 - 4000**

#38 shoulder head, kid body:

14-16in (36-41cm)	$ 800 - 900*
22-23in (56-58cm)	1300 - 1400*

*Allow more for a very pretty doll.
**Not enough price samples to compute a
reliable range.

GEBRÜDER KUHNLENZ *continued*

G.K. child doll: Ca. 1890-on. Perfect bisque socket head with distinctive face, almost a character look, long cheeks, sleep or paperweight-type eyes, open mouth, molded teeth; jointed composition body, sometimes French; dressed; all in good condition.

#41, 44, 56:

9-10in (23-25cm)	$	700
16-19in (41-48cm)		800 - 900
24-26in (61-66cm)		1200 - 1400

#165:

18in (46cm)	425 - 450
22-24in (56-61cm)	525 - 575
34in (86cm)	1200 - 1300

#61, 47 shoulder head:

19-22in (48-56cm)	650 - 750

15in (38cm) 44 child. *H & J Foulke, Inc.*

23in (58cm) 165 child. *H & J Foulke, Inc.*

G.K. Tiny Dolls: Perfect bisque socket head, wig, stationary glass eyes, open mouth with molded teeth; 5-piece composition body with molded shoes and socks; all in good condition. Usually mold #44.
7-8in (18-20cm):

Crude body	$	**185 - 210**
Better body		**225 - 275**

All-Bisque Child: 1895-on. Socket head with glass eyes, open mouth, nice mohair wig; pegged shoulders and hips, white painted stockings, light blue boots, black straps or two-strap shoes. Usually mold #44, #31, or #41.

5in (13cm)	$	**500 - 600**
7-1/2in (19cm)		**850 - 1000**
8-1/2in (22cm)		**1250 - 1400**

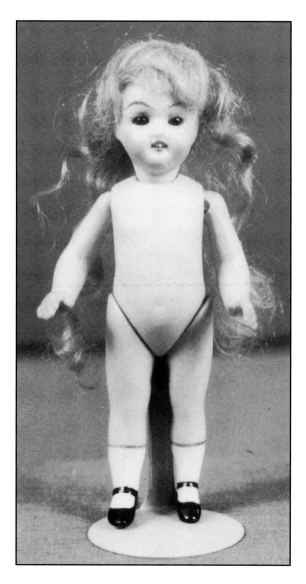

5in (13cm) 31 all-bisque child. *H & J Foulke, Inc.*

LANTERNIER

Marked Lanternier Child: Ca. 1915. Perfect bisque head, good or original wig, large stationary eyes, open mouth, pierced ears; papier-mâché jointed body; pretty clothes; all in good condition.

Cherie, Favorite or **La Georgienne:**
16-18in (41-46cm)	$ **675 - 775***
22-24in (56-61cm)	**900 - 1000***
28in (71cm)	**1400 - 1600***

*Allow extra for lovely face and bisque.

Lanternier Lady: Ca. 1915. Perfect bisque head with adult look, good wig, stationary glass eyes, open/closed mouth with molded teeth; composition lady body; dressed; all in good condition. (For photograph see *7th Blue Book*, page 271.)
Lorraine,
16-18in (41-46cm)	$ **850 - 1250***

*Depending upon costume and quality.

Characters, "Toto" and others: Ca. 1915. Perfect bisque smiling character face, good wig, glass eyes, open/closed mouth with molded teeth, pierced ears; jointed French composition body; dressed; all in good condition. (For photograph see *10th Blue Book*, page 231.)
17-19in (43-48cm)	$ **900 - 1100**

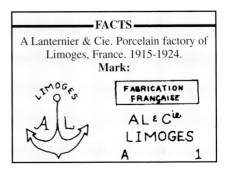

── FACTS ──
A Lanternier & Cie. Porcelain factory of Limoges, France. 1915-1924.
Mark:

22in (56cm) child marked "Limoges." *H & J Foulke, Inc.*

LEATHER, FRENCH

Leather Doll: Baby or child doll with molded and painted hair, painted features, jointed shoulders and hips; original clothes; excellent condition.

Baby, 5in (13cm) $ **2250**
Child, 6in (15cm)   **3000****

**Not enough price samples to compute a reliable average.

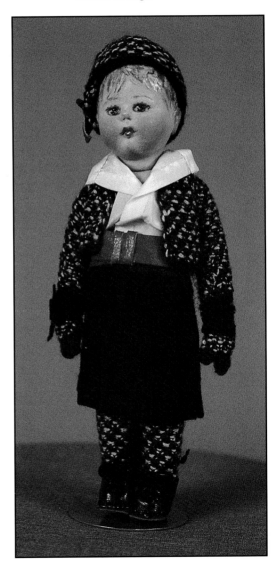

6in (15cm) French leather child all original. *Jan Foulke Collection.*

LENCI

Lenci: All-felt (sometimes cloth torso); pressed felt head with painted features; swivel head, jointed shoulders and hips; painted features, eyes usually side-glancing; original clothes, often of felt or organdy; in excellent condition.

Miniatures and Mascottes:
8-9in (20-23cm) Regionals $ **300 - 350**
Children or unusual costumes **400 - 500**
Flower Vendor, at auction **1300**
Mozart (see photograph on page 268) and
Maria-Teresa **1300 - 1500 pair**
Children #300, 109, 149, 159, 111:
13in (33cm) $ **850 up**
16-18in (41-46cm) **1000 up**
20-22in (51-56cm) **1600 up**
#300 children, 17in (43cm):
Mozart $ **3700**
Russian Boy **3000**
Russian Girl **2400**
Albanian Boy **3500**

Albanian Girl	**2500**
Orientals	**3500 up**
Boy with Golf Bag	**2700**
Sport Series	**2200 up**
Boy in Sweater	**2000**
Indian Girl with Papoose	**5000**

─── FACTS ───

Enrico & Elenadi Scavini, Turin, Italy. 1920-on.
Mark: "LENCI" on cloth and various paper tags; sometimes stamped on bottom of foot.

16in (41cm) 300 series face, all original. *Private Collection.*

1930s Children:
"Benedetta" face,
19in (48cm) $ **1500 up**
"Mariuccia" face,
17in (43cm)   **1200 up**
"Henriette" face,
25in (63cm)   **2000 up**
"Laura" face, 16in (41cm)   **1000 - 1500**
(For photograph see *11th Blue Book*,
page 9.)
"Lucia" face, 14in (36cm):
Child clothes   **800 - 1200**
Regional outfits   **700 - 900**
Ladies and long-limbed novelty dolls,
24-28in (61-71cm)   **1800 up**
40in (102cm)   **3000**
"Valentine"
glass eyes,
20in (51cm)   **2800 - 3000**
"Surprised Eye" (round painted
eyes), fancy clothes. (For photograph see page 268.)
20in (51cm)   **2200 - 2600**
#1500, scowling face,
17-19in (43-48cm) **1800 - 2000**
Baby:
14-18in (36-46cm)
2000 - 2200
21in (53cm)   **2500**
Teenager, long legs,
17in (43cm)   **1200 up**
Margarita with rooster,
21in (53cm), at auction **4200**
Valentino, as "Sheik,"
25in (63cm), at auction **7000**
Googly, watermelon mouth,
22in (56cm)   **1600 - 2000**
Winkers,
12in (31cm)   **750 - 950**
1935 Round face,
11in (28cm)   **500 up**
1950 Characters   **300 up**
Catalogs   **900 - 1200**
Purse   **300**
Fascist Boy,
13in (33cm)   **1200 - 1400**
Brown South Seas,
16in (41cm)   **1800 - 2000**
Mask face, disc eyes,
23in (58cm)   **600 - 700**
Hand Puppet   **400 - 500**

Celluloid-type, 6in (15cm)   **60 - 75**

Collector's Note: Mint examples of rare dolls will bring higher prices. To bring the prices quoted, Lenci dolls must be clean and have good color. Faded and dirty dolls bring only about one-third to one-half these prices

14in (36cm) *"Lucia"* face, all original. *H & J Foulke, Inc.*

20in (51cm) "surprised eye" girl, all original. *H & J Foulke, Inc.* (For further information see page 267.)

9in (23cm) *Mozart,* all original. *H & J Foulke, Inc.* (For further information see page 266.)

21in (53cm) girl, Ca. 1930, all original. *Private Collection.* (For further information see page 267.)

LENCI-TYPE

━━FACTS━━

Various Italian, French and English firms . 1920-1940. 6in (15cm) up.
Mark: Various paper labels, if any.

Felt or Cloth Doll: Mohair wig, painted features; stuffed cloth body; original clothes or costume; excellent condition.
Child dolls, 16-18in (41-46cm) up to **$750** depending upon quality

Regional costume, very good quality:
7-1/2–8-1/2in (19-22cm) $	**40 - 50**
12in (31cm)	**90 - 110**

Alma, Turin, Italy,
16in (41cm)	**400 - 500**

12in (31cm) Italian girl in regional costume.   *H & J Foulke, Inc.*

18in (46cm) ***Alma*** character, all original. *H & J Foulke, Inc.*

LENCI-TYPE *continued*

Dean's Rag Book Company,
England:
  14-16in (36-41cm) $ **500 - 600**
  Compositiion face, 18in (46cm) **600 - 700**
Farnell's Alpha Toys, London, England:
  Alpha Imp, 10in (25cm)   **250**
Coronation Doll of King George VI, 1937.
  16in (41cm)   **400 - 450**

Eugenie Poir, Gre-Poir French Doll Makers, Paris and New York. (For photograph see

11th Blue Book, page 270.) 17-21in (43-46cm):
  Mint condition $ **500 - 600**
  Good condition   **300 - 400**
Raynal, Venus, Marina, Clelia. Paris, France: (For photograph see *9th Blue Book,* page 339.)
  17-18in (43-46cm) mint $ **550 - 600**

20in (51cm)
Venus girl, all
original.
*Courtesy of
Richard W.
Withington,
Inc.*

LIBERTY OF LONDON

FACTS

Liberty & Co. of London, England.
1906-on.
Mark: Cloth label or paper tag "Liberty of London."

British Coronation Dolls: 1939. All-cloth with painted and needle-sculpted faces; original clothes; excellent condition. The **Royal Family** and **Coronation Participants**.

9-9-1/2in (23-24cm)	$ 150 - 165
6in (15cm), Princess Margaret	400
7in (17cm), Princess Elizabeth	400

Other English Historical and Ceremonial Characters: All-cloth with painted and needle-sculpted faces; original clothes; excellent condition.

9-10in (23-25cm)	$ 125 - 135
Beefeater (Tower Guard)	85

Princesses Elizabeth and *Margaret Rose* dressed for their father's coronation, all original. *H & J Foulke, Inc.*

Sir Walter Raleigh, all original. *H & J Foulke, Inc.*

LIMBACH

All-Bisque Child: Ca. 1900. Child all of bisque (sometimes pink bisque) with wire jointed shoulders and hips; molded hair (often with a blue molded bow) or bald head with mohair wig, painted eyes, closed mouth, white stockings, blue garters, brown slippers or strap shoes.

Mark:

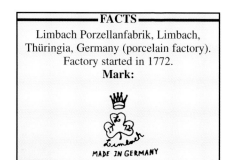

4-5in (10-13cm)	$	**75 - 95**
6in (15cm)		**125**
6-1/2in (16cm) swivel neck		**225**
Glass eyes:		
5in (13cm)		**160 - 185**
8in (20cm)		**275 - 325**
Character, jointed arms only,		
4-5in (10-13cm)		**85 - 95**

All-Bisque Baby: Ca. 1910. Baby with painted hair and facial features; wire jointed shoulders and hips, bent arms and legs; bare feet. (For photograph see *8th Blue Book*, page 299.)

Mark: Clover and number with "P."

4-5in (10-13cm)	$	**85 - 100***
7in (18cm)		**135 - 165***
11-12in (28-31cm) fine quality		**550 - 650**
Black #8675, 6in (15cm)		**800 - 900****

*Allow more for fine quality.
**Not enough price samples to compute a reliable range.

━━━━━ FACTS ━━━━━

Limbach Porzellanfabrik, Limbach,
Thüringia, Germany (porcelain factory).
Factory started in 1772.
Mark:

MADE IN GERMANY

5-1/2in (14cm) P.45 boy.
H & J Foulke, Inc.

LIMBACH *continued*

Limbach Child Doll: 1893-1899; 1919-on. Perfect bisque head, good wig, glass eyes, open mouth with teeth; composition jointed body; dressed; all in good condition.

Wally, Rita, or **Norma** after 1919:

17-19in (43-48cm)	$ 550 - 600*
23-24in (58-61cm)	700 - 750*

Incised with clover (1893-1899):

open mouth,

14-17in (36-43cm)	900 - 1200**
22in (56cm)	1500**
closed mouth, 27in (69cm)	2100 - 2300

#8682 Character Baby: open/closed mouth,

15in (38cm)	$ 900 - 1000**

*Allow 30-40% more for fine quality.
**Not enough price samples to compute a reliable range.

22-1/2in (57cm) girl with incised cloverleaf. *H & J Foulke, Inc.*

ARMAND MARSEILLE (A.M.)

Child Doll: 1890-on. Perfect bisque head, nice wig, set or sleep eyes, open mouth; composition ball-jointed body or jointed kid body with bisque lower arms; pretty clothes; all in good condition.

#390, (larger sizes marked only "A. [size] M."), Florodora (composition body):

9-10in (23-25cm)	$	235 - 265*
12-14in (31-36cm)		225 - 275*
16-18in (41-46cm)		325 - 375*
20in (51cm)		400 - 425*
23-24in (58-61cm)		450 - 475*
28-29in (71-74cm)		650 - 700
30-32in (76-81cm)		750 - 850
35-36in (89-91cm)		1000 - 1200+
38in (96cm)		1500 - 1800+
40-42in (102-107cm)		2000+

5-piece composition body, (excellent quality body),

6-7in (15-18cm)	175 - 200
9-10in (23-25cm)	235 - 265
Closed mouth, 5-5-1/2in (12-14cm)	
	250 - 275

#1894 (composition body):

12-14in (31-36cm) stick body	$ 275 - 325
14-16in (36-41cm)	450 - 550
21-23in (53-58cm)	750 - 850
26in (66cm)	950

#370, 3200, 1894, Florodora, Anchor 2015, Rosebud shoulder heads:

11-12in (28-31cm)	$	165 - 185
14-16in (36-41cm)		200 - 250
22-24in (56-61cm)		375 - 425

* Add $100 for factory original clothes; subtract $50-75 for cardboard and stick body.
+ Allow more for an exceptionally pretty doll.

——————FACTS——————

Armand Marseille of Köppelsdorf, Thüringia, Germany (porcelain and doll factory). 1885-on.

Marks:

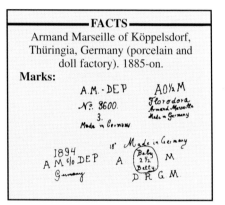

14-1/2in (37cm) 2015 shoulder head girl. *H & J Foulke, Inc.*

ARMAND MARSEILLE (A.M.) *continued*

#2000: 14in (36cm) $ 900**
Queen Louise, Rosebud
(composition body):
12in (31cm) $ 340 - 365
23-25in (58-64cm)   525 - 575
28-29in (71-74cm)   700 - 775
Baby Betty:
14-16in (36-41cm)
  composition body $ 525 - 575
19-21in (48-53cm) kid body   525 - 575
#1894, 1892, 1896, 1897 shoulder heads (excellent quality):
19-22in (48-56cm) $ 475 - 525
Name shoulder head child: 1898 to World War I. Perfect bisque shoulder head marked with doll's name, jointed kid or cloth body, bisque lower arms; good wig, glass eyes, open mouth; well dressed; all in good condition. Names include Rosebud, Lilly, Alma, Mabel, Darling, Beauty and Princess.
Marks:

12-14in (31-36cm) $ 185 - 215
20-22in (51-56cm)   325 - 375
25in (64cm)   450 - 500
Character Children: 1910-on. Perfect bisque head, molded hair or wig, glass or painted eyes, open or closed mouth; composition body; dressed; all in good condition. (For photographs of dolls not shown here, see previous *Blue Books*.)
#230 Fany (molded hair):
15-16in (38-41cm) $ 5200 - 6000
19in (48cm)   7500 - 8000
16in (41cm) piece glued at neck   2600
#231 Fany (wigged) (See photograph on page 277.):
14-15in (36-38cm)   4800 - 5200
18in (46cm)   7500 - 8000
#250, 11-13in (28-33cm)   750
#251/248 (open/closed mouth),
12in (31cm)   1650
16-18in (41-46cm)   2600 - 3000
#340, 13in (33cm)   2600**
#372 Kiddiejoy shoulder head, "mama" body, 19in (48cm)   850 - 900
#400 (child body),
13in (33cm)   1300 - 1500
17in (43cm)   2600 - 2800**
#500, 600, 13-15in (33-38cm)   650 - 750

#550 (glass eyes):
12in (31cm)   2200
18-20in (46-51cm)   3450 - 3750**
#560, 11-13in (28-33cm)   750 - 850
#590, 13-15in (33-38cm)   1200 - 1500
#620 shoulder head, 16in (41cm)   1250**
#640 shoulder head (same face as 550 socket), 20in (51cm)   1500 - 1650**
#700:
13in (33cm) painted eyes   2000
14in (36cm) glass eyes   3000 - 3500
A.M. (intaglio eyes),
16-17in (41-43cm)   4500 up

**Not enough price samples to compute a reliable range.

12-1/2in (32cm) G.B. 251/A.M. 248, open/closed mouth, character child. *H & J Foulke, Inc.*

24in (61cm) early A.M. girl, no mold number. *H & J Foulke, Inc.* (For further information see page 274.)

13in (33cm) A.M. 231 *Fany. H & J Foulke, Inc.* (For further information see page 275.)

23in (58cm) G.B. 256/ A.M. 259, character baby. *H & J Foulke, Inc.* (For further information see page 278.)

13in (33cm) G.B. 251/ A. M. 248, open mouth, character baby. *H & J Foulke, Inc.* (For further information see page 275.)

278

Character Babies and Toddlers: 1910-on. Perfect bisque head, good wig, sleep eyes, open mouth some with teeth; composition bent-limb body; suitably dressed; all in nice condition.

Marks:

Armand Marseille
Germany
990
A 7/0 M

Germany
326

A 11 M

Mold #990, 985, 971, 996, 1330, 326, (solid dome), 980, 991, 327, 329, 259 and others: (See photograph on page 277.)

10-11in (25-28cm)	$	325 - 350
13-15in (33-38cm)		375 - 425
18-20in (46-51cm)		500 - 550
22in (56cm)		650 - 700
24-25in (61-64cm)		750 - 850
#233:		
13-15in (33-38cm)		500 - 550
20in (51cm)		700 - 800

#251/248 (open mouth), (For photograph see page 277.)

12-15in (31-38cm)	750 - 850
#410 (two rows of teeth),	
15-16in (38-41cm)	1200 - 1500**
#518:	
16-18in (41-46cm)	600 - 700
25in (64cm)	1000 - 1200
#560A:	
12in (31cm)	525 - 550
15-17in (38-43cm)	650 - 700
#580, 590 (open/closed mouth):	
9in (23cm)	650 - 750
15-16in (38-41cm)	1200 - 1500
#590 (open mouth):	
12in (31cm)	600
16-18in (41-46cm)	850 - 950
#920 shoulder head, "mama" body,	
21in (53cm)	900**
Melitta, 19in (48cm) toddler	850 - 900
#995, painted bisque toddler	
18in (46cm)	500 - 600

** Not enough price samples to compute a reliable range.

13in (33cm) A.M. 980 character baby. *H & J Foulke, Inc.*

ARMAND MARSEILLE (A.M.) *continued*

Infant: 1924-on. Solid-dome bisque head with molded and/or painted hair, sleep eyes; composition body or hard-stuffed jointed cloth body or soft-stuffed cloth body; dressed; all in good condition.

Mark:
A. M.
Germany.
351.14K

#351, 341, Kiddiejoy and Our Pet: (See photograph on page 280.)
Head circumference:

8-9in (20-23cm)	$ 225 - 250*
10in (25cm)	275 - 300*
12-13in (31-33cm)	350 - 425*
15in (38cm)	600*
6in (15cm) compo body	225 - 250
24in (61cm) wigged toddler	950
Hand Puppet	200 - 225

#352 (For photograph see page 280.)

17-20in (43-51cm) long	575 - 625

#347:
Head circumference:

12-13in (31-33cm)	475 - 525

Baby Phyllis:
Head circumference:

9in (23cm) black	500
12-13in (31-33cm)	425 - 475

Baby Gloria, RBL, New York: (For photograph see page 280.)

15-16in (38-41cm)	700 - 800

*Allow $25-75 extra for composition body.

Marked "Just Me" Character: Ca. 1925. Perfect bisque socket head, curly wig, glass eyes to side, closed mouth; composition body; dressed; all in good condition. Some of these dolls, particularly the painted bisque ones, were used by Vogue Doll Company in the 1930s and will be found with original Vogue labeled clothes. (For photograph see *11th Blue Book*, page 278.)

Mark:

Just ME
Registered
Germany
A 310/5/0 M

7-1/2in (19cm)	$ 1000 - 1100
9in (23cm)	1450
11in (28cm)	1600 - 1800
13in (33cm)	2200

Painted bisque:

7-8in (18-20cm) all original	800 - 900
10in (25cm) all original	1000 - 1100

Lady: 1910-1930. Bisque head with mature face, mohair wig, sleep eyes, open or closed mouth; composition lady body with molded bust, long slender arms and legs; appropriate clothes; all in good condition. (For photograph see *9th Blue Book*, page 304.)

#401 and 400 (slim body), 12-13in (31-33cm):

Open mouth	$ 1050 - 1250
Closed mouth	2000 - 2500

#300 (naked M.H.): (For photograph see *11th Blue Book*, page 277.)

9in (23cm)	1400 - 1500**
All original	1650**

** Not enough price samples to compute a reliable range.

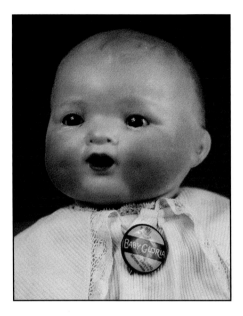

14in (31cm) *Baby Gloria* with pin. *H & J Foulke, Inc.* (For further information see page 279.)

19in (48cm) A.M. 352 infant. *H & J Foulke, Inc.* (For further information see page 279.)

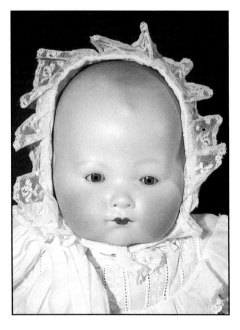

20in (51cm) long A.M. 345 *Kiddiejoy* infant. *H & J Foulke, Inc.* (For further information see page 279.)

MASCOTTE

Bébé Mascotte: Bisque socket head, good wig, closed mouth, paperweight eyes, pierced ears; jointed composition and wood body; appropriate clothes; all in good condition.

11-12in (28-31cm)	$	**2250 - 2500**
17-19in (43-48cm)		**3800 - 4200**
24-26in (61-66cm)		**5300 - 5800**

FACTS

May Freres Cie, 1890-1897; Jules Nicolas Steiner, 1898-on. Paris, France. 1890-1902.

Mark:

"BÉBÉ MASCOTTE
PARIS"

11-1/2in (29cm) *Bébé Mascotte,* signed head and body. *H & J Foulke, Inc.*

METAL DOLLS (AMERICAN)

Metal Child: All metal, body fully jointed at neck, shoulders, elbows, wrists, hips, knees and ankles; sleep eyes, open/closed mouth with painted teeth; dressed; all in good condition. (Body may be jointed composition with metal hands and feet.)

16-20in (41-51cm)   **$ 325 - 425**

Metal Baby: All metal (with bent limbs) jointed at shoulders and hips with metal springs; molded and painted hair and facial features, painted or sleep eyes, closed or open mouth; appropriate clothes; all in good condition.

11-13in (28-33cm)   **$ 100 - 125**
18-20in (46-51cm) metal head, cloth body
with composition lower limbs   **165 - 185**

━━━━━ FACTS ━━━━━

Various U.S. companies, such as Atlas Doll & Toy Co. and Giebeler-Falk, N.Y., U.S.A. Ca. 1917-on.

18in (46cm) unmarked metal head. *H & J Foulke, Inc.*

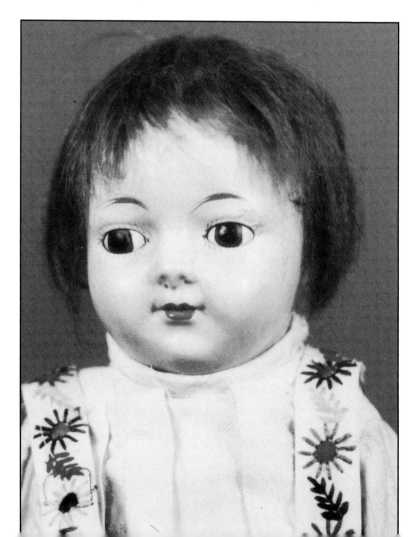

METAL HEADS (GERMAN)

FACTS

Buschow & Beck, Germany (Minerva): Karl Standfuss, Germany (Juno); Alfred Heller, Germany (Diana). Ca. 1888-on.

Mark:

Mark may often be found on front of shoulder plate.

Marked Metal Head Child: Metal shoulder head on cloth or kid body, bisque or composition hands; dressed; very good condition, not repainted.

Molded hair, painted eyes:

12-14in (31-36cm)	$ 110 - 135
23in (58cm)	200

Molded hair, glass eyes:

12-14in (31-36cm)	150 - 175
20-22in (51-56cm)	225 - 250

Wig and glass eyes:

14-16in (36-41cm)	225 - 250
20-22in (51-56cm)	275 - 325

15in (38cm) German metal head, all original. *H & J Foulke, Inc.*

MOLLY-'ES

Molly-'es Composition Dolls: All-composition, jointed at neck, shoulders and hips; molded hair or wig, sleep eyes; beautiful original outfits; all in good condition.

Babies, 15-18in (38-46cm) $	**225 - 250**
Girls, 12-13in (31-33cm)	**125 - 150**
Toddlers, 14-16in (36-41cm)	**275 - 300**
Ladies, 18-21in (46-53cm)	**500 - 550**

Internationals: All-cloth with mask faces, mohair wigs (sometimes yarn), painted features; variety of costumes, all original clothes; in excellent condition with wrist tag. (For photograph see *10th Blue Book*, page 330.)

13in (33cm)	**75 - 95**
Mint-in-box	**100 - 125**

Thief of Baghdad Series:
Sabu, composition. (For photograph see *10th Blue Book*, page 3.)

15in (38cm)	**550 - 600**
Sultan, 19in (48cm)	**650 - 750**
Princess, 15in (38cm) composition or	
18in (46cm) cloth	**600 - 650**

━━━FACTS━━━

International Doll Co., Philadelphia, Pa., U.S.A. Made clothing only. Purchased undressed dolls from various manufacturers. 1920s-on.

Clothes Designer: Mollye Goldman.

Mark: Usually a cardboard tag, dolls unmarked except for vinyl.

13in (33cm)
Molly-'es
composition
Dutch girl,
all original.
*H & J
Foulke, Inc.*

MOTHEREAU

Bébé Mothereau: Perfect bisque head, beautiful blown glass eyes, eye shadow, closed mouth, chin dimple, pierced ears, good wig; wood and composition jointed body; beautifully dressed; all in good condition.

27-29in (69-74cm) $ **25,000up****

**Not enough price samples to compute a reliable average.

─── FACTS ───

Alexandre Mothereau, Paris, France.
1880-1895.
Trademark: Bébé Mothereau
Mark:
B M
11..13

29in (74cm) B.M.//11..13. *Kay & Wayne Jensen Collection.*

MULTI-FACED DOLLS

ABOVE & BELOW: 12in (31cm) Bru *poupée Surprise Doll* with sleeping and awake faces. *Doelman Collection. Courtesy of Richard W. Withington, Inc.*

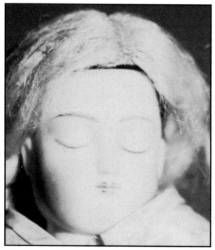

Marked **C.B. Doll:** Carl Bergner, Sonneberg, Germany. Perfect bisque head with two or three different faces, usually sleeping, laughing and crying, papier-mâché hood hides the unwanted face(s); a ring through the top of the hood attached to a dowel turns the faces; cloth torso, composi-

tion limbs; dressed; all in good condition.

13in (33cm) three-faced	$	**1300 - 1500**
13in (33cm) two-faced black and		
white 202 dep		**1800 - 2200**
13in (33cm) Red Riding Hood,		
Grandmother and Wolf		**6000****
14in (31cm) two-faced, frowning and		
hint of a smile,		
Simon & Halbig-type		**3500****

Character Babies: German. Ca. 1910. Perfect bisque head with two faces, usually crying, sleeping or smiling; swivel neck; composition or cloth body; dressed; all in good condition. Some have papier-mâché hoods to cover unwanted faces, while some use cloth bonnets.

17in (43cm) HvB (von Berg)	
two-faced baby	**$1200 - 1400**
13in (33cm) Gebr. Heubach	
three-faced baby	**1800 - 2000**
13in (33cm) Kley & Hahn	
two-faced baby	**2000 - 2200**
9in (23cm) Max Schelhorn	
two-faced baby	**650 - 750**

French Dolls:
Bru *Poupée*, Surprise Doll awake and sleeping. Ca. 1867.

12in (31cm)	**$9,000 - 10,000**

Jumeau, laughing and crying character faces (#211 & 203),

18in (46cm), boxed	**12,000 - 15,000**

American Composition Dolls:
Trudy. 3-in-1 Doll Corp., New York. Sleeping, crying, smiling. All original.

14in (36cm)	$	**250 - 295**

Johnny Tu-Face. Effanbee, New York. Crying and smiling.

16in (41cm)	**300****

**Not enough price samples to compute a reliable average.

— FACTS —

Various German, French and American companies. 1888 and perhaps earlier. One head with two or three different faces.

MUNICH ART DOLLS

Munich Art Dolls: Molded composition character heads with hand-painted features; fully-jointed composition bodies; dressed; all in good condition.

13in (33cm)	$	**2200 - 2500**
18-19in (46-48cm)		**3000 - 4000****
12in (31cm) fair condition		**1100 - 1300**

**Not enough price samples to compute a reliable range.

16in (41cm) Munich Art Doll. *CC Collection.*

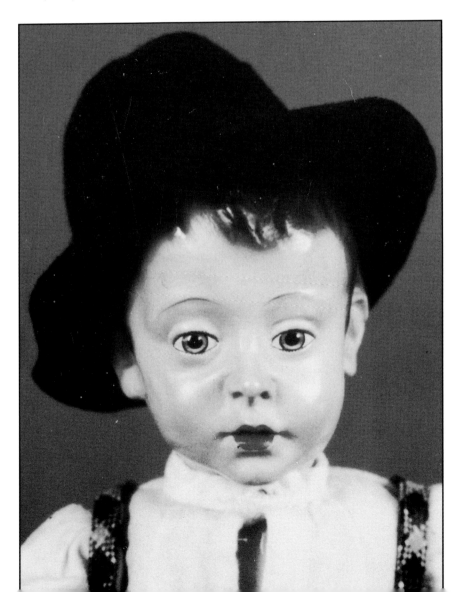

Painted Bisque Marked Storybook Doll:
Mohair wig, painted eyes; one-piece body and head, jointed legs and arms; original clothes; excellent condition with sticker or wrist tag and box. 5-1/2–7in (13-19cm).

1936: Babies only. Gold sticker on front of outfit; sunburst box. **Mark:** "88 Made in Japan" or "87 Made in Japan" **$ 400 up**

1937-1938: Gold sticker on front of outfit; sunburst box, gold label. **Mark:** "Made in Japan 1146," "Made in Japan 1148," "Japan," "Made in Japan" or "AMERICA" **300 - 500**

1938-1939: Gold sticker on front of skirt; sunburst transition to silver dot box. **Mark:** "JUDY ANN USA" (crude mark), "STORYBOOK USA" (crude mark). Molded socks/molded bangs. **Mark:** "StoryBook Doll USA" **300 - 400**

Judy Ann in storybook box with extra outfits, sticker on dress **600 up**

1940: Gold sticker on front of skirt; colored box with white polka dots. Molded socks. **Mark:** "StoryBook Doll USA" **200 up**

1941-1942: Gold wrist tag; white box with colored polka dots; jointed legs. **Mark:** "StoryBook Doll USA" **70 up**

1943-1947: Gold wrist tag; white box with colored polka dots; frozen legs. **Mark:** "StoryBook Doll USA" (some later dolls with plastic arms) **50 up**
Socket head **80 up**

Hard Plastic Marked Storybook Doll:
Swivel head, mohair wig, painted eyes, jointed legs; original clothes, gold wrist tag; white box with colored polka dots, excellent condition.
Mark: "Story Book Doll USA"
5-1/2-7in (13-19cm) **$ 40 up**

━━━ FACTS ━━━

Nancy Ann Storybook Dolls Co., South San Francisco, CA., U.S.A. 1936-on.
Mark: Various as indicated.

Painted bisque *"Judy Ann" Bo-Peep,* all original. *H & J Foulke, Inc.*

Bent-limb Baby:
Star hand baby $ **125 up**
Bisque with closed fist,
open mouth **135 up**
Painted bisque, hard plastic arms **90 up**
Hard Plastic **75 up**
Boxed furniture **300 up**
Special Dolls:
Painted bisque with white
painted socks $ **150 up**
Glow-in-Dark **100 up**
Series Dolls:
Flower Girl $ **200 up**
Masquerade, bisque jointed legs **250 up**
Pirate, colored box with sticker **600 up**
Around the World, bisque **200 up**
Sports, skiing, boxed with sticker **600 up**
Family, Margie Ann in pink felt coat
and hat, white boots, colored box with
white dots. **325 up**
Powder & Crinoline, bisque **150 up**
Operetta, bisque **150 - 175**
All Time Hit Parade, bisque **150 - 175**
Topsy and Eva, bisque pair **500 up**
Special Holiday inserts:
Bisque **100 up**
Hard plastic **75 up**
Nancy Ann Style Show, hard plastic,
17in (43cm) $ **425 - 600**

Muffie, all hard plastic, wig, sleeping eyes,
8in (12cm) tall:
Mark: "StoryBook Dolls USA" some with
"Muffie."
1953: straight leg nonwalker, painted lashes, no brows, dynel wig (side part with flip); 54 complete costumes. Original clothes, excellent condition. $ **175 up**
1954: walker, molded eyelashes, eyebrows after 1955, side part flip or braided wig; 30 additional costumes. Original clothes, excellent condition. **150 up**
1955-1956: hard plastic walker or bent-knee walker, rooted Saran wig (ponytail, braids or side part flip); vinyl head and hard plastic body; molded or painted upper lashes. $ **140 up**
1968: reissued, unmarked, **Muffie Around the World**, straight leg walker, molded eyelashes, glued on wig. 12 dolls in cellophane see-through boxes **100 up**

8in (12cm) **Muffie,** all original. *Doodlebug Dolls.*

17in (43cm) Nancy Ann Style Show, original dress. *H & J Foulke, Inc.*

OHLHAVER

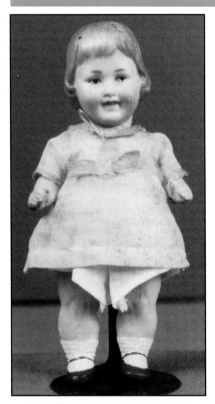

Revalo Character Baby or **Toddler:** Perfect bisque socket head, good wig, sleep eyes, hair eyelashes, painted lower eyelashes, open mouth; baby bent-limb body; dressed; all in good condition.
#22:

15-17in (38-41cm)	**$**	**550 - 600**
22in (56cm)		**800 - 850**
Toddler:		
17-19in (41-48cm)		**850 - 950**

Revalo Child Doll: Bisque socket head, good wig, sleep eyes, hair eyelashes, painted lower eyelashes, open mouth; ball-jointed composition body; dressed; all in good condition. Mold **#150** or **#10727.** (For photograph see *11th Blue Book*, page 287.)

15in (38cm)	**$**	**500 - 550**
18-20in (46-51cm)		**650 - 700**
24-25in (61-64cm)		**800 - 900**

Revalo Character Doll: Bisque head with molded hair, painted eyes, open/closed mouth; composition body; dressed; all in good condition.

Coquette 8in (20cm)	**$**	**550 - 600**
12in (31cm)		**750 - 800**
Coquette with hairbows,		
14in (36cm)		**950**

FACTS

Gebrüder Ohlhaver, doll factory, Sonneberg, Thüringia, Germany. Heads made by Gebrüder Heubach, Ernst Heubach and Porzellanfabrik Mengersgereuth. 1912-on.
Trademarks: Revalo.
Mark:

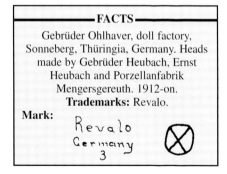

Revalo
Germany
3

TOP: 8in (20cm) character girl *Coquette.* *H & J Foulke, Inc.*

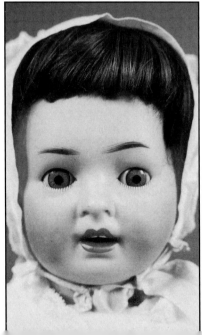

17in (43cm) 22 character toddler. *H & J Foulke, Inc.*

OLD COTTAGE DOLLS

FACTS
Old Cottage Toys, Allargate, Rustington, Littlehampton, Sussex, Great Britain. 1948.
Designers: Greta Fleischmann and her daughter Susi.
Mark: Paper label - "Old Cottage Toys" - handmade in Great Britain.

Old Cottage Doll: Composition or hard plastic head with hand painted features, wig, stuffed cloth body; original clothing; excellent condition.

8-9in (20-23cm)	**$ 135 - 165**
12-13in (31-33cm), mint-in-box	**300****

**Not enough price samples to compute a reliable average.

9in (23cm) *Old Cottage Doll. H & J Foulke, Inc.*

ORIENTAL DOLLS

Japanese Traditional Dolls:
Ichimatsu (play doll): 1868-on. Papier-mâché swivel head on shoulder plate, hips, lower legs and feet (early ones have jointed wrists and ankles); cloth midsection, cloth (floating) upper arms and legs; hair wig, dark glass eyes, pierced ears and nostrils; original clothes; all in very good condition.

Meiji Era (1868-1912):

3-5in (8-13cm)	$	**200 - 250**
12-14in (31-36cm)		**350 - 400**
18-20in (46-51cm)		**500 - 600**
Boy, 18-20in (46-51cm)		**650 - 750**
Early three-bend body (Mitsuore):		
14-16in (36-41cm)	$	**1500 up**
Early exceptional quality,		
24in (61cm)		**1600 up**
Ca. 1920s:		
13-15in (33-38cm)		**150 - 175**
17-18in (43-46cm)		**210 - 250**
Ca. 1940s, 12-14in (31-36cm)		**85 - 95**

Traditional Lady (Kyoto or Fashion Doll):

Ca. 1900, 12in (31cm)	$	**500 up**
1920s:		
10-12in (25-31cm)		**150 - 175**
16in (41cm)		**235 - 265**
1940s, 12-14in (31-36cm)		**85 - 95**

Traditional Warrior:

1880s, 16-18in (41-46cm)	$	**800 up**
1920s, 11-12in (28-31cm)		**250 up**

Royal Personages:

Ca. 1890, 10in (25cm)	$	**800 up**
1920s-1930s:		
4-6in (10-15cm)		**100 - 125**
12in (31cm)		**350 up**

Baby with bent limbs:

Ca. 1910, 11in (28cm)	$	**250 up**
Ca. 1930s, souvenir dolls,		
8-10in (20-25cm)		**65 - 85**

Oriental Bisque Dolls: Ca. 1900-on. Made by German firms such as Simon & Halbig, Armand Marseille, J.D. Kestner and others. Bisque head tinted yellow; matching ball-jointed or baby body; original or appropriate clothes; all in excellent condition. (See previous *Blue Books* for photographs of dolls not pictured here.)

B.P. #220,

16-17in (41-43cm)	$	**3200 - 3500****

Belton-type,

10in (25cm)		**1200 - 1500****

BSW #500:

11in (28cm)	$	**1100 - 1300**
14-15in (36-38cm)		**1800 - 2200**

Tête Jumeau, closed mouth,

19-20in (48-51cm)	$	**48,000 - 62,000**

JDK 243:

13-14in (33-36cm)	$	**4000 - 4500**
18-20in (46-51cm)		**5200 - 5700**

A.M. 353:

12-14in (31-36cm)	$	**1000 - 1150**
10in (25cm) cloth body		**700**

A.M. Girl: 8-9in (20-23cm) **650**

S&H 1329:

14in (36cm)	$	**1800 - 2200**
18-19in (46-48cm)		**2700 - 2800**

**Not enough price samples to compute a reliable average.

12in (30cm) early three-bend boy. *Private Collection.*

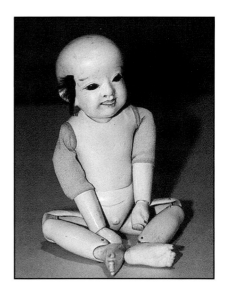

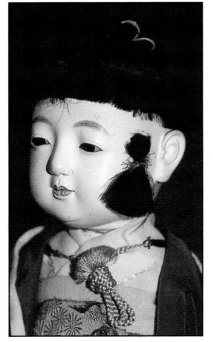

18in (46cm) traditional Japanese boy. *Private Collection.*

16-1/2in (41cm) J.D. Kestner 243 Oriental baby. *Kay & Wayne Jensen Collection.*

ORIENTAL DOLLS *continued*

S&H 1099, 1129, and 1199:
  15in (38cm) $ **2700 - 2800**
  19-20in (48-51cm)   **3200 - 3500**

S PB H, 9in (23cm) $ **650**

#164, 16-17in (41-43cm) $ **2300 - 2500**
Unmarked:
  4-1/2in (12cm) painted eyes   **175**
  6in (15cm) glass eyes   **500**
  11-12in (28-31cm) glass eyes   **850 - 950**

All-Bisque JDK Baby:
  5-1/2in (14cm) $ **1250 - 1350**
  8in (20cm)   **1650 - 1750**

All-Bisque S&H Child:
  5-1/2in (14cm) $ **650 - 750**
  7in (18cm)   **850 - 950**

#419 Papier-Mâché Man: Molded hat
  and mustache, cloth body,
  composition arms. $ **250 - 300**

7in (18cm) Simon & Halbig all-bisque Oriental. *H & J Foulke, Inc.*

12in (30cm) Oriental #419 papier-mâché man. *H & J Foulke, Inc.*

Unknown origin:
Lady with molded headband, wood jointed body, 13in (33cm) $ 650 - 750**
Character man with molded mustache, jointed body 11in (28cm) $ 1100**

Baby Butterfly: 1911-1913. Made by E.I. Horsman. Composition head and hands, cloth body; painted black hair, painted features. (For photograph see *9th Blue Book*, page 320.)
    13in (33cm) $ 300**

Ming Ming Baby: Quan-Quan Co., Los Angeles and San Francisco, Calif., U.S.A. Ca. 1930. All-composition baby, jointed at shoulders and hips; painted facial features; sometimes with black yarn hair, original costume of colorful taffeta with braid trim; feet painted black or white for shoes.
    10-12in (25-31cm) $ 175 - 200

**Not enough price samples to compute a reliable average.

10in (25cm) *Ming Ming Baby,* all original. *H & J Foulke, Inc.*

PAPIER-MÂCHÉ
(So-Called French-Type)

French-type Papier-mâché: Shoulder head with painted black pate, brush marks around face, nailed on human hair wig (often missing), set-in glass eyes, closed or open mouth with bamboo teeth, pierced nose; pink kid body with stiff arms and legs; appropriate old clothes; all in good condition, showing some wear.

12-14in (31-36cm)	$	1000 - 1100
18-20in (46-51cm)		1800 - 2000
24-26in (61-66cm)		2200 - 2500
32in (81cm)		3100
Painted eyes:		
14-16in (36-41cm)		850 - 950
6-8in (15-20cm)		375 - 475

Wood-jointed body, 6in (15cm) **750 - 800**
Shell decoration:
  4-1/2in (12cm) **500 - 600**
  8in (20cm) pair **1000 - 1200**
Poupard, molded bonnet and clothes,
  18in (46cm) **400 - 500**

━━━━ FACTS ━━━━

Heads by German firms such as Johann Müller of Sonneberg and Andreas Voit of Hildburghausen, were sold to French and other doll makers. 1835-1850.
Mark: None.

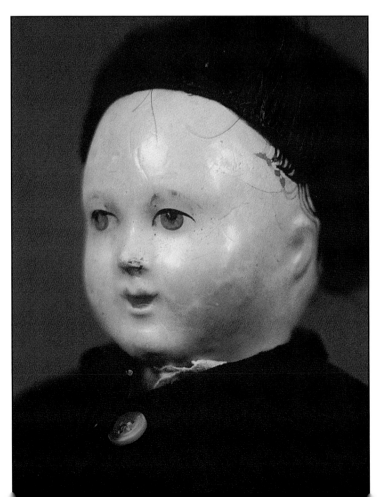

16in (41cm) French-type papier-mâché with painted eyes. *H & J Foulke, Inc.*

PAPIER-MÂCHÉ (German)

Papier-mâché Shoulder Head: Ca. 1840s to 1860s. Unretouched shoulder head, molded hair, painted eyes; some wear and crazing; cloth or kid body; original or appropriate old clothing; entire doll in fair condition.

16-18in (41-46cm)	$	900 - 1000
22-24in (56-61cm)		1100 - 1300
32in (81cm)		1900 - 2200

Glass eyes, short hair:

19in (48cm)	1650 - 1850
24in (61cm)	2400

Glass eyes, long hair,

22in (56cm)	**1700 - 2000**

Flirty eyes, long hair,

23in (58cm)	**2700 - 3000**

FACTS

Various German firms of Sonneberg such as Johann Müller, Müller & Strasburger, F.M. Schilling, Heinrich Stier, A. Wislizenus, and Cuno & Otto Dressel. 1816 - on. Papier-mâché shoulder head, cloth body, sometimes leather arms or kid body with wood limbs.

21in (53cm) papier-mâché with flirty eyes. *Nancy A. Smith Collection.*

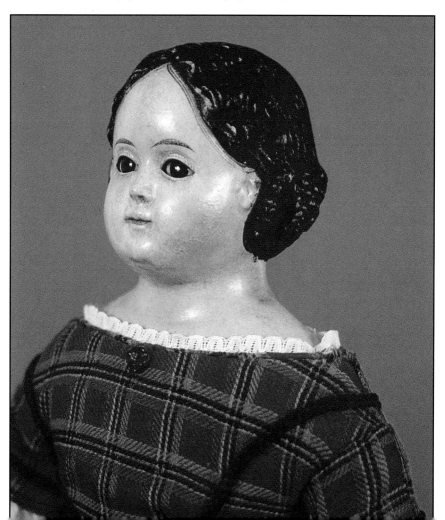

PAPIER-MÂCHÉ (German) *continued*

Molded Hair Papier-mâché: (so-called "milliners' models") 1820s-1860s. Unretouched shoulder head, various molded hairdos, eyes blue, black or brown, painted features; original kid body, wooden arms and legs; original or very old handmade clothing; entire doll in fair condition.

Long curls:
9in (23cm) $ 550
13in (33cm)   675 - 725
23in (58cm)   1400 - 1500
Covered wagon hairdo:
7in (18cm)   275 - 325
11in (28cm)   450 - 500
15in (38cm)   675 - 775

Side curls with braided bun:
9-10in (23-25cm)   750 - 850
13-15in (31-38cm)   1300 - 1500
Center part with molded bun:
7in (18cm)   525
11in (28cm)   950 - 1000
Wood-jointed body   1200 - 1350
Side curls with high beehive (Apollo knot):
11in (28cm)   950 - 1000
18in (46cm)   1900 - 2100
Coiled braids at ears, braided bun,
20in (51cm)   2000 - 2200
Braided coronet, molded comb, painted side curls, all original, very good condition,
14-1/2in (37cm) at auction   3850

Three molded hair papier-mâché dolls. *Joanna Ott Collection.*

PAPIER-MÂCHÉ (GERMAN) *continued*

Sonneberg-type Papier-mâché: Ca. 1880-1910. Shoulder head with molded and painted black or blonde hair, painted eyes, closed mouth; cloth body sometimes with leather arms; old or appropriate clothes; all in good condition, showing some wear.

Mark: Usually unmarked. Some marked:

M & S
Superior
2015

13-15in (33-38cm)	$	250 - 300*
18-19in (46-48cm)		350 - 400*
23-25in (58-64cm)		500 - 600*
Glass eyes, 13in (33cm)		475

*Allow extra for an unusual hairdo.

Papier-mâché: Ca. 1920-on. Papier-mâché head, hard stuffed body, good wig, painted features; original clothes, all in good condition.

10-12in (25-31cm)	$	90 - 110

Above: 17in (43cm) Sonneberg-type papier-mâché. *H & J Foulke, Inc.* **Left:** 12in (31cm) 1920s German papier-mâché, marked Ed.P., all original. *H & J Foulke, Inc.* **Below:** 26in (66cm) Sonneberg-type papier-mâché. *H & J Foulke, Inc.*

PARIAN-TYPE (Untinted Bisque)

Unmarked Parian: Pale or untinted shoulder head, sometimes with molded blouse, beautifully molded hairdo (may have ribbons, beads, comb or other decoration), painted eyes, closed mouth; cloth body; lovely clothes; entire doll in fine condition.
Common, plain style:

8-10in (20-25cm)	$	**135 - 185**
16in (41cm)		**300 - 350***
24in (61cm)		**475 - 525***

Very fancy hairdo and/or elaborately decorated blouse **800 - 2500**
Very fancy with glass eyes **1500 - 3250**

Pretty hairdo, simple ribbon or comb:

14in (36cm)	**425 - 475**
18-20in (46-51cm)	**650 - 750**

Simple hairdo with applied flowers,
20in (51cm) **850**

*Allow $100 for glass eyes.

```
━━━━━━━━━━━ FACTS ━━━━━━━━━━━
        Various German firms.
       Ca. 1860s through 1870s.
       Mark: Usually none,
          sometimes numbers.
```

19in (48cm) parian lady with glass eyes. *H & J Foulke, Inc.*

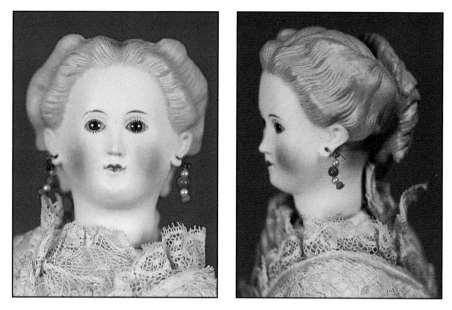

17-1/2in (44cm) parian lady with removable cluster of curls in back. *Richard Wright Antiques.* (For further information see page 302.)

16-1/2in (42cm) parian lady with molded hat. *Private Collection.*

Man, molded collar and tie,
16-17in (41-43cm) $ 750
Boy:
19in (48cm) short black hair   1800
23in (58cm) brown hair, glass eyes   3000
"Augusta Victoria,"
17in (43cm)   1200 - 1300
Molded plate, blonde curls, ribbon, glass
eyes 14in (36cm)   1300 - 1500
Alice hairdo, 21in (53cm)   750 - 800
"Countess Dagmar," 19in (48cm)   950
Molded blonde hair, blue ribbon, glass eyes,
fashion face, swivel neck,
21in (53cm)   4000
Blonde hair, blue glass eyes,
21in (53cm)   900 - 1000
"Irish Queen," Limbach 8552,
16in (41cm)   600 - 700
Brown hair, snood,
24in (61cm)   1200
Pink lustre hat or snood,
17in (43cm)   1700 - 1800

Light brown hair, removable cluster of curls.
(For photographs see page 301.)
17-1/2in (44cm)   6000 - 7000
Blonde hair, molded rose, molded gilt earrings, 16in (41cm)   1600
Decorated shoulder plate, molded yellow
straw hat, glass eyes,
18in (41cm)   4300
Light brown hair, molded black hat with
applied flowers, molded red ribbon tied
under chin, glass eyes,
17in (43cm) (hairlines)   4500

All-Parian, pink lustre boots,
5-1/2in (14cm)   185 - 200

Blonde hair pulled back into individual curls,
glass eyes, swivel neck, pierced ears, 23in
(58cm)   2900

"Dolley Madison," glass eyes, swivel neck,
20in (51cm)   1600

Pink lustre tiara, gold earrings,
12in (31cm)   900

Short blonde hair, wavy curls
combed to front, wide black
hairband,
21in (53cm)   1350

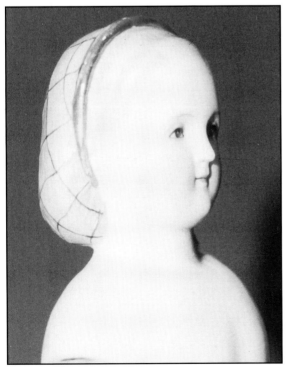

14in (36cm) parian lady with
lustre snood and boots. *Private
Collection.*

P.D.

FACTS
Probably Petit & Dumontier, Paris, France. Some heads made by Francois Gaultier. 1878-1890.

Mark:

P.2.D

P.D. Bébé: Perfect bisque head with paperweight eyes, closed mouth, pierced ears, good wig; jointed composition body (some have metal hands); appropriate clothes; all in good condition.

19-23in (48-58cm)	$	**15,000 - 20,000**
16in (41cm) hairline		**6500**

PHILADELPHIA BABY

FACTS
J.B. Sheppard & Co., Philadelphia, Pa., U.S.A. Ca. 1900. All-cloth.
Mark: None.

Philadelphia Baby: All-cloth with treated shoulder-type head, lower arms and legs; painted hair, well-molded facial features, ears; stocking body; very good condition.

18-22in (46-56cm)	$	**4000**
Mint condition		**5000**
Fair, showing wear		**2500**
Very worn		**1600 - 1800**

Rare style face (see *6th Blue Book*, page 302 for exact doll), at auction **9350**

25in (64cm) P 3 D. *Private Collection.*

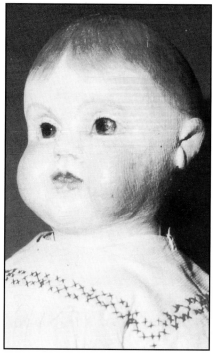

20in (51cm) Philadelphia Baby. *Doelman Collection. Courtesy of Richard W. Withington, Inc.*

PRE-GREINER (So-called)

Unmarked Pre-Greiner: Papier-mâché shoulder head; molded and painted black hair, pupil-less black glass eyes; stuffed cloth body, mostly homemade, wood, leather or cloth extremities; dressed in good old or original clothes; all in good condition.

18-22in (46-56cm)	$	**1000 - 1350**
28-32in (71-81cm)		**2000 - 2300**
Fair condition, much wear,		
20-24in (51-61cm)		**700 - 800**
Flirty eye, 30in (76cm)		**3000**

FACTS
Unknown and various. Ca. 1850. **Mark:** None.

27-1/2in (70cm) Pre-Greiner, all original. *Becky & Jay Lowe.*

RABERY & DELPHIEU

Marked R.D. Bébé: Ca. 1880s. Bisque head, lovely wig, paperweight eyes, closed mouth; jointed composition body; beautifully dressed; entire doll in good condition. Very good quality bisque:

12-14in (31-36cm)	$ **2200 - 2700**
18-19in (46-48cm)	**3000 - 3500**
24-25in (61-64cm)	**3700 - 4200**
28in (71cm)	**4500 - 5000**
13in (33cm) doll in boxed trousseau set	**6000 - 7000**
Lesser quality bisque (uneven coloring or much speckling), 16-18in (41-46cm)	**2250 - 2350**
Open mouth, 19-22in (48-56cm)	**1900 - 2200**
Two rows of teeth, 18in (46cm)	**2500**

FACTS

Rabery & Delphieu of Paris, France. 1856 (founded)-1899, then with S.F.B.J.

Mark:

On back of head: R 5/0 D

Body mark: BÉBÉ RABERY S

(Please note last two lines illegible)

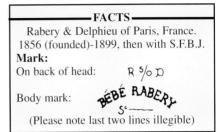

23-1/2in (60cm) R 2 D. *H & J Foulke, Inc.*

RAGGEDY ANN AND ANDY

Early Raggedy Ann or **Andy:** Volland. All-cloth with movable arms and legs; brown yarn hair, button eyes, painted features; legs or striped fabric for hose and black for shoes; original clothes; all in good condition. **Mark:** "PATENTED SEPT. 7, 1915"

16in (41cm)	**$1200 - 1300**
Wear, stains, not original clothes	**750 - 850**
Mint condition pair	**5500**
36in (91cm) much wear at auction	**2875**

Molly-'es Raggedy Ann or **Andy:** 1935-1938, manufactured by Molly-'es Doll Outfitters. Same as above, but with red hair and printed features; original clothes; all in good condition. **Mark:**
"Raggedy Ann and Raggedy Andy Dolls, Manufactured by Molly'es Doll Outfitters" (printed writing in black on front torso)

18-22in (46-56cm)$	**1000**

━━━ FACTS ━━━
Various makers. 1915 to present. All-cloth.
Creator: Johnny B. Gruelle.

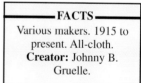

Top: 16in (41cm) *Raggedy Ann* with patent date and wooden heart. *H & J Foulke, Inc. Left:* 16in (41cm) Volland *Raggedy Andy*, all original. *H & J Foulke, Inc.*

Georgene Raggedy Ann or Andy: 1938-1963, manufactured by Georgene Novelties. Same as above, but with red hair and printed features; original clothes; all in good condition, some wear and fading acceptable.

Mark: Cloth label sewn in side seam of body.

15-18in (38-46cm)	$	225 - 275
Fair condition		125 - 150

Asleep/Awake,
13in (33cm)	700 - 800 pair

Black outlined nose,
19in (48cm)	600 - 650
Pair, mint condition with individual name labels and tags	2000 - 2200
Beloved Belindy	1400 - 1500

Knickerbocker Toy Co. Raggedy Ann or Andy: 1963 to 1982. Excellent condition.

12-15in (28-38cm)	$	40
24in (61cm)		95 - 110
36in (91cm)		150 - 200
Beloved Belindy		700
Camel with Wrinkled Knees		150 - 175

19in (48cm) Georgene *Raggedy Ann & Andy*. *Kay & Wayne Jensen Collection.*

21in (53cm) Molly-'es *Raggedy Ann & Andy. H & J Foulke, Inc.*

RALEIGH

Raleigh Doll: Composition head, molded hair or wig, sleep or painted eyes; composition or cloth body; appropriate clothes; all in good condition.

Child:

11in (28cm) wigged	$	**450 - 500**
13in (33cm) molded hair		**600 - 650**
18in (46cm) molded hair		**900 - 950**

Baby:

12in (30cm)	**400**

FACTS

Jessie McCutcheon Raleigh, Chicago, Ill., U.S.A. 1916-1920.
Designer: Jessie McCutcheon Raleigh.
Mark: None.

18in (46cm) Raleigh girl, rare large size. *H & J Foulke, Inc.*

RAVCA

Bernard Ravca Doll: Stockinette face individually needle sculpted; cloth body and limbs; original clothes; all in excellent condition.

Mark: Paper label: "Original Ravca Fabrication Française."

10in (25cm) $ 90 - 110

Ravca-type fine quality peasant man or lady

17in (43cm)   **$225 - 265 each**

Note: The dolls shown in the *9th Blue Book*, page 338, and the *7th Blue Book*, page 256 should have been captioned as Ravca-type dolls. These dolls were not made by Mr. Ravca.

Frances Diecks Ravca Doll:

36in (91cm) 1952. Queen Elizabeth II and others $ 650 - 850

12in (30cm) "Easter Sunday" 1973, black child   250

FACTS

Bernard Ravca, Paris, France. After 1939, New York, N.Y., U.S.A. 1924-on. Frances Diecks Ravca, New York. 1935-on.

10in (25cm) Ravca pair, all original. *H & J Foulke, Inc.*

RECKNAGEL

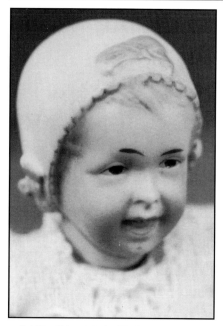

8-1/2in (21cm) R.A. 22 character baby.
H & J Foulke, Inc.

R.A. Child: Ca. 1890s-World War I. Perfect marked bisque head, jointed composition or wooden body; good wig, set or sleep eyes, open mouth; some dolls with molded painted shoes and socks; all in good condition.

1907, 1909, 1914:

8-9in (20-23cm)	$ 160 - 185
16-18in (41-46cm)	325 - 375*
24in (61cm)	500 - 550*

*Fine quality bisque only.

R.A. Character Baby: 1909-World War I. Perfect bisque head; cloth baby body or composition bent-limb baby body; painted or glass eyes; nicely dressed; all in good condition.

#121, 126, 127, 1924 Infants,

8-9in (20-23cm) long	$	235 - 285
#23 character babies		
7-8in (18-20cm)		300 - 350
#22, 28, and **44** bonnet babies,		
8-9in (20-23cm)		550 - 600
11in (28cm)		800
Character children:		
6-8in (15-20cm) composition body		300 - 350

#31 Max and **#32 Moritz,**
molded hair, painted features,

8in (20cm)	$ 650 - 700**

#45 and **46,** Googlies,

7in (18cm)	450 - 500
#43, molded hat, 7in (18cm)	500 - 550

**Not enough price samples to compute a reliable average.

── FACTS ──

Th. Recknagel, porcelain factory, Alexandrienthal, Thüringia, Germany. 1886-on.

Mark:

1907
R/A DEP
I 9/0

7in (18cm) R.A. 43 googly with molded hat. *H & J Foulke, Inc.*

ROHMER FASHION

Rohmer Poupée: China or bisque swivel or shoulder head, jointed kid body, bisque or china arms, kid or china legs; lovely wig, set glass eyes, closed mouth, some ears pierced; fine costuming; entire doll in good condition.

16-18in (41-46cm)   **$4500 - 5500***

*Allow extra for original clothes.

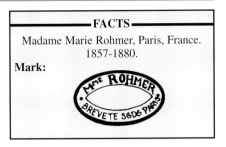

FACTS

Madame Marie Rohmer, Paris, France.
1857-1880.

Mark:

18in (46cm) Rohmer *poupée* with swivel neck. *Private Collection.*

ROLLINSON DOLL

Marked Rollinson Doll: All molded cloth with painted head and limbs; painted hair or human hair wig, painted features (sometimes teeth also); dressed; all in good condition.

Chase-type with molded hair,
  18-22in (46-51cm)   **$**   **800 - 1200**
Child with wig. (For photograph see *8th Blue Book*, page 346.)
  26in (66cm)   **1500 - 2000**
Toddler with wig. (For photograph see *10th Blue Book*, page 311.)
  16in (41cm)   **800 - 1200**

━━━ FACTS ━━━

Utley Doll Co., Holyoke, Mass., U.S.A. 1916-on.
Designer: Gertrude F. Rollinson.
Mark: Stamp in shape of a diamond with a doll in center, around border: "Rollinson Doll Holyoke, Mass."

Rollinson with unusual pierced nose. *Nancy A. Smith Collection.*

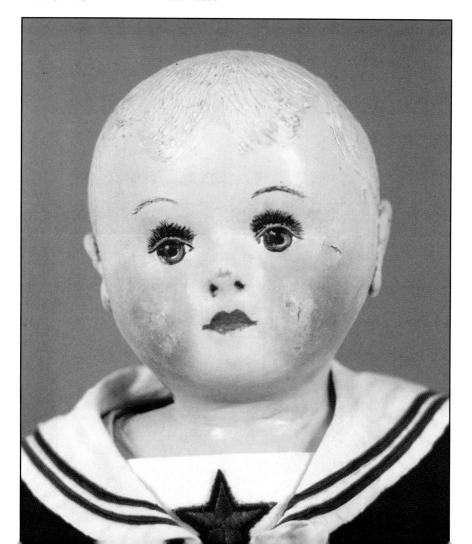

S.F.B.J.

Child Doll: 1899-on. Perfect bisque head, good French wig, set or sleep eyes, open mouth, pierced ears; jointed composition body; nicely dressed; all in good condition.

Jumeau-type, paperweight eyes (no mold number), 1899-1910:

14-16in (36-41cm)	$	1100- 1250
21-23in (53-58cm)		1700 - 1900
25-27in (64-69cm)		2200 - 2500

#301:

12-14in (31-36cm)	$	800 - 900
20-23in (51-58cm)		1150 - 1250
28-30in (71-76cm)		1700 - 1900
37in (94cm)		3000
16in (41cm) white face clown, all original		700
22in (56cm), lady body		1200 - 1400

#60, end of World War I on:

12-14in (31-36cm)	$	650 - 700
19-21in (48-53cm)		850 - 900
28in (71cm)		1300

Bleuette #301. (For photograph see *8th Blue Book*, page 347.):

10-1/2–11in (27-29cm)	$	825 - 925

Walking, kissing and flirting:

22in (56cm)	1700 - 1800
All original	2400

Papier-mâché head #60, fully-jointed body:

17in (43cm)	325 - 375
22in (56cm)	500
11in (28cm) elaborate silk and lace outfit, original box, mint	1000

----FACTS----

Société Française de Fabrication de Bébés & Jouets, Paris, France. 1899-on.

Mark:

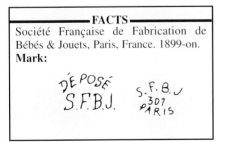

30in (76cm) S.F.B.J. 301 child. *H & J Foulke, Inc.*

10in (25cm) S.F.B.J. 248 character child. *Doelman Collection. Courtesy of Richard W. Withington, Inc.* (For further information see page 315.)

S.F.B.J. *continued*

Character Dolls: 1910-on. Perfect bisque head, wig, molded, sometimes flocked hair on mold numbers 237, 266, 227 and 235, sleep eyes, composition body; nicely dressed; all in good condition. (See previous *Blue Books* for illustrations of mold numbers not shown here.)

Mark:

#226,	20in (51cm)	$	2100
#227,	17in (43cm)		1850
#239,	16in (41cm)		2000 - 2200
#230 (sometimes Jumeau):			
	12-14in (30-36cm)		1200 - 1400
	19-22in (48-56cm)		1900 - 2100
#233,	16in (41cm)		3000
#234,	18in (46cm) toddler		3200
#235,	16in (41cm)		1850

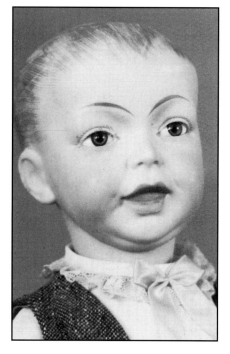

20in (51cm) S.F.B.J. 226 character boy. *Ruth Noden Collection.*

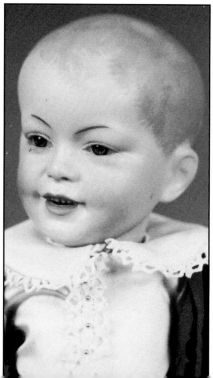

17in (43cm) S.F.B.J. 227 character boy. *H & J Foulke, Inc.*

S.F.B.J. *continued*

#236 Baby:
15-17in (38-43cm)	$ **1100 - 1200**
20-22in (51-56cm)	**1500 - 1700**
25in (64cm)	**2000**

Toddler:
15-16in (38-41cm)	**1600 - 1800**
27-28in (69-71cm)	**2200 - 2500**
#237, 15-16in (38-41cm)	**2000 - 2200**

#238 Child,
15-16in (38-41cm)	**2200 - 2400**
Lady, 18-19in (46-48cm)	**2400 - 2600**

#239, 13in (33cm)
all original	**5500 - 6500**

#242 Nursing baby,
13-14in (33-35cm)	**3250****

#245 Googly. (See page 186.)

#247 Baby,
20-22in (51-56cm)	**2300 - 2500**

Toddler:
13-15in (33-38cm)	$ **2300 - 2400**
25-27in (64-69cm)	**3200 - 3700**

#248 (For photograph see page 313.)
10-12in (25-30cm)	**7500 - 8500**

#250, 13-15in (33-38cm) **1500 - 1700****
In original trousseau box,
12in (31cm)	**3300**

#251 Toddler:
14-15in (36-38cm)	**1600 - 1700**
20in (51cm)	**2000**
27-28in (69-71cm)	**2600 - 2800**

#252 Baby, 10in (25cm) **3000**
Toddler:
10in (25cm)	**3600**
13in (33cm)	**4800**
20in (51cm)	**6500**

** Not enough price samples to compute a reliable range.

11-1/2in (29cm) S.F.B.J. 245 googly. *Kay & Wayne Jensen Collection.*

SASHA

Sasha: All-vinyl of exceptionally high quality, long synthetic hair, painted features, wistful, appealing expression; original clothing, tiny circular wrist tag; excellent condition.

16in (41cm)	$	**210 - 225**
Boxed		**250**
In cylinder package		**350**
Gregor (boy)		**210 - 225**
Boxed		**250**
Cora (black girl)		**275 - 300**
Caleb (black boy)		**275 - 300**
Black baby		**200 - 225**
White baby		**165 - 185**
Sexed baby, pre 1979		**250 - 275**

Limited Edition Dolls:

1980 Velvet Dress	$	**350 - 375**
1982 Pintucks Dress		**350 - 375**
1983 Kiltie		**350 - 375**
1985 Prince Gregor		**350 - 375**

"Serie Sasha":

Götz model, 1965 - 69	**800 - 1000**
Boxed	**1000 - 1200**
Early model 1950s	**5000 - 6000**
Fair condition and naked	**2500 - 2850**
1995 Sasha and Gregor, issue price	**300**

FACTS

Trendon Toys, Ltd., Reddish, Stockport, England. 1965-1986. **Designer:** Sasha Morgenthaler.

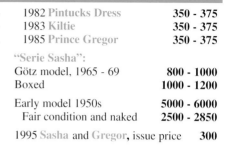

16in (41cm) *Serie Sasha* by Götz, all original. *H & J Foulke, Inc.*

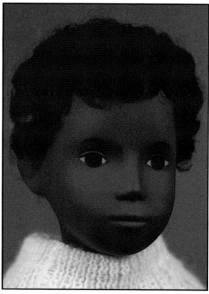

16in (41cm) *Caleb,* all original. *H & J Foulke, Inc.*

BRUNO SCHMIDT

FACTS

Bruno Schmidt, doll factory, Waltershausen, Thüringia, Germany. Heads by Bähr & Pröschild, Ohrdruf, Thüringia, Germany. 1898-on.

Mark:

Marked B. S. W. Child Doll: Ca. 1898-on. Bisque head, good wig, sleep eyes, open mouth; jointed composition child body; dressed; all in good condition.

18-20in (46-51cm)	$	550 - 650
24-26in (61-66cm)		800 - 900
22in (56cm) flirty eyes		825 - 850

26in (67cm) B.S.W. child. *H & J Foulke, Inc.*

318

BRUNO SCHMIDT *continued*

Marked B. S. W. Character Dolls: Bisque socket head, glass eyes; jointed composition body; dressed; all in good condition.

#2048, 2094, 2096 (so-called "Tommy Tucker"), molded hair, open mouth. (For photograph see *10th Blue Book*, page 373.)

13-14in (33-36cm)	$	**1100 - 1200**
19-21in (48-53cm)		**1400 - 1500**
25-26in (64-66cm)		**1900 - 2000**

#2048 (closed mouth),
16-18in (41-46cm)	$	**2500****

#2042, 20in (51cm) at auction   **2800**

#2072:
23in (58cm) toddler	**$4500 - 5000****
17in (43cm)	**3000 - 3500****

(For photograph see *7th Blue Book*, page 335.)

#2033 (so-called "Wendy") (537). (For photograph see *9th Blue Book*, page 347.)
12-13in (30-33cm)	$	**12,000 - 13,000**
20in (51cm)		**25,000**

#2025 (529) closed mouth, wigged,
22in (56cm)	$	**5000 - 6000****

#2026 (538), 22in (56cm)   **$4500 - 5000****

#2097, character baby open mouth. (For photograph see *9th Blue Book*, page 347.)
13-14in (33-36cm)	$	**500 - 550**
18in (46cm)		**750 - 850**
15in (38cm) toddler		
		1050 - 1150

#425 all-bisque baby,
5-1/2–6in (13-15cm)	**250 - 300**

** Not enough price samples to compute a reliable range.

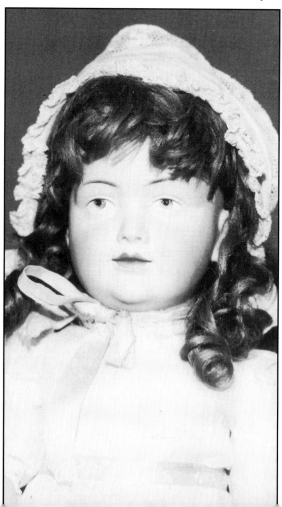

21in (53cm) B.S.W. 2025/529 character child. *Kay & Wayne Jensen Collection.*

FRANZ SCHMIDT

Marked F.S. & Co. Character Baby: Ca. 1910. Perfect bisque character head, good wig, sleep eyes, open mouth, may have open nostrils; jointed bent-limb composition body; suitably dressed; all in good condition.

#1271, 1272, 1295, 1296, 1297, 1310: Baby. (See also photograph on page 320.)

12-14in (31-36cm)	$	**500 - 600**
20-21in (51-53cm)		**800 - 850**
26-27in (66-69cm)		**1400 - 1600**
Toddler:		
7in (18cm), 5-piece body		**650 - 675**
10in (25cm), 5-piece body		**700 - 800**
13-15in (33-38cm)		**800 - 1000**
19-21in (48-53cm)		**1300 - 1500**

#1286, molded hair with blue ribbon, glass eyes, open smiling mouth,

16in (41cm) toddler	$	**4000****

**Not enough price samples to compute a reliable averge.

--- **FACTS** ---

Franz Schmidt & Co., doll factory, Georgenthal near Waltershausen, Thüringia, Germany. Heads by Simon & Halbig, Gräfenhain, Thüringia, Germany. 1890-on.

15in (38cm) F.S. & Co. 1271 character baby. *H & J Foulke, Inc.*

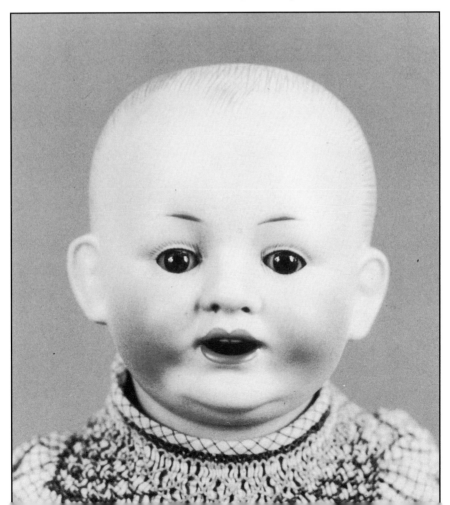

FRANZ SCHMIDT *continued*

#1263 Character Child, closed pouty mouth, painted eyes, wig,
   21in (53cm) at auction   **$**   **19,500**

#1267 Character, open/closed mouth, painted eyes
   24in (61cm) at auction   **$**   **2800**

Mark:

Marked S & C Child Doll: Ca. 1890-on. Perfect bisque socket head, good wig, sleep eyes, open mouth; jointed composition child body; dressed; all in good condition. Some are Mold **#293**.

6in (15cm)	**$** **275 - 325**
16-18in (41-46cm)	**500 - 550**
22-24in (56-61cm)	**650 - 750**
29-30in (74-76cm)	**1050 - 1200**
42in (107cm)	**3200 - 3600**

Shoulder head, kid body,
   26in (66cm)   **650**

Mark:

$$S \& C$$
$$SIMON \& HALBIG$$
$$28$$

20in (51cm) F.S. & Co. 1295 character baby. *H & J Foulke, Inc.* (For further information see page 319.)

SCHMITT

Marked Schmitt Bébé: Ca. 1879. Perfect bisque socket head with skin or good wig, large paperweight eyes, closed mouth, pierced ears; Schmitt-jointed composition body; appropriate clothes; all in good condition.

Long face: (For photograph see *11th Blue Book*, page 321.)

16-18in (41-46cm) $	12,000 - 14,000
23-25in (58-64cm)	22,000 - 23,000

Short face (parted lips):

16-18in (41-46cm)	16,500 - 17,500
22in (56cm)	20,000 - 22,000

Oval/round face: (For photograph see *11th Blue Book*, page 321.)

11-13in (28-33cm)	**9000 - 10,000***
15-17in (38-43cm)	**12,000 - 14,000***

Cup and saucer neck,
13-14in (33-36cm)	**15,000 up****

Open/closed mouth, two rows of teeth,
24in (61cm)	**25,000****

Papier-mâché head,
16in (41cm) $	**2600**

* Allow one-third less for dolls that do not have strongly molded faces.
**Not enough price samples to compute a reliable average.

FACTS
Schmitt & Fils, Paris, France. 1854-1891.
Mark: On both head and body:

18in (46cm) Schmitt "2" with short face. *Kay & Wayne Jensen Collection.*

SCHOENAU & HOFFMEISTER

Child Doll: 1901-on. Perfect bisque head; original or good wig, sleep eyes, open mouth; ball-jointed body; original or good clothes; all in nice condition. #1906, 1909, 5700, 5800.

14-16in (36-41cm)	$	350 - 400
21-23in (53-58cm)		550 - 600
28-30in (71-76cm)		850 - 950
33in (84cm)		1200 - 1300
39in (99cm)		2400 - 2500

#4000, 4600, 5000, 5500:

15-17in (38-43cm)	$	450 - 500
22in (56cm)		600 - 650

#Künstlerkopf:

24-26in (61-66cm)	$	850 - 950

FACTS

Schoenau & Hoffmeister, Porzellanfabrik Burggrub, Burggrub, Bavaria, Germany, porcelain factory, 1901-on. Arthur Schoenau also owned a doll factory. 1884-on.
Trademarks: Hanna, Burggrub Baby, Bébé Carmencita, Viola, Kunstlerkopf, Das Lachende Baby.
Mark:

22in (56cm) 5500 child. *H & J Foulke, Inc.*

Character Baby: 1910-on. Perfect bisque socket head, good wig, sleep eyes, open mouth; composition bent-limb baby body; all in good condition. #169, 769, "Burggrub Baby" or "Porzellanfabrik Burggrub." (For photograph see *8th Blue Book*, page 355.)

13-15in (33-38cm)	$	375 - 475
18-20in (46-51cm)		550 - 650
23-24in (58-61cm)		750 - 800
28in (71cm)		1000 - 1100

Princess Elizabeth, 1929. Chubby 5-piece body. (For photograph see *11th Blue Book*, page 323.)

17in (43cm)	$	1900 - 2100
20-23in (51-58cm)		2200 - 2500

Pouty Baby: Ca. 1925. Perfect bisque solid dome head with painted hair, tiny sleep eyes, closed pouty mouth; cloth body with composition arms and legs; dressed; all in good condition. (For photograph see *8th Blue Book*, page 355.)

11-12in (28-31cm)	$	750 - 800**

Hanna: (For photograph see *11th Blue Book*, page 323.)
Baby:

14-16in (36-41cm)	$	700 - 750
20-22in (51-56cm)		900 - 1100
26in (66cm)		1500
Toddler, 14 16in (36-41cm)		900 - 1100
Brown, 7-1/2in (19cm) toddler		350 - 400

OX: 15in (38cm) toddler $ 1200

Das Lachende Baby, 1930. (For photograph see *8th Blue Book*, page 355.)

23-24in (58-61cm)	$2200 - 2500**

**Not enough price samples to compute a reliable range.

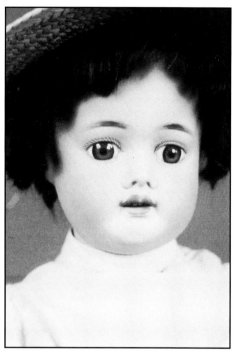

18-1/2in (47cm) 5000 child. *H & J Foulke, Inc.*

15in (38cm) 4000 child. *H & J Foulke, Inc.*

SCHOENHUT

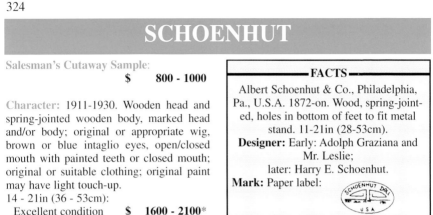

Salesman's Cutaway Sample:
$ 800 - 1000

Character: 1911-1930. Wooden head and spring-jointed wooden body, marked head and/or body; original or appropriate wig, brown or blue intaglio eyes, open/closed mouth with painted teeth or closed mouth; original or suitable clothing; original paint may have light touch-up.

14 - 21in (36 - 53cm):
 Excellent condition $ 1600 - 2100*
 Good, some wear 900 - 1400*

*Allow extra for rare faces.

---FACTS---

Albert Schoenhut & Co., Philadelphia, Pa., U.S.A. 1872-on. Wood, spring-jointed, holes in bottom of feet to fit metal stand. 11-21in (28-53cm).
Designer: Early: Adolph Graziana and Mr. Leslie;
later: Harry E. Schoenhut.
Mark: Paper label:

Incised: SCHOENHUT DOLL
PAT. JAN. 17, '11, U.S.A.
& FOREIGN COUNTRIES

16in (41cm) 301 pouty girl. *H & J Foulke, Inc.*

SCHOENHUT *continued*

Character with carved hair: Ca. 1911-1930. Wooden head with carved hair, comb marks, possibly a ribbon or bow, intaglio eyes, mouth usually closed; spring-jointed wooden body; original or suitable clothes; original paint may have light touch-up. (See photograph in *11th Blue Book*, page 12.)

14-21in (36-53cm):

Excellent condition	$	**2500 - 2800**
Good, some wear		**1800 - 2200**
Early style		**3500 - 4000**
20in (51cm) man		**2200**
Tootsie Wootsie,		
15in (38cm)		**3000****
Snickelfritz, 15in (38cm), wear		**2500****
Carved hat, restored		**2500**

** Not enough price samples to compute a reliable range.

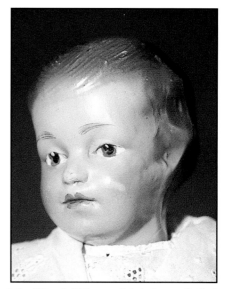

14in (36cm) 205 carved hair boy. *H & J Foulke, Inc.*

15in (38cm) 312 pouty girl, all original. *H & J Foulke, Inc.*

15in (38cm) 101 carved hair girl. *H & J Foulke, Inc.*

SCHOENHUT *continued*

Baby Face: Ca. 1913-1930. Wooden head and fully-jointed toddler or bent-limb baby body, marked head and/or body; painted hair or mohair wig, painted eyes, open or closed mouth; suitably dressed; original paint; all in good condition, with some wear. (For photograph see *10th Blue Book*, page 379.)

Mark:

Baby:

12in (31cm)	$	550 - 600
15-16in (38-41cm)		700 - 800

Toddler:

11in (28cm)	$	800 - 900
14in (36cm)		800 - 850*
16-17in (41-43cm)		850 - 950*

*Allow more for mint condition.

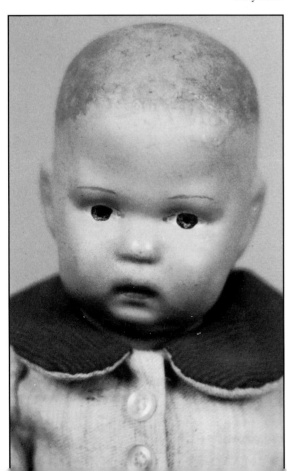

Dolly Face: Ca. 1915-1930. Wooden head and spring-jointed wooden body; original or appropriate mohair wig, decal eyes, open/closed mouth with painted teeth; original paint; original or suitable clothes.

14-21in (36-53cm):

Excellent condition	$	800 - 900
Good condition, some wear		600 - 700

Walker: Ca. 1919-1930. All-wood with "baby face," mohair wig, painted eyes; curved arms, straight legs with "walker" joint at hip; original or appropriate clothes; all in good condition. Original paint. No holes in bottom of feet. (For photograph see *9th Blue Book*, page 355.)

13in (33cm)	$	800 - 900
17in (43cm), excellent with original shoes		1250

Sleep Eyes: Ca. 1920-1930. Used with "baby face" or "dolly face" heads. Mouths on this type were open with teeth or barely open with carved teeth. Original paint. (For photograph see *9th Blue Book*, page 354.)

14-21in (36-53cm):

Excellent condition	$	1200 - 1500
Good condition		800 - 900

All-Composition: Ca. 1924. Jointed at neck, shoulders and hips, right arm bent, molded blonde curly hair, painted eyes, tiny closed mouth; original or appropriate clothing; in good condition. (See photograph in *8th Blue Book*, page 359.)

Paper label on back:

13in (33cm)	$	500 - 600**

**Not enough price samples to compute a reliable range.

14in (36cm) toddler. *H & J Foulke, Inc.*

SCHUETZMEISTER & QUENDT

S & Q Child Doll: Ca. 1900. Perfect bisque head with mohair wig, sleep eyes, open mouth with teeth; jointed composition body; nicely dressed; all in good condition. (For photograph see *9th Blue Book,* page 356.)

Mark: S & Q
                1 0 1
                D o p
                6

#101 Jeanette:

16-18in (41-46cm)	$	375 - 450
24-25in (61-64cm)		550 - 650

S & Q Character Baby: Ca. 1910. Perfect bisque head with mohair wig, sleep eyes, open mouth with tongue and teeth; composition baby body; nicely dressed; all in good condition.

Mark: 301
            (Ⓢ)
            Germany

#201, 301:

13-15in (33-38cm)	$	425 - 475
18-20in (46-51cm)		550 - 650
23-24in (58-61cm)		750 - 850

FACTS

Schuetzmeister & Quendt, porcelain factory, Boilstadt, Thüringia, Germany, made heads for Welsch, Kämmer & Reinhardt, and Wolf & Co. 1889-on. **Distributor:** John Bing Co., New York, U.S.A.

21in (53cm) S & Q 201 character baby. *H & J Foulke, Inc.*

SHIRLEY TEMPLE

FACTS

Ideal Novelty Toy Corp., New York, N.Y., U.S.A. 1934 to present.
Designer: Bernard Lipfert.

All-Composition Child: 1934 through late 1930s. Marked head and body, jointed composition body; all original including wig and clothes; entire doll in very good condition. Sizes 11-27in (28-69cm).

Mark: On body:

SHIRLEY TEMPLE
13

On head:

13
SHIRLEY TEMPLE

On cloth label:

Genuine SHIRLEY TEMPLE DOLL REGISTERED U.S. PAT OFF IDEAL NOVELTY & TOY CO	MADE IN USA

11in (28cm)	$ 850 - 950*
13in (33cm)	850 - 900*
15-16in (38-41cm)	850 - 900*
18in (46cm)	1000*
20-22in (51-56cm)	1200*
25in (64cm)	1400*
27in (69cm)	1800 - 2000*
Button	135
Dress, tagged	150 up
Trunk	175 - 200
Carriage	600 - 650

*Allow 50-100% more for mint-in-box doll. Also allow extra for a doll with unusual outfit, such as *Texas Ranger, Little Colonel,* and *Captain January.*

Baby Shirley. (For photograph see *11th Blue Book*, page 328.)
16-18in (41-46cm)
$1000 - 1200**

Hawaiian Shirley,
18in (46cm)   900 - 1000****

** Not enough price samples to compute a reliable range.

11in (28cm) **Shirley Temple**, all original. *H & J Foulke, Inc.*

SHIRLEY TEMPLE *continued*

Vinyl and Plastic: 1957.
Mark: "Ideal Doll ST—12"
(number denotes size)

Excellent condition, original clothes:

12in (31cm)	$	**175 - 200**
15in (38cm)		**275 - 300**
17in (43cm)		**350 - 375**
19in (48cm)		**400 - 425**
36in (91cm)		**1400 - 1500**
Script name pin		**25 - 30**
Name purse		**20 - 25**

Vinyl and Plastic, 1973:

16in (41cm) size only	$	**100 - 110**
Boxed		**135 - 150**
Boxed dress		**35**

Other Shirley Temples:
Made in Japan composition,
7-1/2in (19cm) $ **275 - 325**
Reliable (Canada) composition, all original and boxed,
18-22in (46-56cm) **1200**

18in (46cm) *Shirley Temple*, all original. *H & J Foulke, Inc.*

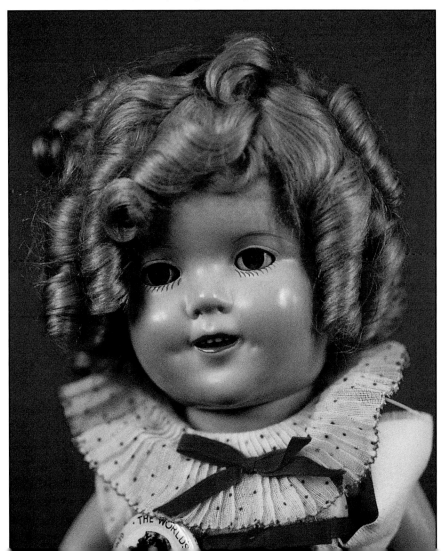

SIMON & HALBIG

Shoulder head with molded hair: Ca. 1870s. Perfect bisque shoulder head, painted or glass eyes, closed mouth, molded hair; cloth body, bisque lower arms; appropriately dressed; all in good condition.

Mark:

$$S \; 7 \; H$$

on front shoulder plate

18-20in (46-51cm)	$	1500 - 2000
9in (23cm) with painted eyes and swivel neck		1250
6in (15cm) shoulder head only		650

Fashion Doll (Poupée): Ca. 1870s. Perfect bisque socket head on bisque shoulder plate, glass eyes, closed mouth, good mohair wig; gusseted kid lady body; appropriately dressed; all in good condition. No marks.

15-16in (38-41cm)	$	3000 - 3200
Twill over wood body:		
9-10in (23-25cm)		4000 - 4500
15-16in (38-41cm)		5800 - 6000

───── FACTS ─────

Simon & Halbig, porcelain factory, Gräfenhain, Thüringia, Germany, purchased by Kämmer & Reinhardt in 1920. 1869-on. Bisque head, kid (sometimes cloth) or composition body.

Mark:

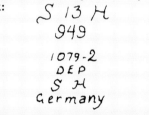

$$S \; 13 \; H$$
$$949$$
$$1079-2$$
$$DEP$$
$$S \; H$$
$$Germany$$

18in (46cm) S 7 H shoulder head. *Courtesy of Richard W. Withington, Inc.*

15in (38cm) S & H fashion lady (*poupée*). *H & J Foulke, Inc.*

SIMON & HALBIG *continued*

Child doll with closed mouth: Ca. 1879. Perfect bisque socket head on ball-jointed wood and composition body; good wig, glass set or sleep eyes, closed mouth, pierced ears, dressed; all in good condition. (See *Simon & Halbig Dolls, The Artful Aspect* for photographs of mold numbers not shown here.)

#719, 19-21in (48-53cm)	$ 3000 - 3500
#749, 20-22in (51-56cm)	3500**
#905, 908, 14-17in (36-43cm)	2500 - 3000
#929, 18-21in (46-53cm)	3500 - 4500**
#939:	
14-15in (36-38cm)	2500 - 2700
19-22in (48-56cm)	3100 - 3600
27in (69cm)	4700
#949:	
15-16in (38-41cm)	1900 - 2300
22-23in (56-58cm)	2700 - 2900
28in (71cm)	3700
#979, 15-16in (38-41cm)	3000**
#919, 17in (43cm) at auction	6750

** Not enough price samples to compute a reliable range.

All-Bisque Child: 1880-on. All-bisque child with swivel neck, pegged shoulders and hips; appropriate mohair wig, glass eyes, open or closed mouth; molded stockings and shoes.

#886 and 890:

Over-the-knee black or blue stockings:

5-1/2–6in (14-15cm)	$ 700 - 800*
7-7-1/2 (18-19cm)	900 - 1000*
8-1/2in (22cm)	1400 - 1600*

Early model with 5-strap bootines, closed mouth:

7in (18cm)	1600 - 1800*
9in (23cm)	2200 - 2400*

Open mouth with square cut teeth:

6in (15cm)	1200 - 1300*
8in (20cm)	1600 - 1800*

*Allow extra for original clothes.

Kid or **Cloth Body:**

#720, 740, 940, 950:

9-10in (23-25cm)	$ 550 - 650
16-18in (41-46cm)	1450 - 1650
22in (56cm)	1800 - 2000
#949, 18-21in (46-53cm)	$ 1800 - 2200
#920, shoulder head only,	
4in (10cm)	1000

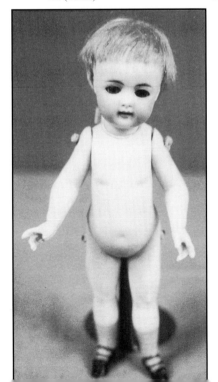

9in (23cm) S & H all-bisque with square cut teeth. *H & J Foulke, Inc.*

14in (35cm) S & H 1170 shoulder head.
H & J Foulke, Inc.

18in (46cm) S & H 1009,
French body. *H & J Foulke,
Inc.*

22in (56cm) S & H 570.
H & J Foulke, Inc.

SIMON & HALBIG *continued*

Child doll with open mouth and composition body: Ca. 1889 to 1930s. Perfect bisque head, good wig, sleep or paperweight eyes, open mouth, pierced ears; original ball-jointed composition body; very pretty clothes; all in nice condition. (See *Simon & Halbig Dolls, The Artful Aspect* for photographs of mold numbers not shown here.)

#719, 739, 749, 759, 769, 939, 949, 979:

12-14in (31-36cm)	$ 1150 - 1450*
19-22in (48-56cm)	2000 - 2300*
29-30in (74-76cm)	2800 - 3000*

*Allow $200-300 extra for square cut teeth.

#939, 40in (102cm)	$	4000 - 4400
#905, 908, 12-14in (31-36cm)		1500 - 1800

#1009:

15-16in (38-41cm)	$ 900 - 1000
19-21in (48-53cm)	1200 - 1500
24in (61cm)	1800

#1039:

16-18in (41-46cm)	$750 - 850*
23-25in (58-64cm)	
	1050 - 1250*

*Allow extra for flirty eyes.

#1039, key-wind walking body,
16-17in (41-43cm) **$1700 - 1800**

#1039, walking, kissing,
20-22in (51-56cm) **$1050 - 1250**

#1078, 1079:

10-12in (25-31cm)	$	500 - 600
14-15in (36-38cm)		650 - 675
17-19in (43-48cm)		700 - 750
22-24in (56-61cm)		850 - 950
28-30in (71-76cm)		1200 - 1400
34-35in (86-89cm)		1800 - 2100
42in (107cm)		3800 - 4200

#1248, 1249, Santa:

13-15in (33-38cm)	$	900 - 1000
21-24in (53-61cm)		1300 - 1500
26-28in (66-71cm)		1700 - 1900
32in (81cm)		2200 - 2300
38in (96cm)		3200

#540, 550, 570, Baby Blanche.

22-24in (56-61cm)	$	750 - 850
#600, 14in (36cm)		950 - 1100

15in (38cm) S & H 905, papier-mâché shoulder plate, kid fashion body. *H & J Foulke, Inc.*

SIMON & HALBIG *continued*

7in (18cm) S & H 1079, all original. *H & J Foulke, Inc.*

Child doll with open mouth and kid body:
Ca. 1889 to 1930s. Perfect bisque swivel head on shoulder plate or shoulder head with stationary neck, sleep eyes, open mouth, pierced ears; kid body, bisque arms, cloth lower legs; well costumed; all in good condition.

#1010, 1040, 1080, 1260:

9-1/2in (24cm) cloth body	$	325
14-16in (36-41cm)		500 - 600
21-23in (53-58cm)		700 - 800
#1009, 17-19in (43-48cm)	$	950 - 1050
#1250:		
14-16in (36-41cm)	$	550 - 650
22-24in (56-61cm)		800 - 900
29in (74cm)		1000 - 1100
#949, 19-21in (48-53cm)	$	1400 - 1500
#969, 20in (51cm) at auction	$	2700

Tiny Child Doll: Ca. 1889 to 1930s. Usually mold number 1079 or 1078. Perfect bisque head, nice wig, sleep eyes, open mouth; composition body with molded shoes and socks; appropriate clothes; all in good condition.

7-8in (18-20cm)	$	425 - 475
10in (25cm) walker,		
5-piece body		600 - 625
Fully-jointed,		
8-10in (20-25cm)		500 - 550

So-called "Little Women" type: Ca. 1900. Mold number 1160. Shoulder head with fancy mohair wig, glass set eyes, closed mouth; cloth body with bisque limbs, molded boots; dressed; all in good condition. (For photograph see *9th Blue Book*, page 365.)

5-1/2–7in (14-18cm)	$	350 - 400
10-11in (25-28cm)		425 - 475

SIMON & HALBIG *continued*

Character Child: Ca. 1909. Perfect bisque socket head with wig or molded hair, painted or glass eyes, open or closed mouth, character face, jointed composition body; dressed; all in good condition. (See *Simon & Halbig Dolls, The Artful Aspect* for photographs of mold numbers not shown here.)

#120, 28-30in (71-76cm)	$3000 - 4000**
#150:	
14in (36cm)	$ 12,000**
20in (51cm)	23,000**
25in (63cm)	42,000**
#151:	
14-15in (36-38cm)	$ 4500 - 5000
18in (46cm)	7000 - 8000
24in (61cm)	11,000
#153, 17in (43cm)	$ 40,000**
#1279:	
14-17in (36-43cm)	$ 2000 - 2400
19-21in (48-53cm)	2700 - 3200
27in (69cm)	5500 - 6000
#1299, 14-17in (36-43cm)	$ 1200 - 1600
#1339:	
18in (46cm)	$1000 - 1100**
28-32in (71-81cm)	1900 - 2100**
#1388, 23in (58cm)	$ 30,000**
#1398, 23in (58cm)	$ 20,000**
IV, #1448,	
13-14in (33-36cm)	$ 15,000**
17-18in (43-46cm)	$ 24,000**

**Not enough price samples to compute a reliable range.

Character Baby: Ca. 1909 to 1930s. Perfect bisque head, molded hair or wig, sleep or painted eyes, open or open/closed mouth; composition bent-limb baby or toddler body; nicely dressed; all in good condition. (See *Simon & Halbig Dolls, The Artful Aspect* for photographs of mold numbers not shown here.)

#1294:	
Baby, 17-19in (43-48cm)	$ 750 - 850
23-25in (58-64cm)	1100 - 1300
Toddler, 20in (51cm)	1500 - 1600
28in (71cm) with clockwork eyes	2500**
#1428:	
Baby:	
13-14in (33-36cm)	$ 1500 - 2000
21in (53cm)	3000
Toddler: (See photograph on page 336.)	
15-18in (38-46cm)	2400 - 2600
24in (61cm)	3750
#1488:	
Baby, 20in (51cm)	$ 5000
Toddler, 16-18in (41-46cm)	4500

#1489 Erika. (For photograph see *10th Blue Book*, page 352.)

Baby, 21-22in (53-56cm)	$3300 - 3700**

#1498,

Toddler, 17in (43cm)	$3800 - 4200**

#172 Baby. (For photograph see *10th Blue Book*, page 353.)

	$ 3500

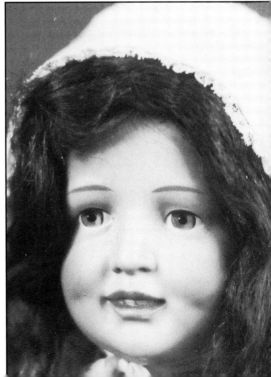

22in (56cm) S & H 151 character.
Mary Barnes Kelley Collection.

SIMON & HALBIG *continued*

24-1/2in (62cm) 1428 toddler. *Carol Green Collection.* (For further information see page 335.)

Lady doll: Ca. 1910. Perfect bisque socket head, good wig, sleep eyes, pierced ears; lady body, molded bust, slim arms and legs; dressed; all in good condition.

#1159 (may have an H. Handwerck body):

12in (31cm)	$	1100 - 1200
16-18in (41-46cm)		1800 - 2000
24in (61cm)		2500 - 2700
28in (71cm)		3000 - 3500

#1468, 1469:

13-15in (33-38cm)

naked	$	2000 - 2300
Original clothes		3000 - 4200

#1303 Lady,

20in (51cm) **$15,000 - 17,000****

#152:

18in (46cm)	$	**15,000 up****
25in (64cm)		**25,000****

#1308 Man,

13in (33cm), at auction **$ 13,000**

#1307, 21in (53cm) **$ 20,000****

#1303 Indian,

21in (53cm) **$ 17,000****

#1305 Polichinelle Candy

Container **26,000****

**Not enough price samples to compute a reliable range.

12in (31cm) S & H 1159 flapper. *H & J Foulke, Inc.*

SNOW BABIES AND SANTAS

Snow Babies: All-bisque with snowsuits and caps of pebbly-textured bisque; painted features; various standing, lying or sitting positions.

1-1/2in (4cm)	$	50
2-1/2in (6cm)		125
3in (9cm) huskies pulling sled with snow baby		250 - 300
2-1/2in (6cm) snowman		95 - 110
3in (8cm) baby riding snow bear		250 - 300
2-1/2in (6cm) tumbling snow baby		165 - 175
2in (5cm) musical snow baby		85
2in (5cm) baby on sled		125
3in (8cm) baby on sled		175 - 200
2in (5cm) reindeer pulling snow baby		250
2in (5cm) twins		100
2in (5cm) early fine quality babies with high hoods		165 - 175
Three small babies on sled		150 - 175
Santa on snow bear		350 - 400
3-1/2in (9cm) jointed snow baby		350
1-1/2in (4cm) seated dressed snow girl		125
2-1/2in (6cm) babies sliding on cellar door		250 - 300
2in (5cm) snow dog and snowman on sled		250 - 300
2-1/2in (6cm) Santa going down chimney		350
Snow bears		40 - 75
Snow boy or girl on sled		150 - 165
Shoulder head, cloth body:		
4-1/2in (11cm)		185
10in (25cm)		225 - 250
Train engine with coal car and Santa		400

"No Snows":

Boy and girl on sled, 2in (5cm)	$	165
Skiing boy, 2-1/2in (6cm)		95

FACTS
Various German firms including Hertwig & Co. and Bähr & Pröschild after 1910.
Mark: Sometimes "Germany."

Top: A single snow baby with snow baby twins. *H & J Foulke, Inc.* **Middle:** Group of snow bears. *H & J Foulke, Inc.* **Above:** 2-1/2in (6cm) and 3in (8cm) houses with Santas. *H & J Foulke, Inc.*

SONNEBERG TÄUFLING
(SO-CALLED MOTSCHMANN BABY)

Sonneberg Täufling: Papier-mâché or wax-over-composition head with painted hair or wig, dark pupil-less glass eyes; closed mouth or open mouth with bamboo teeth; composition lower torso; composition and wood arms and legs jointed at ankles and wrists, cloth covered midsection with voice box, upper arms and legs cloth covered, called floating joints; dressed in shift and bonnet. (For body photograph see *11th Blue Book*, page 336.)

Very good condition:

12-14in (31-36cm)	**$ 1000 - 1200**	
18-20in (46-51cm)	**1600 - 2000**	
24in (61cm)	**2200 - 2500**	

Fair condition, with wear:

12-14in (31-36cm)	**500 - 600**
18-20in (46-51cm)	**800 - 900**

Note: For many years it was thought that these dolls were made by Ch. Motschmann because some were found stamped with his name; hence, they were called Motschmann Babies by collectors. However, research has shown that they were made by various factories and that Motschmann was the holder of the patent for the voice boxes, not the manufacturer of the dolls.

FACTS

Various Sonneberg factories such as Heinrich Stier; many handled by exporter Louis Lindner & Söhn, Sonneberg, Thüringia, Germany. 1851-1880s.
Mark: None.

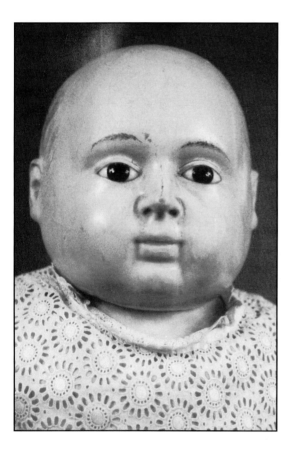

26-1/2in (67cm) Sonneberg Täufling. *H & J Foulke, Inc.*

STEIFF

Steiff Doll: Felt, plush or velvet, jointed; seam down middle of face, button eyes, painted features; original clothes; most are character dolls, many have large shoes to enable them to stand; all in excellent condition.

Children (Character Dolls):
11-12in (28-31cm)	**$**	**900 - 1250**
16-17in (41-43cm)		**1500 - 1650**
Black child, 17in (43cm)		**2100**
Adults*:		**2000 - 4000**
Gnome, 12in (31cm)		**900**
Record Moritz, at auction		**1715**

*Fewer women are available then men.

Mickey & Minnie Mouse #411 & 412,
5in (13cm) at auction	**4000**

Collector's Note: To bring the prices quoted, Steiff dolls must be clean and have good color. Faded and dirty dolls bring only one-third to one-half of these prices.

FACTS
Fräulein Margarete Steiff, Würtemberg, Germany. 1894-on.
Mark: Metal button in ear.

11-1/2in (29cm) Steiff character boy. *H & J Foulke, Inc.*

JULES STEINER

Round face with open mouth: Ca. 1870s. Perfect very pale bisque socket head, appropriate wig, bulgy paperweight eyes, open mouth with pointed teeth, round face, pierced ears; jointed composition body; dressed; all in good condition.

Mark: None, but sometimes body has a label.

Two rows of teeth,
16-19in (41-48cm) $ 6000**

Gigoteur: Kicking, crying bébé, mechanical key-wind body with composition arms and lower legs. (For photograph see *11th Blue Book*, page 341.)
17-18in (43-46cm) $ **2100 - 2300**
23in (58cm)   **2600 - 2750**

Täufling-type body with bisque shoulders, hips and lower arms and legs.
18-21in (46-53cm) $ 6500**

**Not enough price samples to compute a reliable range.

FACTS

Jules Nicolas Steiner and successors, Paris, France. 1855-1908.

14in (36cm) Sie A Bourgoin Steiner. *H & J Foulke, Inc.*

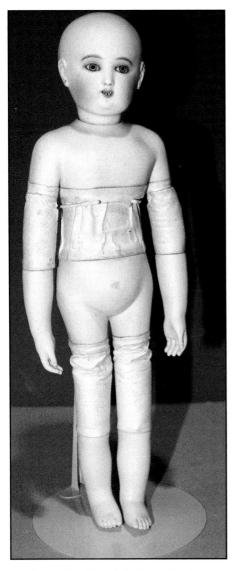

Above: 19in (49cm) Steiner with täufling body and rare swivel neck. *Private Collection.* **TOP: Right:** 16-1/2in (42cm) Flre C on lady body, all original. *Kay & Wayne Jensen Collection.* **Middle:** 10in (25cm) Sie F 3/0, rare Steiner. *Doelman Collection. Courtesy of Richard W. Withington, Inc.* **Bottom:** 29in (74cm) Flre A-19. *Kay & Wayne Jensen Collection.* (Descriptions of Steiner dolls are continued on page 342.)

JULES STEINER *continued*

Marked C or A Series Steiner Bébé: 1880s. Perfect socket head, cardboard pate, appropriate wig, sleep eyes with wire mechanism or bulgy paperweight eyes with tinting on upper eyelids, closed mouth, round face, pierced ears with tinted tips; jointed composition body with straight wrists and stubby fingers (sometimes with bisque hands); dressed; all in good condition. Sizes 4/0 (8in) to 8 (38in). Series "C" more easily found than "A."

Mark: (incised)

SIE A 0

(red script)

(incised)

SIE C 4

(red stamp)

J STEINER B. S. G.D.G.

8-10in (20-25cm)	**$ 3500 - 4000**
15-16in (38-41cm)	**5000 - 6000**
21-24in (53-61cm)	**6900 - 7500**
28in (71cm)	**9500**
33in (84cm) wire eyes	**12,000**

Wax plate with inset hair, 15-1/2in (39cm) **25,000****

Figure A or C Steiner Bébé: Ca. 1887-on. Perfect bisque socket head, cardboard pate, appropriate wig, paperweight eyes, closed mouth, pierced ears; jointed composition body; dressed; all in good condition. Figure "A" more easily found than "C."

Mark: (incised)

J. STEINER
BTE S.G.D.G.
PARIS
FIRE A 15

Body and/or head may be stamped:

"Le Petit Parisien
BEBE STEINER
MEDAILLE d'OR
PARIS 1889"

or paper label of doll carrying flag

8in (20cm)	**$ 2600 - 3000**
10in (25cm)	**3000**
15-16in (38-41cm)	**4200 - 4700**
22-24in (56-61cm)	**5500 - 6500**
28-30in (71-76cm)	**7500**
9in (23cm) fully-jointed with trunk and trousseau, at auction	**6000**

Open mouth, 17in (43cm)	**2500**
22in (56cm)	**2900**

*Allow 20-30% more for Figure C.

Figure B: Open mouth with two rows of teeth,

23-25in (58-64cm)	**$ 5000 - 5250**

Bébé Le Parisien: 1892-on. Pefect bisque socket head, cardboard pate, appropriate wig, paperweight eyes, closed or open mouth, pierced ears; jointed composition body; dressed; all in good condition. (For photograph see *11th Blue Book*, page 9.)

Mark: head (incised):

A-19
PARIS

(red stamp):

"LE PARISIEN"
body (purple stamp):
"BEBE 'LE PARISIEN'
MEDAILLE D'OR
PARIS"

Closed mouth:

13-15in (33-38cm)	**$ 3500 - 4000**
18-20in (46-51cm)	**4500 - 5000**
23-25in (58-64cm)	**5500 - 6000**
30in (76cm)	**8000**

Open mouth:

20-22in (51-56cm)	**2600 - 2800**

SWAINE & CO.

Swaine Character Babies: Ca. 1910-on. Perfect bisque head; composition baby body with bent limbs; dressed; all in good condition. (See previous *Blue Books* for photographs of specific models.)

Incised Lori, molded hair, glass eyes, open/closed mouth,

   22-24in (56-61cm) $ 2800 - 3200

#232, (open-mouth Lori):

   8-1/2in (21cm) $ 750
   12-14in (31-36cm)   1000 - 1100
   20-22in (51-56cm)   1700 - 1800

DIP (wig, glass eyes, closed mouth):

   8-1/2–9-1/2in (21-24cm) $ 800
   11in (28cm)   900 - 950
   15in (38cm)   1450 - 1550
   17-18in (43-46cm) toddler   2000 - 2200

DV (molded hair, glass eyes, open/closed mouth):

   13in (33cm) $ 1450
   16in (41cm)   1650

DI (molded hair, intaglio eyes, open/closed mouth):

   12-13in (31-33cm) $ 850 - 900

B.P., B.O. (smiling character):

   16-18in (41-46cm)   **$ 5000****

F.P.:

   8-9in (20-23cm)
        $ 900 - 1250**

**Not enough price samples to compute a reliable range.

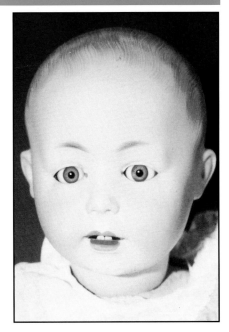

FACTS

Swaine & Co., porcelain factory, Hüttensteinach, Sonneberg, Thüringia, Germany. Ca. 1910-on for doll heads.

Mark: Stamped in green:

Top: 20in (51cm) 232 *Lori. H & J Foulke, Inc.*
Right: 15in (38cm) DV. *H & J Foulke, Inc.*

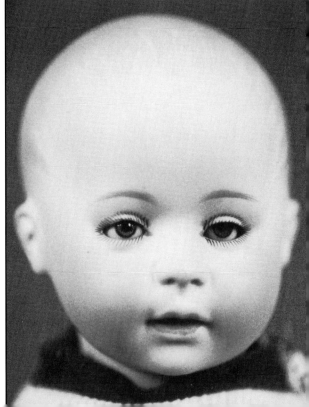

TERRI LEE

16in (41cm) *Jerri Lee,* all original. *H & J Foulke, Inc.*

Terri Lee Child Doll: Original wig, painted eyes; jointed at neck, shoulders and hips; all original tagged clothing and accessories; very good condition. (For photographs see *10th Blue Book*, pages 356 and 396.)

16in (41cm)

Pat. Pending	**$325 - 350***
Terri Lee only	**275 - 325***
Mint-in-box	**500***
Patty-Jo (black)	**500 - 600****
Jerri Lee, 16in (41cm)	**300**

Benjie (black). (For photograph see *11th Blue Book*, page 343.) **500 - 600****

Tiny Terri Lee, inset eyes. (For photograph see *8th Blue Book*, page 381.)

10in (25cm)	**165 - 185**
Tiny Jerri Lee, inset eyes,	
10in (25cm)	**185 - 210**
Connie Lynn	**350 - 400**
Gene Autry	**1500 - 1800****

Linda Baby. (For photograph see *8th Blue Book*, page 381.)

10in (25cm)	**185 - 195**
Ginger Girl Scout,	
8in (20cm)	**150**
Mint-in-box, at auction	**350**

*Allow extra for special outfits or gowns.

** Not enough price samples to compute a reliable range.

FACTS

TERRI LEE Sales Corp., V. Gradwohl, Pres., U.S.A. 1946- Lincoln, Neb.; then Apple Valley, Calif., from 1952-Ca. 1962. First dolls, rubbery plastic composition; later, hard plastic. **Mark:** embossed across shoulders
First dolls:
"TERRI LEE
PAT. PENDING"
raised letters
Later dolls: "TERRI LEE"

THUILLIER

Marked A.T. Child: Perfect bisque head, cork pate, good wig, paperweight eyes, pierced ears, closed mouth; body of wood, kid or composition in good condition; appropriate old wig and clothes, excellent quality.

12-13in (31-33cm)	$ **22,000 - 30,000**
16-18in (41-46cm)	**35,000 - 43,000**
22-24in (56-61cm)	**47,000 - 52,000**

Open mouth, two rows of teeth:

20-22in (51-56cm)	$ **9000 - 12,000**
36in (91cm)	**25,000**

Approximate size chart:
1 = 9in (23cm)
3 = 12in (31cm)
7 = 15-1/2in (39cm)
9 = 18in (46cm)
12 = 22-23in (56-58cm)
15 = 36-37in (91-93cm)

— FACTS —
A. Thuillier, Paris, France. Some heads by F. Gaultier. 1875-1893.
Mark:

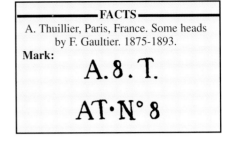

18-1/2in (47cm) A.T.
Private Collection.

UNIS

Unis Child Doll: Perfect bisque head, wood and composition jointed body; good wig, sleep eyes, open mouth; pretty clothes; all in nice condition.

#301 or 60 (fully-jointed body):

8-10in (20-25cm)	$	425 - 475
15-17in (38-43cm)		650 - 700
23-25in (58-64cm)		900 - 1000
28in (71cm)		1200

5-piece body:

5in (13cm) painted eyes	150 - 175
6-1/2in (17cm) glass eyes	240 - 265
11-13in (28-33cm)	325 - 350

Black or brown bisque,

11-13in (28-33cm)	375 - 425

Bleuette,

11in (28cm)	$	800 - 850*

Princess (See page 226.):

#251 character toddler:

14-15in (36-38cm)	$	1400 - 1500

28in (71cm)		2200 - 2400

Composition head 301 or 60:

11-13in (28-33cm)	$	150 - 175
20in (51cm)		350 - 400

Composition head #251 or #247 toddler,

22in (56cm)	650 - 750

*Brings a much higher price in France.

── FACTS ──

Société Française de Fabrication de Bébés et Jouets. (S.F.B.J.) of Paris and Montreuil-sous-Bois, France. 1922-on. Bisque head, composition body. 5in (13cm) and larger.

Mark:

18-1/2in (47cm) Unis 301. *Kiefer Collection.*

VOGUE

All-Composition Toddles: 1937-1948. Jointed neck, shoulders and hips; molded hair or mohair wig, painted eyes looking to side; original clothes; all in good condition. **Mark:** "VOGUE" on head "DOLL CO." on back "TODDLES" stamped on sole of shoe

7-8in (18-20cm)	**$**	**200 - 225***
Mint condition		**350***

* Allow extra for unusual outfits, such as cowboy.

Hard Plastic Ginny: All-hard plastic, jointed at neck, shoulders and hips (some have jointed knees and some walk); nice wig, sleep eyes (early ones have painted eyes, later dolls have molded eyelashes); original tagged clothes; all in excellent condition with perfect hair and pretty coloring. **Mark:** On strung dolls: "VOGUE DOLLS" On walking dolls: "GINNY//VOGUE DOLLS"

7-8in (18-20cm):

1948-1949:

Painted eyes	**$**	**350 - 400***
Miss 1920, mint,		
at auction		**2300**

1950-1953:

Painted eyelashes,		
strung **$**		**325 - 425***
Caracul wig		**350 - 450***

1954:

Painted eyelashes,	
walks	**250 - 300***

1955-1957:

Molded eyelashes, walks	**175 - 225***
Davy Crockett with original outfit box, gun and patch, at auction	**850**

1957-1962:

Molded eyelashes, walks,	
jointed knees	**125 - 150***

*Allow extra for mint-in-box dolls and desirable outfits, such as **Tiny Miss Series**

FACTS

Vogue Dolls, Inc., Medford, Mass., U.S.A.
Creator: Jennie Graves.
Clothes Designer: Virginia Graves Carlson.
Clothes Label: "Vogue," "Vogue Dolls," or

VOGUE DOLLS, INC.
MEDFORD, MASS. USA
® REG U.S. PAT OFF

8in (20cm) Vogue composition *Toddles,* all original. *H & J Foulke, Inc.*

348

VOGUE *continued*

Black Ginny	**700 up**
Crib Crowd Baby,	
1950	**650***
Queen	**700 up**
Wee Imp,	
red hair	**275 - 300**

*Allow extra for mint-in-box dolls.

Accessories – all in excellent condition:

Ginny's Pup	**$ 150 - 175**
Cardboard suitcase with	
contents	**50**
Parasol	**15 - 18**
Gym set	**250 - 300**
Dresser, bed, rocking chair,	
wardrobe	**55 each**
School bag	**75 - 85**
"Hi I'm Ginny"	
pin	**75**
Ginny's First Secret	
book	**125**
Swag bag, hat box, auto bag	
and garment bag	**35 each**
Roller skates	
in cylinder	**15**
Hats	**5 - 10**
Dress and panties,	
tagged	**35-45**
Glasses	**4 - 5**
Shoes, center snap	**20**
Shoes, plastic	**8**

Top: 8in (20cm) *Ginny* with painted eyelashes. *H & J Foulke, Inc.* **Left:** 11in (28cm) *Lil Imp,* tagged dress. *Rhoda Shoemaker Collection.*

All Composition Girl: Jointed neck, shoulders and hips; sleeping eyes, open or closed mouth, mohair wig; original clothes; all in good condition.
Mark: None on doll; round silver sticker on front of outfit.

13in (33cm)	$	**300 - 325**
19in (48cm)		**400 - 425**

Jill: 1957. All hard plastic, adult body. All original and excellent.

10in (25cm)	$	**175 - 225**

Jeff: 1957. Vinyl head, all original and excellent.

10in (25cm)	$	**125 - 150**

Ginnette: 1957. All vinyl baby. All original and excellent.

8in (20cm)	$	**150 - 175**

Lil Imp: Vinyl head, hard plastic body with bent knees. Original clothing. Excellent condition.

11in (28cm)	$	**200 - 225**

Baby Dear: 1959. Designed by Eloise Wilken. Vinyl head and limbs, cloth body. All original and excellent.

18in (46cm)	$	**125 - 150**
Mint-in-box, at auction		**300**

19in (48cm) all composition Vogue girl, all original. *H & J Foulke, Inc.*

IZANNAH WALKER

Izannah Walker Doll: Stockinette, pressed head, features and hair painted with oils, applied ears, treated limbs; muslin body; appropriate clothes; in good condition.

17-19in (43-48cm) $ **16,000 - 18,000**
  Fair condition   **8500 - 9500**
  Very worn   **3000 - 4000**

FACTS

Izannah Walker, Central Falls, R.I., U.S.A. 1873, but probably made as early as 1840s.
Mark: Later dolls are marked:

Patented Nov. 4th 1873

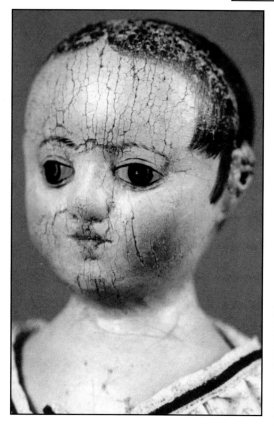

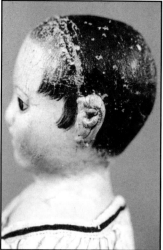

Two views of a 16in (41cm) Izannah Walker doll. *Private Collection.*

WAX DOLL, POURED

Poured Wax Doll: Head, lower arms and legs of wax; cloth body; set-in hair, glass eyes; lovely elaborate original clothes or very well dressed; all in good condition.

Baby:

17-19in (43-48cm)	**$ 1350 - 1650***
24-26in (61-66cm)	**1900 - 2300***
Lady, 22-24in (56-61cm)	**2500 - 3500**
Child, 17-18in (43-46cm)	**1500 - 1800***
Man, 18in (46cm)	
inset mustache	**1650 - 1750****

(For additional photograph see *11th Blue Book*, page 8.)

Baby or child, lackluster ordinary face,
20-22in (51-56cm)   **800 - 1000**

*Greatly depending upon appeal of face.
**Not enough samples to compute a
   reliable range.

FACTS

Various firms in London, England, such as Montanari, Pierotti, Peck, Meech, Marsh, Morrell, Cremer and Edwards. 1850s through the early 1900s.
Mark: Sometimes stamped on body with maker or store.

23in (58cm) poured wax doll. *Private Collection.*

WAX (REINFORCED)

Reinforced Poured Wax Doll: Poured wax shoulder head lined on the inside with plaster composition, glass eyes (may sleep), closed mouth, open crown, pate, curly mohair or human hair wig nailed on (may be partially inset into the wax around the face); muslin body with wax-over-composition lower limbs (feet may have molded boots); appropriate clothes; all in good condition, but showing some nicks and scrapes.

11in (28cm)	$	**225 - 250**
14-16in (36-41cm)		**325 - 375**
19-21in (48-53cm)		**500 - 550**
Lady, 23in (58cm)		**800 - 1000**
with molded shoulder plate		**2500****
with molded gloves, all original		**2500****

Socket head on ball-jointed composition body (Kestner-type):

13in (33cm)	$	**700 - 800**
19in (48cm)		**1200 - 1300**

**Not enough price samples to compute a reliable average.

FACTS
Various firms in Germany. 1860-1890. Poured wax shoulder head lined on the inside with plaster composition to give strength and durability, (not to be confused with wax-over-composition which simply has a wax coating).
Mark: None.

15in (38cm) reinforced wax. *H & J Foulke, Inc.*

WAX-OVER-COMPOSITION

FACTS
Numerous firms in England, Germany or France. During the 1800s.
Mark: None.

English Slit-head Wax: Ca. 1830-1860. Wax-over-composition shoulder head with round face, not rewaxed; human hair wig, glass eyes (may open and close by a wire), faintly smiling; original cloth body with leather arms; original or suitable old clothing; all in fair condition, showing wear. (For photograph see *9th Blue Book*, page 387.)

14-15in (36-38cm)	$	**650 - 750**
18-22in (46-56cm)		**900 - 1100**
26-28in (66-71cm)		**1300 - 1500**

Molded Hair Doll: Ca. 1860-on. German wax-over-composition shoulder head, not rewaxed; molded hair sometimes with bow, glass sleep or set eyes; original cloth body; wax-over or wooden extremities with molded boots or bare feet; nice old clothes; all in good condition, good quality.

14-16in (36-41cm)	$	**275 - 325**
22-25in (56-64cm)		**450 - 500**

Alice hairdo, 16in (41cm), early model, squeaker torso **550 - 650**

Continued on page 353.

WAX-OVER-COMPOSITION *continued*

Wax Doll with Wig: Ca. 1860s to 1900. German. Wax-over-shoulder head, not re-waxed; blonde or brown human hair or mohair wig, blue, brown or black glass eyes, sleep or set, open or closed mouth; original cloth body, any combination of extremities mentioned above, also arms may be made of china; original clothing or suitably dressed; entire doll in nice condition.

Standard quality:

11-12in (28-31cm)	$	**125 - 150**
16-18in (41-46cm)		**250 - 300**
22-24in (56-61cm)		**350 - 400**

Superior quality (heavily waxed):

11-12in (28-31cm)	**200 - 225**
16-18in (41-46cm)	**350 - 400**
22-24in (56-61cm)	**550 - 600**
30in (76cm)	**750**
17in (43cm) all original and excellent	**575**

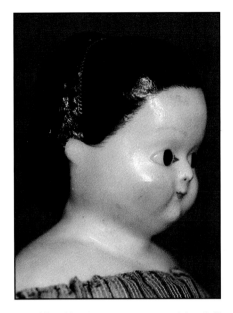

15-1/2in (40cm) wax-over-composition doll with *Alice* hairdo. *Kay & Wayne Jensen Collection.*

Bonnet Wax Doll: Ca. 1860-1880. Wax-over-shoulder head, with molded bonnet; molded hair may have some mohair or human hair attached, blue, brown or black set eyes; original cloth body and wooden extremities; nice old clothes; all in good condition.

16-17in (41-43cm)

common model	$	**350**
20in (51cm) boy with cap		**550 - 600**
28in (71cm) early round face with molded poke bonnet		**3000****
16in (41cm) molded hat perched on forehead		**2500****
24in (61cm) molded blue derby-type hat		**2000****

Double-Faced Doll: 1880-on. Fritz Bartenstein. One face crying, one laughing, rotating on a vertical axis by pulling a string, one face hidden by a hood. Body stamped "Bartenstein."

15-16in (38-41cm)	$	**850**

**Not enough price samples to compute a reliable average.

18in (46cm) wax-over-composition doll, all original. *Rhoda Shoemaker Collection.*

NORAH WELLINGS

Wellings Doll: All-fabric, stitch-jointed shoulders and hips; molded fabric face (also of papier-mâché, sometimes stockinette covered), painted features; all in excellent condition. Most commonly found are sailors, Canadian Mounties, Scots and Black Islanders.

Characters (floppy limbs):

8-10in (20-25cm)	$	75 - 100
13-14in (33-36cm)		150 - 200
Glass eyes, 14in (36cm) black		250
Old Couple, 26in (66cm)		1500 pair

Children:

12-13in (31-33cm)	$	400 - 500
16-18in (41-46cm)		600 - 700
23in (58cm)		1000 - 1200
26in (66cm)		1500
Glass eyes, 16-18in (41-46cm)		700 - 800

Bobby, 16in (41cm) glass eyes	**800 - 1000**
Harry the Hawk, 10in (25cm)	**200**
Nightdress Case	**400**
Baby, 11in (28cm)	**350 - 400**

FACTS

Victoria Toy Works, Wellington, Shropshire, England, for Norah Wellings. 1926-Ca. 1960. Fabric: felt, velvet and velour, and other material, stuffed. **Designer:** Norah Wellings **Mark:** On tag on foot: "Made in England by Norah Wellings."

20in (51cm) Wellings Gypsy Nightdress Case, all original. *H & J Foulke, Inc.*

12in (31cm) Wellings girl, all original. *H & J Foulke, Inc.*

WOOD, ENGLISH

William & Mary Period: Ca. 1690. Carved wooden face, painted eyes, tiny lines comprising eyebrows and eyelashes, rouged cheeks, flax or hair wig; wood body, cloth arms, carved wood hands (fork shaped), wood-jointed legs. Appropriate clothes; all in fair condition. (For photograph see *9th Blue Book*, page 223.)

12-17in (31-43cm) $ **50,000 up**

Queen Anne Period: Ca. early 1700s. Carved wooden face, dark glass eyes (sometimes painted), dotted eyebrows and eyelashes; jointed wood body, cloth upper arms; appropriate clothes; all in fair condition. (For photograph see *11th Blue Book*, page 8.)

24in (61cm) $ **25,000 up**

Georgian Period: Mid to late 1700s. Round wooden head with gesso covering, inset glass eyes (later sometimes blue), dotted eyelashes and eyebrows, flax or hair wig; jointed wood body with pointed torso; appropriate clothes; all in fair condition.

12-13in (31-33cm) $ **2500**
16-18in (41-46cm)   **4500**
24in (61cm)   **6000**

Early 19th Century: Wooden head, gessoed, painted eyes, pointed torso, flax or hair wig; old clothes (dress usually longer than legs); all in fair condition.

13in (33cm) $ **1300 - 1600**
16-21in (41-53cm)   **2000 - 3000**

— FACTS —
English craftsmen. Late 17th to mid 19th century.
Mark: None.

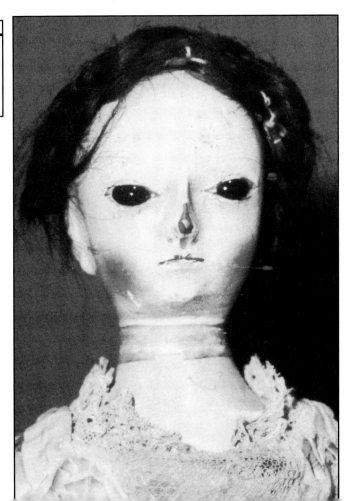

17in (43cm)
Queen Anne
Period wood,
all original.
*Private
Collection.*

WOOD, GERMAN (PEG WOODENS)

Early to Mid 19th Century: Delicately carved head, varnished, carved and painted hair and features, with a yellow tuck comb in hair, painted spit curls, sometimes earrings; mortise and tenon peg joints; old clothes; all in fair condition. (For photograph see *11th Blue Book*, page 356.)

6-7in (15-18cm)	$	650 - 750
12-13in (31-33cm)		1350 - 1450
17-18in (43-46cm)		1800 - 2000
9in (23cm) exceptional all		
original condition		1700 - 1750
Fortune tellers,		
17-20in (43-51cm)		2500 - 3000
Shell dolls,		
8-1/2in (28cm)		1200 - 1300 pair

Late 19th Century: Wooden head with painted hair, carving not so elaborate as previously, sometimes earrings, spit curls; dressed; all in good condition.

4in (10cm)	$	125 - 135
7-8in (18-20cm)		175 - 225
12in (31cm)		350 - 400
Turned red torso,		
10in (25cm)		150 - 200

Wood shoulder head, carved bun hairdo, cloth body, wood limbs:

9in (23cm) all original	350 - 400
17in (43cm)	500 - 550
24in (61cm)	800 - 900

Early 20th Century: Turned wood head, carved nose, painted hair, peg-jointed, painted white lower legs, painted black shoes.

11-12in (28-31cm)	$	60 - 80

FACTS

Craftsmen of the Grodner Tal, Austria, and Sonneberg, Germany, such as Insam & Prinoth (1820-1830) Gorden Tirol and Nürnberg verlagers of pegwood dolls and wood doll heads. Late 18th to 20th century. **Mark:** None.

12in (31cm) Mid 19th Century German wood doll. *Richard Wright Antiques.*

357

WOOD, German (20th Century)

"Bébé Tout en Bois" (Doll All of Wood): All of wood, fully jointed; wig, inset glass eyes, open mouth with teeth; appropriate clothes; all in fair to good condition.
Child:

13in (33cm)	$	425 - 475
17-19in (43-48cm)		650 - 750
22-24in (56-61cm)		950
18in (46cm) mint, all original		1100

Baby:

16-1/2in (42cm)	$	400 - 500

— FACTS —
Various companies, such as Rudolf Schneider and Schilling, Sonneberg, Thüringia, Germany. 1901-1914. For French trade.
Mark: Usually none; sometimes Schilling "winged angel" trademark.

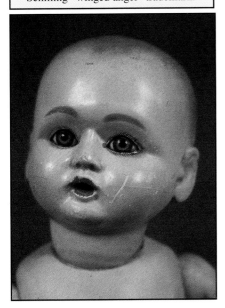

16-/12in (42cm) *Tout en Bois* baby. *H & J Foulke, Inc.*

WOOD, Swiss

Swiss Wooden Doll: Wooden head with hand-carved features and hair with good detail (males sometimes have carved hats); all carved wood jointed body; original, usually regional attire; excellent condition.

6in (15cm)	$	300 - 350
9-10in (23-25cm)		250 - 275
12in (31cm)		350 - 400
17-18in (43-46cm)		750 - 850
12in (31cm) boy with carved hat		500
15in (38cm) lady		500 - 600

— FACTS —
Various Swiss firms. 20th century.
Mark: Usually a paper label on wrist or clothes.

15in (38cm) Swiss wood lady. *H & J Foulke, Inc.*

GLOSSARY

Applied Ears: Ears molded independently and affixed to the head. (On most dolls the ear is included as part of the head mold.)

Bald Head: Head with no crown opening, could be covered by a wig or have painted hair.

Ball-jointed Body: Usually a body of composition or papier-mâché with wooden balls at knees, elbows, hips and shoulders to make swivel joints; some parts of the limbs may be wood.

Bébé: French child doll with "dolly face."

Belton-type: A bald head with one, two or three small holes for attaching wig.

Bent-limb Baby Body: Composition body of five pieces with chubby torso and curved arms and legs.

Biscaloid: Ceramic or composition substance for making dolls; also called imitation bisque.

Biskoline: Celluloid-type substance for making dolls.

Bisque: Unglazed porcelain, usually flesh tinted, used for dolls' heads or all-bisque dolls.

Breather: Doll with an actual opening in each nostril; also called open nostrils.

Breveté (or Bté): Used on French dolls to indicate that the patent is registered.

Character Doll: Dolls with bisque or composition heads, modeled to look life-like, such as infants, young or older children, young ladies and so on.

China: Glazed porcelain used for dolls' heads and *Frozen Charlottes.*

Child Dolls: Dolls with a typical "dolly face," which represents a child.

Composition: A material used for dolls' heads and bodies, consisting of such items as wood pulp, glue, sawdust, flour, rags and sundry other substances.

Contemporary Clothes: Clothes not original to the doll, but dating from the same period when the doll would have been a plaything.

Crown Opening: The cut-away part of a doll head.

DEP: Abbreviation used on German and French dolls claiming registration.

D.R.G.M.: Abbreviation used on German dolls indicating a registered design or patent.

Dolly Face: Typical face used on bisque dolls before 1910 when the character face was developed; "dolly faces" were used also after 1910.

Embossed Mark: Raised letters, numbers or names on the backs of heads or bodies.

Feathered Eyebrows: Eyebrows composed of many tiny painted brush strokes to give a realistic look.

Fixed Eyes: Glass eyes that do not move or sleep.

Flange Neck: A doll's head with a ridge at the base of the neck which contains holes for sewing the head to a cloth body.

Flapper Dolls: Dolls of the 1920s period with bobbed wig or molded hair and slender arms and legs.

Flirting Eyes: Eyes which move from side to side as doll's head is tilted.

Frozen Charlotte: Doll molded all in one piece including arms and legs.

Ges.(Gesch.): Used on German dolls to indicate design is registered or patented.

Googly Eyes: Large, often round eyes looking to the side; also called roguish or goo goo eyes.

Hard Plastic: Hard material used for making dolls after 1948.

Incised Mark: Letters, numbers or names impressed into the bisque on the back of the head or on the shoulder plate.

Intaglio Eyes: Painted eyes with sunken pupil and iris.

JCB: Jointed composition body. See *ball-jointed body.*

Kid Body: Body of white or pink leather.

Lady Dolls: Dolls with an adult face and a body with adult proportions.

Mama Doll: American composition and cloth doll of the 1920s to 1940s with "mama" voice box.

Mohair: Goat's hair widely used in making doll wigs.

Molded Hair: Curls, waves and comb marks which are actually part of the mold and not merely painted onto the head.

Motschmann-type Body: Doll body with cloth midsection and upper limbs with floating joints; hard lower torso and lower limbs.

Open-Mouth: Lips parted with an actual opening in the bisque, usually has teeth either molded in the bisque or set in separately and sometimes a tongue.

Open/Closed Mouth: A mouth molded to appear open, but having no actual slit in the bisque.

Original Clothes: Clothes belonging to a doll during the childhood of the original owner, either commercially or homemade.

Painted Bisque: Bisque covered with a layer of flesh-colored paint which has not been baked in, so will easily rub or wash off.

Paperweight Eyes: Blown glass eyes which have depth and look real, usually found in French dolls.

Papier-mâché: A material used for dolls' heads and bodies, consisting of paper pulp, sizing, glue, clay or flour.

Pate: A shaped piece of plaster, cork, cardboard or other material which covers the crown opening.

Pierced Ears: Little holes through the doll's earlobes to accommodate earrings.

Pierced-in Ears: A hole at the doll's earlobe which goes into the head to accommodate earrings.

Pink Bisque: A later bisque of about 1920 which was pre-colored pink.

Pink-toned China: China which has been given a pink tint to look more like real flesh color; also call lustered china.

Poupée: French lady doll, Ca. 1860-on.

Poupée Bois: French lady doll, Ca. 1860-on, with wood body.

Poupée Peau: French lady doll, Ca. 1860-on, with kid body.

Rembrandt Hair: Hair style parted in center with bangs at front, straight down sides and back and curled at ends.

S.G.D.G.: Used on French dolls to indicate that the patent is registered "without guarantee of the government."

Shoulder Head: A doll's head and shoulders all in one piece.

Shoulder Plate: The actual shoulder portion sometimes molded in one with the head, sometimes a separate piece with a socket in which a head is inserted.

Socket Head: Head and neck which fit into an opening in the shoulder plate or the body.

Solid-dome Head: Head with no crown opening, could have painted hair or be covered by wig.

Stationary Eyes: Glass eyes which do not move or sleep.

Stone Bisque: Coarse white bisque of a lesser quality.

Toddler Body: Usually a chubby ball-jointed composition body with chunky, shorter thighs and a diagonal hip joint; sometimes has curved instead of jointed arms; sometimes is of five pieces with straight chubby legs.

Topsy-Turvy: Doll with two heads, one usually concealed beneath a skirt.

Turned Shoulder Head: Head and shoulders are one piece, but the head is molded at an angle so that the doll is not looking straight ahead.

Vinyl: Soft plastic material used for making dolls after 1950s.

Watermelon Mouth: Closed line-type mouth curved up at each side in an impish expression.

Wax Over: A doll with head and/or limbs of papier-mâché or composition covered with a layer of wax to give a natural, lifelike finish.

Weighted Eyes: Eyes which can be made to sleep by means of a weight which is attached to the eyes.

Wire Eyes: Eyes that can be made to sleep by means of a wire which protrudes from doll's head.

BIBLIOGRAPHY

Anderton, Johana.
Twentieth Century Dolls. North Kansas City, Missouri: Trojan Press, 1971.
More Twentieth Century Dolls. North Kansas City, Missouri: Athena Publishing Co., 1974.
Angione, Genevieve. *All-Bisque & Half-Bisque Dolls.* Exton, Pennsylvania: Schiffer Publishing Ltd., 1969.
Borger, Mona. *Chinas, Dolls for Study and Admiration.* San Francisco: Borger Publications, 1983.
Cieslik, Jürgen and Marianne.
German Doll Encyclopedia 1800-1939. Cumberland, Maryland: Hobby House Press, Inc., 1985.
Coleman, Dorothy S., Elizabeth Ann and **Evelyn Jane.** *The Collector's Book of Dolls' Clothes.* New York: Crown Publishers, Inc., 1975.
The Collector's Encyclopedia of Dolls, Vol. I & II. New York: Crown Publishers, Inc., 1968 & 1986.
Corson, Carol. *Schoenhut Dolls, A Collector's Encyclopedia.* Cumberland, Maryland: Hobby House Press, Inc., 1993.
Foulke, Jan.
Blue Books of Dolls & Values, Vol. I-XI. Cumberland, Maryland: Hobby House Press, Inc., 1974-1991.
Doll Classics. Cumberland, Maryland: Hobby House Press, Inc., 1987.
Focusing on Effanbee Composition Dolls. Riverdale, Maryland: Hobby House Press, 1978.
Focusing on Gebrüder Heubach Dolls. Cumberland, Maryland: Hobby House Press, Inc., 1980.
Kestner, King of Dollmakers. Cumberland, Maryland: Hobby House Press, Inc., 1982.
Simon & Halbig Dolls, The Artful Aspect. Cumberland, Maryland: Hobby House Press, Inc., 1984.
Treasury of Madame Alexander Dolls. Riverdale, Maryland: Hobby House Press, 1979.

Gerken, Jo Elizabeth.
Wonderful Dolls of Papier-Mâché. Lincoln, Nebraska: Doll Research Associates, 1970.
Hillier, Mary.
Dolls and Dollmakers. New York: G. P. Putnam's Sons, 1968.
The History of Wax Dolls. Cumberland, Maryland: Hobby House Press, Inc.; London: Justin Knowles, 1985.
King, Constance Eileen.
The Collector's History of Dolls. London: Robert Hale, 1977; New York: St. Martin's Press, 1978.
Mathes, Ruth E. and **Robert C.** *Dolls, Toys and Childhood.* Cumberland, Maryland: Hobby House Press, Inc., 1987.
McGonagle, Dorothy A. *The Dolls of Jules Nicolas Steiner.* Cumberland, Maryland: Hobby House Press, Inc., 1988.
Merrill, Madeline O. *The Art of Dolls, 1700-1940.* Cumberland, Maryland: Hobby House Press, Inc., 1985.
Noble, John. *Treasury of Beautiful Dolls.* New York: Hawthorn Books, 1971.
Pardella, Edward R. *Shirley Temple Dolls and Fashions.* West Chester, Pennsylvania: Schiffer Publishing, Ltd., 1992.
Richter, Lydia. *Heubach Character Dolls and Figurines.* Cumberland, Maryland: Hobby House Press, Inc., 1992.
Schoonmaker, Patricia N.
Effanbee Dolls: The Formative Years 1910-1929. Cumberland, Maryland: Hobby House Press, Inc., 1984.
Patsy Doll Family Encyclopedia. Cumberland, Maryland: Hobby House Press, Inc., 1992.
Tarnowska, Maree. *Fashion Dolls.* Cumberland, Maryland: Hobby House Press, Inc., 1986.

ABOUT THE AUTHOR

The name Jan Foulke is synonymous with accurate information. As the author of the *Blue Book of Dolls & Values*®, she is the most quoted source on doll information and the most respected and recognized authority on dolls and doll prices in the world.

Born in Burlington, New Jersey, Jan Foulke has always had a fondness for dolls. She recalls, "Many happy hours of my childhood were spent with dolls as companions, since we lived on a quiet county road, and until I was ten, I was an only child." Jan received a B.A. from Columbia Union College, where she was named to the *Who's Who in American Colleges & Universities* and was graduated with high honors. Jan taught for twelve years in the Montgomery County school system in Maryland, and also supervised student teachers in English for the University of Maryland, where she did graduate work.

Jan and her husband, Howard, who photographs the dolls presented in the *Blue Book*, were both fond of antiquing as a hobby, and in 1972 they decided to open a small antique shop of their own. The interest of their daughter, Beth, in dolls sparked their curiosity about the history of old dolls—an interest that quite naturally grew out of their love of heirlooms. The stock in their antique shop gradually changed and evolved into an antique doll shop.

Early in the development of their antique doll shop, Jan and Howard realized that there was a critical need for an accurate and reliable doll identification and price guide resource. In the early 1970s, the Foulkes teamed up with Hobby House Press to produce (along with Thelma Bateman) the first *Blue Book of Dolls & Values*, originally published in 1974. Since that time, the Foulkes have exclusively authored and illustrated the eleven successive editions, and today the *Blue Book* is

regarded by collectors and dealers as the definitive source for doll prices and values.

Jan and Howard Foulke now dedicate all of their professional time to the world of dolls: writing and illustrating books and articles, appraising collections, lecturing on antique dolls, acting as consultants to museums, auction houses and major collectors, and selling dolls both by mail order and through exhibits at major shows throughout the United States. Mrs. Foulke is a member of the United Federation of Doll Clubs, Doll Collectors of America, and the International Doll Academy.

Mrs. Foulke has appeared on numerous television talk shows and is often quoted in newspaper and magazine articles as the ultimate source for doll pricing and trends in collecting. Both *USA Today* and *The Washington Post* have stated that the *Blue Book of Dolls & Values* is "the bible of doll collecting."

In addition to her work on the twelve editions of the *Blue Book of Dolls & Values*, Jan Foulke has also authored: *Focusing on Effanbee Composition Dolls; A Treasury of Madame Alexander Dolls; Kestner, King of Dollmakers; Simon & Halbig, The Artful Aspect; Focusing on Gebrüder Heubach Dolls; Doll Classics;* and *Focusing on Dolls.*

INDEX

A

A.M., 183, 274-280, 292
A.T., 345
A.T. Type, 235, 238
Action Kewpie, 245
Action Marine, 175
Action Pilot, 175
Action Soldier, 175
Adams, Emma and Marietta, 133
Adelina Patti, 126
Admiral Dewey and Officers, 150
Adrienne, 204
Adventure Team, 175
Agnes, 128
Alabama Baby, 17
Alabama Indestructible Doll, 17
Albanian Boy, 266
Albanian Girl, 266
Alexander-Kins, 30
Alexander, Madame, 15, 18
Alice, 18
Alice-in-Wonderland, 23, 26
Amy, 26
Annabelle, 26
Armed Forces Dolls, 22
Babies, 22, 27, 31
Babs, 26
Baby Brother, 31
Baby Clown, 30
Baby Genius, 27
Baby Jane, 23
Baby Lynn, 31
Baby McGuffey, 22
Ballerina, 30
Beth, 26
Betty, 19
Betty face, 22
Billy, 30
Binnie, 29
Birthday Dolls, 19
Bitsey, 22
Black Baby Ellen, 31
Black Pussy Cat, 31
Bobby Q., 18
Brenda Starr, 31, 33
Bride, 19, 22, 26, 27, 30
Bridesmaids, 19, 22
Brigitta, 34
Brother, 31
Bunny Belle, 18
Butch, 22
Carmen, 22
Caroline, 31
Cherry Twin, 30
Cinderella, 22, 26
Cissette, 30
Cissy, 27, 28
Cloth Baby, 18
Cloth Character Dolls, 18
Cloth Dionne Quintuplet, 18
Coco, 34

Composition, 19-25
Cynthia, 26
Dionne Quintuplets, 19
Annette, 19
Cecile, 19
Emelie, 19
Marie, 19
Yvonne, 19
Disney, 22
Disney Snow White, 31
Dr. Dafoe, 23
Easter Girl, 31
Edith, 31
Elise, 30, 31, 32, 34
Fairy Princess, 22
Fairy Queen, 22, 26
First Ladies, 34
Flora McFlimsey, 22
Foreign Countries, 19
Friedrich, 34
Gibson Girl, 30
Glamour Girls, 26
Godey Ladies, 26
Godey Man, 26
Godey Portrait, 27
Gold Ballerina, 30
Gold Rush, 30
Gretl, 34
Groom, 30
Hard Plastic, 26-30
Jacqueline, 30-31
Jane Withers, 23
Janie, 31
Jeannie Walker, 23
Jenny Lind, 31
Jo, 26
John Powers Models, 26
Kamkins-type, 18
Karen Ballerina, 23
Kate Greenaway, 30
Kathy, 26
Katie, 31
Kelly, 30-31
Kelly Face, 31
Kurt, 34
Lady in Red, 27
Laurie, 30
Leslie, 31, 33
Liesl, 34
Lissy, 30
Lissy Beth, 29
Little Colonel, 19
Little Genius, 20, 22
Little Lady, 30
Little Men, 26
Little Minister, 26
Little Shaver, 18
Little Women, 18, 20, 26, 30
Louisa, 34
Lucinda, 31
Maggie, 26, 34
Maggie Face, 26
Maggie Mixup, 30
Margaret Face, 23, 26

Margaret O'Brien, 23-24, 26
Margaret Rose, 26
Margot, 30
Margot Ballerina, 26
Maria, 34
Marionettes, 22
Marlo, 34
Marme, 26- 27
Marta, 34
Martha Face, 34
Mary Ann Face, 31, 34
Mary Cassatt Baby, 31
Mary Ellen, 29
Mary Martin, 26
Marybel, 31
McGuffey Ana, 21-22, 30
Me and My Shadow, 26
Meg, 26
Michael, 34
Miss America, 22
My Shadow, 30
Nancy Drew, 34
Nancy Drew Face, 34
Nina Ballerina, 26
Nurse, 19, 30
Pamela, 30, 34
Parlor Maid, 30
Peter Pan, 26, 34
Peter Pan Set, 34
Pinky, 22
Polly, 31
Polly Face, 31
Polly Pigtails, 26
Pollyana, 31
Portrait Dolls, 22, 34
Portrettes, 30
Precious, 22
Prince Charles, 30
Prince Charming, 26
Prince Philip, 26
Princess Ann, 30
Princess Elizabeth, 20, 22
Princess Elizabeth Face, 22
Queen, 27
Queen Elizabeth, 26
Quizkin, 30
Renoir Child, 34
Romantic Couple, 34
Rosamund Bridesmaid, 26
Rozy, 31
Scarlet O'Hara, 22
Scarlett, 31
Shari Lewis, 30
Sleeping Beauty, 22, 30
Slumbermate, 31
Smarty, 31
Snow White, 21-22, 25-26
Sonja Henie, 23
Sound of Music, 34
Southern Belle, 30

Special Face Dolls, 23
Special Girl, 21, 23
Special Outfits, 19
Story Princess, 26
Storybook Characters, 8, 19
Susie Q., 18
Suzy, 31
Sweet Violet, 29
Tinker Bell, 34
Tony Sarg, 22
Topsy Turvy, 19-20
Vinyl, 31-34
Wendy, 26, 30, 34
Wendykins, 12
Wendy Ann, 22
Wendy Ann Face, 22
Wendy Ballerina, 30
Wendy Bride, 25-26
Wendy-Ann, 26
Winnie, 29
Alexander-type, 138-139
Alexandre, Henri, 35
Alice, 18, 166, 172, 302
Alice-in-Wonderland,23, 26, 65
Alice Roosevelt, 65
All Time Hit Parade, 289
All-bisque, 8, 15, 36-47, 172, 182, 196, 242, 244, 251, 263, 272, 294, 331
Allen, 82
Alma, 269
Alpha Imp., 270
Alt, Beck & Gottschalck, 37, 48-51, 67, 71, 85, 107, 122
Aman, 146
Amberg, Louis & Son, 37, 52-55
American Character Doll Co., 56-59
American Family Series, 62
American Heartland Dolls, 204
American Pioneer Children, 62
American Schoolboy, 88
Amy, 26, 62-63
Anchor, 274
Angel, 132
Angela, 63
Annabelle, 26
Annette, 19
Anne Shirley, 161-162
Armed Forced Dolls, 22
Armstrong-Hand, Martha, 62
Around the World, 289
Arranbee Doll Co., 60-61
Artcraft Toy Product Co., 134
Artist Dolls, 62
Atlas Doll & Toy Co., 282
Augusta Victoria, 302
Aunt Jemima Family, 130

Australian Jungle Fighter, 175
Averill, Georgene, 66-70
Averill Mfg. Co, 66, 148
Ayoka, 204

B

B.L. Bébé, 223
B.P. Character Baby, 76
Babs, 26
Baby Aero, 108
Baby Betty, 275
Baby Blanche, 333
Baby Blossom, 111
Baby Bo Kaye, 71, 110
Baby Bokaye, 51, 202
Baby Bright Eyes, 158
Baby Brother, 31
Baby Bud, 43
Baby Bumps, 205
Baby Butterfly, 295
Baby Clown, 30
Baby Dainty, 158
Baby Dear, 349
Baby Dimples, 206
Baby Effanbee, 158
Baby Genius, 27
Baby Georgene, 66
Baby Gloria, 280
Baby Grumpy, 155-156, 158
Baby Hendren, 66
Baby Jane, 23
Baby Jean, 242
Baby Lynn, 31
Baby McGuffey, 22
Baby Mine, 112
Baby Peggy, 52, 54
Baby Petite, 56
Baby Ruth, 94
Baby Sandy, 171
Baby Shirley, 328
Baby Snooks, 215
Baby Stuart, 203
Baby Tinyette, 159
Babyette, 157
Babyland Rag, 72-73
Babyland Rag-type, 73
Bähr & Pröschild, 37, 74-76, 249, 254, 317
Ballerina, 30
Bambino, 118
Barbara Ann, 163-164
Barbara Joan, 163
Barbara Lou, 163
BARBIE® 14-15, 77-82
Baby Sits, 79
Bendable Leg, 79
Bloomingdales Special, 82
Bob Mackie BARBIE® dolls, 81-82
Bubble Cut, 79-80
Christmas, 82
Color Magic, 79
Dogs & Duds, 79
Easter Parade, 77, 79
Empress Bride, 82

Enchanted Evening, 79
Fashion Queen, 79
Francie (black), 80
Gay Parisienne, 77, 79
Gift Sets, 79
Gold, 81-82
Golden Jubilee Special, 82
Hair Happenin's, 79
Hallmark Special, 82
Here Comes the Bride, 79
Living, 79
Masquerade Ball, 82
Miss, 79
Montgomery Ward, 79
Neptune Fantasy, 82
"No Bangs" Francie, 81
Pan Am Stewardess, 79
Platinum, 82
Ponytail, 77-78
Queen of Hearts, 82
Roman Holiday, 77, 79
Round the Clock Giftset, 80
Shimmering Magic, 79
Standard, 81
Starlight Splendor, 82
Swirl Ponytail, 79-80
Talking, 79
Truly Scrumptious, 82
Twist & Turn, 79
Twist Francie, 81
1600 Series, 79
Barefoot Children, 204
Barrie, Mirren, 62
Barrois, E., 3, 168
Bashful, 253
Bastian, 204
Bébé Gourmand, I, 102-103
Bébé Le Parisien, 342
Bébé Mascotte, 281
Bébé Motherean, 285
Bébé Phénix, 35
Bébé Têteur, 102-103
Bébé Tout en Bois, 357
Becassine, 106
Beckett, Bob & June, 62
Becky, 62
Beefeater, 271
Beloved Belindy, 307
Belton-type, 74, 84, 95
Benedetta, 267
Benjie, 344
Bergmann, C.M., 85
Bergner, Carl, 286
Bertha, 128
Bester Doll Co., 134
Beth, 26
Betsy, 63
Betsy McCall, 59, 218
Betsy Wetsy, 213
Betty, 19
Betty Boop, 111
Betty Boop-type, 47
Betty Brite,163
Betty face, 22
Betty Jane, 214
Billiken, 205, 246

Billy, 30
Billy Boy, 155
Bing Art Dolls, 259
Bing, John, 327
Binnie, 29
Birthday Dolls, 19
Bisque Dolls, 8, 86-93, 246, 292
Bitsey, 22
Black Dolls, 3, 17 31, 72, 95-99, 120, 171, 173, 186, 199, 205-206, 244, 316, 348
Action Soldier, 175-176
Alabama Baby, 17
Aunt Jemima Family, 130
Baby Bumps, 205
Baby Ellen, 31
Babyland Rag,
Barrois, 3, 168
Belton-type, 95
Benjie, 344
Bru, 95
Character Girl, 47
Cotton Joe, 205
E.D., 95
E. Heubach, 95-96
F.G. Fashion, 177
Gebr. Heubach, 95
Ginny, 348
Goo Goo Topsy, 171
H. Handwerch, 95
Hard Plastic Character, 98
Hilda, 95
Hottentot, 244
Jumeau, 95
K & R, 95-96
Kestner, 95
Kuhnlenz, 95
Leslie, 31, 33
Mammy, 97-98, 120
Papier-Mâché, 98
Paris Bébé, 95
Patsy-type, 98
Pussy Cat, 31
Rufus, 67
S.F.B.J., 186
S PB H Hanna, 95
Simon & Halbig, 95, 97
Snowball, 206
Steiner, 95
Stockinette, 98
Toddler, 98
"Topsy" Baby, 98
W.P.A., 98
Van Rosen, 95
Blakeley, Halle, 62
Bleuette, 313, 346
Blink, 206, 208
Bobby, 354
Bobby Q., 18
Body Twists, 69
Bonnet Wax Doll, 353
Bonnie Babe, 67, 202
Bonny Braids, 218
Bonomi, 192
Bo-Peep, 288

Borgfeldt, George, 67, 71, 76, 107, 244
Boudoir Doll, 100
Brandon, Elizabeth, 62
Brenda Starr, 31, 33
Breveté Bébé, 102, 104
Bride, 19, 22, 26-27, 30, 47, 146
Bridesmaids, 19, 22
Bright Star, 207
Brigitta, 34
Bringloe, Frances, 62
British Commando, 175
Brother, 31, 61
Brownies, 130
Brown South Seas, 267
Bru, I, 95, 101-105, 168, 286
Bru Jne & Cie., 101
Bru Jne Bébé, 103-105
Bru Type, 84, 235
Brückner Rag Doll, 73
Bubbles, 157-158, 167
Bucherer, A., 106
Buddy Lee, 140, 190
Buds, 155
Buffalo Bill, 150
Bullard, Helen, 62
Bunnie, 132
Bunny Belle, 18
Bunny Boy, 202
Bunny Girl, 202
Buschow & Beck, 283
Butch, 22
Button Nose, 163
Bye-Lo, 15
Bye-Lo Baby, 9, 107-109
C ■■■■■■■■■■■■■■■■■
C.M. Bergmann, 85
C.O.D. Character Baby, 151-152
Caleb, 316
Cameo Doll Co., 71, 107, 110-112
Campbell, Astry, 62
Campbell Kid, 56, 206-209
Candy Kid, 163
Can't Break'Em Characters, 205
Captain Kiddo, 147
Carlson, Virginia Graves, 347
Carmen, 22
Carol Ann Beery, 58
Caroline, 31
Catterfelder Puppenfabrik, 113
Cecile, 19
Celluloid Dolls, 9, 114-116, 246, 258, 267
Century Doll Co., 117
Chad Valley, 118
Champ. 111
Champagne Lady, 167
Character Baby, 199, 242, 249, 278, 286
Character Children, 151, 249, 275
Character Infant, 279
Character Toddler, 278
Charlie Chaplin, 52-53

Charlie McCarthy, 163
Chase, Martha Jenks, 12, 119-120
Cherie, 264
Cherry Twin, 30
China Head, 14-15, 121-129, 167, 252
Chin-Chin, 202
Cho-Cho San, 47
Chocolate Drop, 147-148
Christopher Robin, 63
Chubby, 43
Cinderella, 22, 26, 166, 214-215
Cindy, 207
Circle Dot Bébé, 103
Circus Set, 47
Cissette, 30
Cissy, 27-28
Clear, Emma, 62
Clelia, 270
Cloth dolls, 18, 70, 98, 130-131, 247, 255-256, 269
Coco, 34
Colonial Toy Mfg. Co., 134
Columbian Doll, 133
Comic characters, 46-47, 106
Composition, 15, 19-25, 70, 98, 132, 134-143, 148, 151, 162, 186, 247, 253, 284, 286, 347, 349
Connie Lynn, 344
Coquette, 155, 202-203, 290
Cora, 316
Cotton Joe, 205
Countess Dagmar, 302
Cremer, 351
Crib Crowd Baby, 348
Crowning Glory, 167
Crystal Faerie, 64-65
Cuddle Kewpie, 247
Cynthia, 26
D ■■■■■■■■■■■■■■■■
Daddy's Girl, 218
Daisy, 128, 238
Dan, 67
Danel, 144
Danel & Cie., 144
Danny, 62
Das Lachende Baby, 323
Däumlinchen, 258
Davy Crockett, 347
Deanna Durbin, 214-215
Dean's Rag Book Co., 270
Debu'Teen, 61
Demalcol, 183
DeNunez, Marianne, 62
DEP, 145, 154
Dewees Cochran, 132
Dimmie, 68-69
Dimples, 209
Dionne Quintuplets, 19, 171
Dionne-type Doll, 138
Disney, 22
Disney Snow White, 31
Doc, 253
Doggi, 258

Dollar Princesses, 250
Doll House Doll, 89
Dolley Madison, 126, 302
Dolly Dear, 130
Dolly Dingle, 67, 148
"Dolly" Face, 91, 326
Dolly Reckord, 66
Dollypop, 73
Donald Duck, 253
Door of Hope Mission, 146
Dopey, 253
Dorothy, 128
Dorothy of the Wizard of Oz, 215
Dr. Dafoe, 23
Drayton, Grace, 147-148
Dressed Animals, 46
Dressed Teddy Bears, 46
Dressel, 149-152
Dressel, Cuno & Otto, 143, 149, 297
Dressel & Kister, 128
Du Mein, 257
Dummy Dan, 171
Dutch Girl, 46
Dwarfs, 118, 255
Dy-Dee Baby, 162
E ■■■■■■■■■■■■■■■■
E.B. Bébé, 83
E.D. Bébé, 95, 153
EJA, 222
E.J. Bébé, 222
E.T. Gibson Girl, 130
Early All-bisque, 242
Easter Girl, 31, 309
Eden Bébé, 154
Edith, 31, 128
Edwards, 351
Edwina, 55
EFFanBEE Doll Co., 155-167
Alice, 166
American Children, 163, 165
Anne Shirley, 161-162
Baby Bright Eyes, 158
Baby Dainty, 158
Baby Effanbee, 158
Baby Grumpy, 155-156, 158
Baby Tinyette, 159
Babyette, 157
Bambino, 118
Barbara Ann, 163-164
Barbara Joan, 163
Barbara Lou, 163
Betty Brite, 163
Billy Boy, 155
Bubbles, 157-158, 167
Buds, 155
Button Nose, 163
Candy Kid, 163
Champagne Lady, 167
Charlie McCarthy, 163
China Head, 167
Cinderella, 166
Coquette, 155
Crowning Glory, 167
Dewees Cochran, 132
Dy-Dee Baby, 162

Fluffy Girl Scout, 167
Gibson Girl, 163
Girl with Watering Can, 167
Harmonica Joe, 155
Historical dolls, 163, 166
Honey, 166
Howdy Doody, 166
Katie Kroose, 155-156
Lambkin, 158
Little Lady, 163
Lovums, 158
Mama doll, 156, 158
Marilee, 158
Mary Ann, 158
Mary Jane, 158
Mary Jane Nurse, 167
Mary Lee, 158
Mickey, 158, 167
Patsy, 12, 15, 159
Patsy Ann, 159-160
Patsy Ann Girl Scout, 167
Patsy Baby, 159, 161
Patsy Joan, 159
Patsy Jr., 159
Patsy Kins, 159
Patsy Lou, 159
Patsy Rae, 159
Patsy Ruth, 159
Patsyette, 158-159
Portrait Dolls,163-164
Pouting Bess, 155
Prince Charming, 166
Princess Diana, 167
Red Boy, 167
Rosemary, 158
Sherlock Holmes, 167
Skippy, 167
Sugar Baby, 158
Susan B. Anthony, 167
Suzanne, 163
Suzette, 163
Sweetie Pie, 157-158
Tinyette, 160
Tommy Tucker, 158
W.C. Fields, 159
Wee Patsy, 159
Whistling Jim, 155
Eleonore, 85
Elin, 140
Elise, 30-32, 34
Ella Cinders, 206
Ellen, 204
Eloise, 59
Emelie, 19
Emma, 65
Erika, 335
Ernst Heubach, 95-96, 149,
183, 197-199, 290
Esther, 128
Ethel, 128
Eugenie Poir, 270
Eva, 70, 289
F ■■■■■■■■■■■■■■■
F.G. Bébé, 178-179
F.G. Fashion Doll, 177
F.S. & Co., 115

Fairy Princess, 22
Fairy Queen, 22, 26
Famlee, 140
Fangel, Maud Tousey, 70
Fany, 275, 277
Farmer, 150
Farnell's Alpha Toys, 270
Fascist Boy, 267
Fashion Lady, 292
Father Christmas, 62, 65
Fatou, 204
Favorite, 264
Felt, 269
Fiene, 204
First Ladies, 34
Flapper, 45
Fleischmann & Bloedel, 154
Fleischmann, Greta, 291
Fleischmann, Susi, 291
Flexy Dolls, 215
Flora McFlimsey, 22
Florence, 128
Florian, Gertrude, 62
Florodora, 274
Flossie Flirt, 213
Flower Girl, 289
Flower Vendor, 266
Fluffy Girl Scout, 167
Fly-Lo Baby, 108
Foreign Countries, 19
Francie, 80-82
Frederike, 204
French Fashion-Type, 168-169
French Resistance Fighter, 175
Freundlich Novelty Corp., 170-
171
Friedebald, 258
Friedrich, 34
Frozen Charlotte, 172-173
Fulper Pottery Co., 174
Furga, 192
G ■■■■■■■■■■■■■■■
G.B., 275, 277
G.I. Joe, 175-176
G.K. doll, 261-263
Gabby, 215
Gaultier, Francois, 168, 177,
180, 303
Gene Autry, 344
Gene Carr Character, 206
General Douglas MacArthur,
170
George Washington, 130
Georgene, 307
Georgene Novelty, 66
German Child, 257
German Soldier, 171
Gesland, 168, 180
Gibson Girl, 30, 163, 241-
242
Giebeler-Falk, 282
Gigateure, 340
Giggles, 111
Gigi, 210
Ginger Girl Scout, 344
Ginnette, 349

Ginny, 347
Girl with Watering Can, 167
Glamour Girls, 26
Globe Baby, 194
Gnome, 339
Godey Ladies, 26
Godey's Little Lady Dolls, 181
Godey Man, 26
Godey Portrait, 27
Goebel, F. & W., 182-183
Gold Ballerina, 30
Gold Rush, 30
Goo Goo Eva, 171
Goo Goo Topsy, 171
Goodnow, June, 62
Googly, 186, 267
Googly-Eyed Dolls, 182-186
Grape Lady, 62, 126
Graves, Jennie, 347
Graziana, Adolph, 324
Gregor, 316
Greiner, Ludwig, 15, 187
Grenier-style, 123
Gretchen, 231
Gretl, 34
Groom, 30, 47
Grumpy, 253
Gypsy Mother, 62
H ■■■■■■■■■■■■■■■
H. Bébé, 86
H. Handwerch, 95, 188
H.A. Bébé, 35
HvB, 91, 93, 286
Handwerck, 4
Handwerck, Heinrich, 95, 188
Handwerck, Max, 189
Hanna, 323
Hanna Kruse Dolls, 258
Hannah, 140
Hans, 231
Happifats, 43
Happy, 253
Hard Plastic, 26-30, 248,
258
Harmonica Joe, 155
Harmus, Carl, 193
Harriet Flanders, 70
Harriet Hubbard Ayer, 216
Harry the Hawk, 354
Hartmann, Carl, 194
Hartmann, Karl, 193
Hasbro, 175-176
Hawaiian Shirley, 328
HEbee,SHEbee, 43, 206
Hedwig/diAngeli, 140
Heine & Schneider Art Dolls,
259-260
Heinrich Stier, 143, 297,
338
Heiser, Dorothy, 62
Helen, 128
Heller, Adolf, 194
Heller, Alfred, 283
Hen and Chicks, 130
Henriette, 267
Hertel, Schwab & Co., 4, 13,

37, 107, 182, 186, 195-
196, 249, 254
Hertwig & Co., 122, 128,
337
Heubach Babies, 203
Heubach Character Child, 200
Heubach, Ernst, 95-96, 149,
183, 197-199, 290
Heubach, Gebrüder, 95, 149,
182-183, 186, 200-203,
286, 290
Hilda, 15, 94-95
Himstedt, Annette, 204
Historical dolls, 163, 166
Hitler Youth, 46
Holly, 63
Holz-Masse Head, 149
Honey, 166
Horsman, E.I. Co., 72, 208
Baby Bumps, 205
Baby Dimples, 206
Billiken, 205, 246
Blink, 206, 208
Campbell Kid, 206-209
Cindy, 207
Ella Cinders, 206
Gene Carr Character, 206
HEbee-SHEbee, 206
Jackie Coogan, 206
Jane, 206
Jeanie, 207
Jo-Jo, 207
Mike, 206
Naughty Sue, 207
Peggy Ann, 206
Peterkin, 206
Polly Pru, 205
Rosebud, 206
Skinney, 206
Snowball, 206
Hotpoint Man, 111
Howdy Doody, 166
Hoyer, Doll Mfg. Co., Mary,
210
Hug Me Kids, 185, 186
Hug-Me-Tight, 147
Huret, Maison, 168, 212
I ■■■■■■■■■■■■■■■
Ichimatsu, 292
Ideal Novelty & Toy Co.,
213-218, 328
Baby Shirley, 328
Baby Snooks, 215
Betsy McCall, 218
Betsy Wetsy, 213
Betty Jane, 214
Bonny Braids, 218
Children, 215
Cinderella, 214-215
Daddy's Girl, 218
Deanna Durbin, 214-215
Dorothy of the Wizard of
Oz, 215
Flexy Dolls, 215
Flossie Flirt, 213
Gabby, 215

Harriet Hubbard Ayer,
216
Hawaiian Shirley, 328
Jiminy Cricket, 215
Judy Garland, 215
King-Little, 215
Little Miss Revlon, 218
Little Princess, 214
Magic Skin Baby, 215,
217
Mama Doll, 213
Mary Hartline, 218
Miss Curity, 218
Miss Ideal, 218
Miss Revlon, 218
Mortimer Snerd, 215
Patti Playpal, 218
Peter Playpal, 218
Pinocchio, 215
Plassie, 215
Sara Ann, 218
Saralee, 218
Saucy Walker, 217-218
Shirley Temple, 213-214
Snoozie, 213
Snow White, 214
Soldier, 215-216
Sparkle Plenty, 215
Toni, 218
Uneeda Kid, 213
Immobiles, 46
Improved Foot Doll, 130
Indian Squaw, 266
Irish Queen, 302
It, 55
Izannah Walker Doll, 350
J ■■■■■■■■■■■■■■■
J.J., 132
J.M. Bébé, 86
Jackie Coogan, 206
Jackie Robinson, 139
Jacqueline, 30-31
Jael, 62
Jane, 206
Jane Withers, 23
Janette, 65
Janie, 31
Janka, 204
Japanese Imperial Soldier,
175-176
JDK, 183, 241-242, 294
Jeanie, 207
Jeannie Walker, 23
Jeff, 349
Jenny Lind, 31, 126
Jerri Lee, 344
Jill, 349
Jiminy Cricket, 215, 253
Jimmie, 69
Jo, 26
John Powers Models, 26
Johnny Tu-Face, 286
Joi Lin, 62
Jo-Jo, 207
Joshua, 62
Joy, 111

Judy, 130
Judy Ann, 288
Judy Garland, 215
Jullien Jeune, 219
Jullien Bébé, 219
Jumeau, 15, 95, 144-145, 153, 168, 202, 220-226
"Jumeau Déposé" Bébé, 145, 223, 225
Just Me, 279
Jutta Child, 150-152
K ▪▪▪▪▪▪▪▪▪▪▪▪▪▪▪▪
K & K Toy Co., 67, 71, 107
K & R, (see Kämmer & Reinhardt)
K * R, 115, 186
K.P.M., 122
Kai, 204
Kallus, Joseph L., 244
Kamkins, 15, 227
Kamkins-type, 18
Kämmer & Reinhardt, 4, 95-96, 116, 142, 182, 228-234, 327, 330
Kampes Studio, Lousie R, 229
Kane, Maggie Head, 62
Karen Ballerina, 23
Karl Hartmann Doll Factory, 193
Kasimir, 204
Kate, 65
Kate Greenaway, 22
Kathe, 204
Käthe Kruse, 4, 10, 256-258
Kathy, 26
Katie, 31
Katie Kroose, 155-156
Kaulitz, Marion, 287
Kelly, 30-31
Kelly Face, 31
Ken #1, 82
Ken-Tuck, 65
Kestner & Co., 4, 122
Kestner, J.D., 37, 40, 42-43, 95, 107, 113, 143, 182, 235-243, 249, 293
Kewpie, 110, 244-248, 255
Kewpie Mountain, 245
Kewpie-type Characters, 139
Kiddiejoy, 275, 279-280
Kindergarten Girl, 146
King-Little, 215
Kitty-Puss, 148
Kley & Hahn, 186, 249-250, 286
Kling & Co., 37, 107, 122, 251-252
Knickerbocker Doll & Toy Co., 253, 307
König & Wernicke, 107, 142, 254
Krueger, Richard G., 255
Kruse-type, 259-260
Kubelka lady, 169
Kuhnlenz, Gebrüder, 95, 261-263, 305
Künstlerkopf, 322

Kurt, 34
Kyoto, 292
L ▪▪▪▪▪▪▪▪▪▪▪▪▪▪▪▪
La Georgienne, 264
Lacmann bodies, 187
Lady Doll, 243, 267
Lady in Red, 27
Lambkin, 158
Land Adventurer, 175
Lanternier, A. & Cie, 264
Lanternier Lady, 264
Laura, 267
Laurie, 30
Leather Doll, 265
Lenci, 100, 266-268
Lenci-Type, 269-270
Leslie, 31, 33
Leslie, Mr., 324
Liberty & Co. of London, 271
Liesl, 34
Li'l Apple, 65
Lil Imp, 348-349
Limbach, 37, 272-273
Limoges, 264
Linda Baby, 344
Lindner, Louis & Söhn, 338
Lisa, 204
Lissy, 30
Lissy Beth, 29
Little Angel Baby, 61
Little Annie Rooney, 111
Little Bright Eyes, 186
Little Cherub, 70
Little Colonel, 19
Little Genius, 20, 22
Little German Child, 257
Little Imp, 43
Little Lady, 30, 163
Little Lulu, 70
Little Men, 26
Little Minister, 30
Little Miss Revlon, 218
Little Miss Sunshine, 65
Little Princess, 214
Little Shaver, 18
Little Women, 18, 20, 26, 30, 63, 181
Little Women Type, 334
Lone Ranger, 139
Lori, 343
Lorraine, 264
Louis Amberg & Son, 52-55
Louisa, 34
Lovums, 158
"Lucia" Face, 267
Lucinda, 31
Lydia, 140
M ▪▪▪▪▪▪▪▪▪▪▪▪▪▪▪▪
M. Bébé, 86
Mabel, 128
Mabel Lucie Attwell, 118
Madame Hendren, 66
Maggie, 26, 34
Maggie Face, 26
Maggie Mixup, 30
Magic Skin Baby, 215, 217

Makimura, 204
Malin, 204
Mama Doll, 56, 66, 117, 136, 138, 156, 158, 206, 213
Mama Katzenjammer Tea Cozy, 131
Mammy, 72, 97-98, 120
Man of Action, 175
Manchu Lady, 146
Margaret Face, 23, 26
Margaret O'Brien, 23-24, 26
Margaret Rose, 26
Margie, 111-112
Margot, 30
Margot Ballerina, 26
Margarita, 267
Maria, 34
Maria-Teresa, 266
Marie, 231
Marilee, 158
Marina, 270
Marion, 128
Marionettes, 22
Mariuccia, 267
Marked "Nippon" Characters, 47
Marlo, 34
Marme, 26-27
Marseille, Armand, 85, 95, 149, 182, 274-280
Marsh, 351
Marta, 34
Martha face, 34
Martha Washington, 130
Mary, 65
Mary Ann, 158
Mary Ann Face, 31, 34
Mary Cassatt Baby, 31
Mary Ellen, 29
Mary Hartline, 218
Mary Hoyer, 210
Mary Jane, 158, 190
Mary Jane Nurse, 167
Mary Lee, 158
Mary Martin, 26
Mary Todd Lincoln, 124
Marybel, 31
Mascotte, 266, 281
Mask face, 267
Masquerade, 289
Mattel, Inc. 77
Maud Tousey Fangel, 70
Max and Moritz, 234, 310
McGuffey Ana, 21-22, 30
McKim child, 63
Me and My Shadow, 26
Meech, 351
Meg, 26
Meiji Era, 292
Meissen and Royal Copenhagen, 122
Merry Marie, 130
Metal Dolls, 282
Metal Heads, 283
Miami Miss, 65
Mibs, 52, 54
Michael, 34

Michiko, 204
Mickey, 158, 167
Mickey Mouse, 47, 253, 339
Midge, 77
Mike, 206
Military Dolls, 170
Ming Ming Baby, 295
Miniatures, 266
Minnie Mouse, 253, 339
Miss America, 22
Miss Curity, 139, 218
Miss Ideal, 218
Miss Peep, 112
Miss Revlon, 218
Mitsvare, 292
Molly-'es, 284, 306
Monica, 140
Montanari, 351
Moritz, 234, 310
Morning Glory, 126
Mortimer Snerd, 215
Mothereau, 285
Mozart, 266, 268
Muffie, 289
Müller & Strasburger, 297
Müller, Johann, 296-297
Multi-Faced Dolls, 286
Munich Art Dolls, 287
My Dearie, 91
My Dream Baby, 60
My Girlie, 91
My Shadow, 30
N ▪▪▪▪▪▪▪▪▪▪▪▪▪▪▪▪
Nancy, 60-61, 70
Nancy Ann Storybook Dolls, 288-289
Nancy Ann Style Show, 289
Nancy Drew, 34
Nancy Drew Face, 34
Nancy Lee, 61
Nanette, 61
Natural Doll Co., 137
Naughty Sue, 207
Nellie Bly, 65
New Era Novelty Co., 134
Nina Ballerina, 26
No Snows, 337
Nodder Characters, 46-47
Norma, 273
Nurse, 19, 30
Nurse Jane, 69-70
O ▪▪▪▪▪▪▪▪▪▪▪▪▪▪▪▪
O.I.C. Baby, 243
Ohlhaver, 290
Old Cottage Doll, 291
Old Rip, 150
Old Woman in Shoe, 47
Oldenburg, Mary Ann, 62-63
O'Neill, Rose, 65
Operatta, 289
Orientals, 47, 266, 292-295
Orphan Annie & Sandy, 171
Orsini, 43, 51
Ottolini, 192
Our Pet, 279

P ▪▪▪▪▪▪▪▪▪▪▪▪▪▪▪▪
P.D. Bébé, 303
P.D. Smith, 139
P.G. Bébé, 87
P.M., 186
Pamela, 30, 134
Pan Bébé, 86
Pansy, 91
Papier-Mâché, 15, 98, 226, 294, 296-299, 338
Parian-type, 300-302
Paris Bébé, 144
Paris Doll Co. Peggy, 140
Park, Irma, 62
Parker, Ann, 62
Parlor Maid, 30
Parsons-Jackson, 116
Patent Washable, 13
Patsy, 12, 15, 159
Patsy Ann, 159-160
Patsy Ann Girl Scout, 167
Patsy Baby, 159-161
Patsy Joan, 159
Patsy Jr., 159
Patsy Kins, 159
Patsy Lou, 159
Patsy Rae, 159
Patsy Ruth, 159
Patsyette, 158-159
Patsy-type, 98
Patsy-Type Girl, 70, 135
Patti Playpal, 218
Patty-Jo, 344
Paula, 204
Pauline, 128
Peck, 351
Peek-a-Boo, 147
Peggy Ann, 70, 206
Peter, 231
Peter Pan, 26, 34
Peter Pan Set, 34
Peter Playpal, 218
Peter Ponsett, 132
Peterkin, 43, 206
Philadelphia Raby, 303
Piano Babies, 202
Pierotti, 351
Pinkie, 111
Pinky, 22, 65
Pinocchio, 140, 215, 253, 255
Pirate, 289
Pitti Sing, 130
Plassie, 215
Plawo Girl, 115
Polly, 31
Polly Face, 31
Polly II, 63
Polly Piedmont, 63-64
Polly Pigtails, 26
Polly Pru, 205
Pollyana, 31
Pop-Eye, 111
Portrait Dolls, 22, 34, 132, 150, 163-164
Portrait Jumeau, 222, 224
Portrait of a Young Girl, 65
Portrettes, 30

Poupée Bois, 177, 220
Poupée Peau Fashion Lady, 168-169, 177, 220
Pouty Baby, 323-325
Powder & Crinoline, 284
Precious, 22
Pre-Grenier, 304
Prince Charles, 30, 63
Prince Charming, 26, 166
Prince Gregor, 316
Prince Philip, 26
Princess, 91, 284, 346
Princess Ann, 30, 63
Princess Caroline, 63
Princess Diana, 167
Princess Elizabeth, 20, 22, 271, 323
Princess Elizabeth Face, 22
Princess Elizabeth Jumeau, 226
Princess Grace, 63
Princess Juliana, 202
Princess Kimimi, 65
Princess Margaret Rose, 63, 271
Prize Baby, 196
Puggy, 56
Punch & Judy, 37, 130
Puppy Pippin, 147
Pussy Cat, 31
Puz, 230
Puzzy, 140
Q ▪▪▪▪▪▪▪▪▪▪▪▪▪▪▪
Queen, 27, 62, 348
Queen Elizabeth, 26, 309
Queen Louise, 275
Queue San, 47
Quizkin, 30
R ▪▪▪▪▪▪▪▪▪▪▪▪▪▪▪
R.A., 183, 310
R.D. Bébé, 305
R.R. Bébé, 223
Rabbit, 46
Rabery & Delphieu, 305
Rag, 69
Raggedy Andy, 306-307
Raggedy Ann, 306-307
Raleigh Doll, 308
Raleigh, Jessie McCutcheon, 308
Ratti, 192
Ravca, Bernard, 309
Ravca, Francis Diecks, 309
Ravca Doll, 309
Raynal, 270
Recknagel,Th., 310
Record Moritz, 339
Red Boy, 167
Red Ridinghood, 171, 286
Redmond, Kathy, 62
Reflections of Youth, 204
Renoir Child, 34
Revalo Character Baby, 290
Revalo Child Doll, 290
Ricky, 62
Rita, 273

Ritzy Chubby Baby, 137
Roche, Lynn & Michael, 62
Rohmer, Madame Marie, 168, 311
Rollinson, Gertrude F., 312
Romantic Couple, 34
Rosamund Bridesmaid, 26
Rose O'Neill, 65
Rosebud, 206, 274-275
Rosemary, 158
Rozy, 31
Rumpumpel Baby, 258
Russian Boy, 266
Russian Cloth Doll, 131
Russian Girl, 266
Russian Infantry Man, 175-176
Ruth Gibbs Doll, 181
S ▪▪▪▪▪▪▪▪▪▪▪▪▪▪▪
S PB H, 294
S.F.B.J., 154, 186, 313-315, 346
S & H (see Simon & Halbig)
Sabu, 284
Sally, 56
Sand Baby, 257
Sandreuter, Regina, 62
Santa, 46, 337
Santa Claus, 140
Sara Ann, 218
Saralee, 218
Sasha dolls, 316
Saucy Walker, 217-218
Scarlet O'Hara, 22
Scarlett, 31, 65
Scavini, Enrico & Elenadi, 266
Schelhorn, Max, 286
Schieler, 186
Schilling, F.M., 297, 357
Schlenkerchen, 257
Schmidt, Bruno, 317-318
Schmidt, Franz & Co., 95, 319-320
Schmitt & Fils, 321
Schneider, Rudolf, 357
Schoenau & Hoffmeister, 322-323
Schoenhut, Albert & Co., 107, 324-326
Schoenhut, Harry E., 324
Schuetzmeister & Quendt, 327
Scootles, 9, 110-112
Screamer, 202
September Morn, 148
Serie Sasha, 316
Seven Dwarfs, 253
Shari Lewis, 30
Sheppard, J.B. & Co., 303
Sherlock Holmes, 167
Sherman Smith, 62
Shirley Temple, 14-16, 47, 213-214, 328-329
Shirley Temple-type, 139,

214
Siegfried, 243
Simon & Halbig, 37, 42, 85, 95, 97, 149, 188, 228, 292, 294, 319, 330-336
Simon & Halbig-type, 40, 42, 286
Sir Walter Raleigh, 271
Sizzy, 140
Skating Doll, 61
Skinney, 206
Skippy, 167
Sleeping Beauty, 22, 30
Sleepy, 253
Sluggo, 70
Slumbermate, 31
Smarty, 31
Smiling, 202, 257
Smith, Sherman, 62
Snickelfritz, 325
Sneezy, 253
Snooks, 70
Snookums, 70
Snoozie, 213
Snow Babies, 337
Snow White, 21-22, 25, 26, 47, 214, 253, 255
Snowball, 206
Société Française de Fabrication de Bébés & Jouets (see S.F.B.J.)
Soldier, 170, 215-216
Sonja Henie, 22
Sonneberg-type, 299
Sonneberg Täufling, 338
Sonny, 69
Sorensen, Lewis, 62
Sound of Music, 34
Southern Belle, 30
Sparkle Plenty, 215
Special Face Dolls, 23
Special Girl, 21, 23
Standfuss, Karl, 107, 283
Standish No Break Doll, 130
Steiff Doll, 339
Steiff, Margarete, 339
Steiner, 95, 182
Steiner, Jules Nicolas, 340-342
Sterling Doll Co. Sports Doll, 140
Stiff Characters, 47
Stier, Heinrich, 143, 297, 338
Stormy, 132
Story Princess, 26
Storybook Characters, 8, 19
Storybook Dolls, 60, 288
Sue, 55
Sugar Baby, 158
Sultan, 284
Sunny Boy, 69
Sunny Girl, 68-69
Sunshine, 65
Superior Doll Mfg. Co., 134

Suprised Eye, 267-268, 286
Susan B. Anthony, 167
Susie Q., 18
Suzanne, 140, 163
Suzette, 163
Suzy, 31
Swaine & Co., 343
Sweet, Elizabeth, 62
Sweet Nell, 51
Sweet Sue, 57, 58
Sweet Sue Sophisticate, 58
Sweet Violet, 29
Sweetie Pie, 157-158
Sweets, 70
Swiss Wooden Lady, 357
T ▪▪▪▪▪▪▪▪▪▪▪▪▪▪▪
Tabby Cat, 130
Tabby's Kittens, 130
Tag, 69
Taki, 204
Talking Action Marine, 175
Talking Action Pilot, 175
Talking Action Sailor, 175
Talking Action Soldier, 175
Talking Astronaut, 175
Talking Man of Action, 175
Teenager, 267
TerriLee, 344
Tête Jumeau, 11, 223, 225-226, 292
Theola, 62
Thinker, 245
Thompson, Martha, 63
Thorp, Ellery, 63
Three Bears, 47
Three Pigs and Wolf, 47, 140
Thuillier, A., 345
Timi, 204
Tinker Bell, 34
Tinty Tots Body Twists, 55
Tiny child doll, 229, 334
Tiny Jerri Lee, 344
Tiny Miss Series, 347
Tiny Tears, 58
Tiny Terri Lee, 344
Tinyette, 160
Tiss Me, 202
Todd, 62
Toddler, 76, 98, 174
Tommy Tucker, 115, 158, 318
Toni, 58, 204, 218
Tony Sarg, 22
Toodles, 58, 347
Tootsie Wootsie, 325
Topsy, 70, 130, 289
Topsy Turvy, 19, 20, 72
Toto, 264
Toymaker, 62
Traditional Warrior, 292
Traumerchen, 257
Trendon Toys, Ltd., 316
Triste Bébé, 221-222
Trousseau, 181

Trudy, 139, 286
Truly Scrumptious, 82
Tutti, 82
Tuttle, Eunice, 63
Two-face Baby, 47
Two-Gun Mickey, 253
Tynie Baby, 207, 209
U ▪▪▪▪▪▪▪▪▪▪▪▪▪▪▪
U.F.D.C. Souvenir Doll, 65
U.S. Zone Germany, 257
Uncle Sam, 150
Uncle Wiggily, 70
Uneeda Kid, 137, 213
Uneeda Rita Hayworth, 140
Unis, 346
Unis Child Doll, 346
Utley Doll Co., 312
Y ▪▪▪▪▪▪▪▪▪▪▪▪▪▪▪
Valentine, 267
Valentino, 267
Van Rosen, 95
Vanta Baby, 55
Venus, 270
Vinyl, 31-34, 248
Vogelsanger, Paul, 287
Vogue Dolls, Inc., 347-349
Voit, Andreas, 296
Volland, 306
W ▪▪▪▪▪▪▪▪▪▪▪▪▪▪▪
WAAC, 170
Walker, 326
Walker, Izannah, 350
Walküre, 259
Wally, 273
Walters, Beverly, 63
WAVE, 170
Wax doll, 351-352
Wax-over-Composition, 352-353
W.C. Fields, 159
Wee Patsy, 159
Wellings, Norah, 354
Welsch, 327
Wendy, 26, 30, 34, 318
Wendykins, 12
Wendy Ann, 22
Wendy Ann Face, 22
Wendy Ballerina, 30
Wendy Bride, 25-26
Wendy-Ann, 26
Whistler, 202
Whistling Doll, 67
Whistling Jim, 155
Winkers, 267
Winnie, 29
Winnie the Pooh, 63
Wislizenus, A., 297
Wood, 355-357
Wolf & Co., 327
World Child Collection, 204
Wright, John, 63
Wyffels, Berdine, 63
Y ▪▪▪▪▪▪▪▪▪▪▪▪▪▪▪
Yvonne, 19
Z ▪▪▪▪▪▪▪▪▪▪▪▪▪▪▪
Zeller, Fawn, 63